God, Creation,
and Contemporary
Physics

THEOLOGY AND THE SCIENCES

Kevin Sharpe, Series Editor

God, Creation, *and* Contemporary Physics

Mark William Worthing

FORTRESS PRESS   MINNEAPOLIS

GOD, CREATION, AND CONTEMPORARY PHYSICS

Library of Congress Cataloging-in-Publication Data

Worthing, Mark William.
    God, creation, and contemporary physics / Mark William Worthing.
      p.   cm.—(Theology and the sciences)
    Includes bibliographical references.
    ISBN 0-8006-2906-X (alk. paper)
    1. Physics—Religious aspects—Christianity.   2. Cosmology.
  3. God.   4. God—Proof.   5. Creation.   6. Providence and government
of God.   7. End of the world.   I. Title.   II. Series.
BL265.P4W67   1995
261.5'5—dc20   95-48973
                                                         CIP

Manufactured in the U.S.A.   AF 1-2906
00   99   98   97   2   3   4   5   6   7   8   9   10

Contents

Acknowledgments

One of the most intriguing and increasingly fruitful areas of interdisciplinary dialogue in which theology has been involved in recent years is that with modern physics and cosmology. The research for this book, which provides an overview of this dialogue with specific focus on the doctrines of God and creation, began during my doctoral studies at the University of Regensburg, Germany. In this regard I am especially indebted to my *Doktorvater,* Hans Schwarz, whose support of my research from beginning to end and whose own commitment to dialogue with the natural sciences has been indispensable. I am also indebted to Christoph Meinel, specialist in the history of science, and Ulrich Rößler, physicist, for their help in this interdisciplinary project. Their many helpful suggestions led to numerous improvements in the text.

I am grateful to Fortress Press for the inclusion of this work in the Theology and the Sciences series. Special thanks go to Timothy Staveteig and to series editor Kevin Sharpe, both of whom read the manuscript and provided suggestions for improving style and focusing the discussion.

I express gratitude also to Jenny Moore, Russell Briese, and Martin Rothgangel, all of whom proofread the manuscript at various stages and contributed to improvement of style and content. Thanks also go to Hildegaard Ferme for assistance with many technical aspects of the production of the text.

Introduction

John Updike's novel *Roger's Version* opens with a meeting between the staid theology professor Roger Lambert and the precocious young scientist Dale Kohler. Aside from demonstrating their mutual inability to understand the code words and concerns of the other's world—symbolic of much of the current relationship between science and religion—their conversation does not contain much of interest to us. It is precisely at this point that the book's unlikely plot develops. The young scientist, hoping of all things for research funds from theology, excitedly informs his theological colleague that something miraculous is taking place. "The physicists," he proclaims, "are getting down to the nitty-gritty, they've really just about pared things down to the ultimate details, and the last thing they ever expected to happen is happening. God is showing through." After his initial and certainly justified skepticism, Roger Lambert asks the crucial question: "What kind of God is showing through, exactly?"[1]

Updike's story is fictional, to be sure. Part of the reason that its plot works, however, is precisely because such a conversation between a theologian and a scientist today is not entirely inconceivable. It was the astrophysicist Robert Jastrow who, in the conclusion to his 1978 book, *God and the Astronomers,* made the now-famous statement: "At this moment it seems as though science will never be able to raise the curtain on the mystery of creation. For the scientist who has lived by his faith in the power of reason, the story ends like a bad dream. He has scaled the mountains of ignorance; he is about to conquer the highest peak; as he pulls himself over the final rock, he is greeted by a band of theologians who have been sitting there for centuries."[2]

If Jastrow's statement raised the hopes of many Christians that science, long perceived to be the enemy of faith, was now prepared to support, if not prove, the existence of God, those hopes were dashed by the 1988 publication of *A Brief History of Time* by the respected Cambridge physicist Stephen Hawking. Jastrow, to be sure, was hardly a mover and shaker in the world of physics, but rather a competent astronomer with a penchant for overstatement. Stephen Hawking, by contrast, is one of the leading theoretical physicists of our time. It was all the more significant, therefore, when he produced a popular work that was not only about "the frontiers of physics, astronomy [and] cosmology" but was "also a book about God."[3] Hawking's tentative conclusion, in light of an anticipated Grand Unified Theory of physics and his proposal of a "no boundary condition" that would apply to time as well as to the three spatial dimensions, is that if there is a God, God's role in the creation and preservation of the universe would be minimal.[4]

For those hoping for a great collaboration between science and theistic faith, Hawking's book was a disillusionment. Perhaps the world of science and the world of faith did not have much to do with each other after all. Yet something very significant was taking place. Hawking's conclusions may not have been what many theists were hoping to hear, but the fact could not be overlooked that a leading physicist was addressing the question of God in a serious manner—and he was by no means the only one. Not since the days of Isaac Newton has the word *God* so frequently graced the pages of so many articles and books about physics.

A question perhaps even more important for theology than the actual position physicists are taking toward the possibility and role of a Creator is, to paraphrase Updike's fictional theologian, What kind of God is being argued for or against? Given the individualistic and existential nature of personal faith, it is unlikely that significant numbers of people would either begin or cease believing in the existence of God as a result of a favorable or disfavorable scientific consensus. A historically informed view, however, of the role of science in shaping the worldview against which philosophy and theology take place would indicate that what physicists are saying now about God may well have a significant impact on the *kind* of God in whom future generations believe or do not believe.

Contemporary physics has taken on more and more of the roles that once belonged exclusively to metaphysics and is producing direct as well as indirect statements concerning the nature of time, space, the universe, ultimate reality, and God, with significant implications for theology. Indeed, one prominent physicist, Frank Tipler, in his latest book *The Physics of Immortality,* goes so far as to contend that theology should be understood as a branch of physics.[5] The specifically scientific conclusions of the new physics cannot, from a theological standpoint, be challenged. Yet the metaphysical and theological implications (both stated and implied) can and must be analyzed critically by theology in a healthy dialogue that avoids the extremes of either unquestioned acceptance or close-minded rejection. In this book, therefore, I pursue a three-fold objective: first, to determine what contemporary physicists (and those in adjacent fields) are saying about God and God's relationship to the space-time world; second, to analyze the validity and significance of this emerging "God-talk" from the perspective of Christian theology, with attention to both the possibilities and pitfalls inherent in the new rapprochement between theology and science; and third, to suggest some necessary presuppositions and a methodological basis for the continuing dialogue with physics.

Two concepts are central to this study: *physics* and *God.* A comprehensive definition of either of these terms that would be completely acceptable to either a majority of physicists or theologians is probably not possible. I will attempt no such definitions. Instead, I will seek to clarify my own functional understanding of both terms.

More than an exposition of how matter and energy are related through motion and force in our everyday environment, or how the laws of gravitational attraction regulate the course of our solar system, contemporary physics (especially theoretical physics) is engaged in the search for a comprehensive theory (or theories) of existence that would explain the functioning, origin, and destiny of the universe, and, if Hawking is to be believed, that would allow us to know "the mind of God."[6] Indeed, no mean task! Of course, not even every theoretical physicist is directly involved in the effort to meld the theories of general relativity and quantum mechanics into a Grand Unified Theory (GUT) that is expected to deliver a comprehensive view of the universe. The many and varied specialists within the compass of physics, and of such related fields as cosmology, astronomy, and theoretical mathematics, however, are seen as participating in this overall search for a theoretically unified understanding of our cosmos.

It should also be noted that it is neither desirable nor possible to take into account the religious and/or metaphysical views of everyone holding a chair of physics somewhere. Physicists are human beings and have a range of human opinions on a diverse number of topics that bear little or no relationship to their work as physicists. That John Houghton,[7] former professor of atmospheric physics at Oxford, is an outspoken evangelical Christian, or that the physicist Hermann Bondi[8] considers religion a "habit-forming evil" that produces the bulk of hatred, war, and intolerance in the world, is interesting but not significant for our study—even though both seek to lend credibility to their views through their positions as physicists. Houghton and Bondi seem to have arrived at their divergent opinions in regard to religion quite independent of their respective scientific studies; in all likelihood, they would have held these opinions with equal vigor if they had studied law or economic theory instead of physics. A distracting and unproductive interest in the religious opinions of various physicists must be scrupulously avoided. What is of interest to us, instead, are the metaphysical/theological conclusions and implications that are, at least ostensibly, rooted in the study of the issues addressed by contemporary physics. That a given physicist goes to church regularly or sees religion as a pervasive evil interests us no more than the religious habits and beliefs of any other member of society. When a physicist claims, however, that certain physical theories, laws, or principles lead necessarily (or even potentially) to the affirmation, rejection, or reformulation of a metaphysical or theological proposition, then we are appropriately interested in what he or she has to say. Here, then, we are dealing with the physicist as physicist—and as metaphysicist.

When one speaks of God, especially in relation to our understanding of the physical world, a wide range of possibilities present themselves. The God of theism, the "Watchmaker" God of Deism, the God of medieval scholasticism, a God-of-the-gaps, the God of process theology, and a host of others continue to present themselves in current discussions of God and the physical world. Which conception (or conceptions) of God is to be found among the various physicists we will treat remains to be seen. When I speak of God, however, I have in mind specifically the transcendent, triune God of Christian theism whom the Christian faith confesses to be the God who created and preserves the physical universe, who was involved personally in human history through Jesus Christ, and whose hands hold the final destiny of the universe. As I believe the following pages will show, such a description of God, however restrictive it may appear, is essential for a productive dialogue between modern physics and Christian theology.

In undertaking this study I am making two key assumptions. The first is that science can legitimately address questions related, at least indirectly, to the existence and role of God in our world. Any form of theological protectionism that attempts to reserve certain areas or questions as the exclusive domain of theology is self-destructive. To draw lines around what is scientifically knowable and claim the remainder as the unknowable realm of God is risky. At best, one ends up supporting a God-of-the-gaps in which the gaps become increasingly smaller. As Ralph Waldo Emerson aptly put it, "the religion that fears science, insults God and commits suicide."[9]

This is not to deny that empirical research has certain inherent, noetic limitations, but only to say that any attempt to declare what questions these limitations would prohibit science from addressing not only discourages interdisciplinary dialogue but commits theology to a course of unending capitulation and retreat. Yet neither do I wish to imply that science can "find" God—that is, conclusively verify either God's existence or nonexistence. Siegfried Müller-Markus's description of God as the "infinite horizon of the creative evolution of our knowledge" rightly reminds us that the being of God will always remain beyond strict scientific verifiability.[10]

It is constructive, at the same time, to recognize that the Christian view of God as Creator, Sustainer, and Redeemer admits of an intrinsic connection between God and the physical world. This, in turn, opens the door for science to address questions related to the existence and nature of God—even if God remains always on the "infinite horizon." As the Swiss theologian Emil Brunner observed, "the theological statement: God is the 'Creator of Heaven and Earth,' brings this affirmation into the sphere of facts which are accessible to our natural knowledge."[11] Similarly, Thomas F. Torrance, the Scottish theologian long noted for his constructive interaction with scientific worldviews, contends that the Christian doctrine of creation out of nothing necessitates such dialogue with the natural sciences. Theology's concept of a creation *ex nihilo* (out of nothing), according to Torrance, "implies that if we are to understand the world of contingent reality we must investigate the world itself, and learn of it out of its own natural processes and interior relations." For Torrance, therefore, any attempt to explicate knowledge of God apart from the structure of space-time which God created is inevitably irrational.[12]

The other major assumption of this study is that, while theology cannot critique the specifically scientific and technical aspects of physics, it is certainly free to analyze the relevance of the results of physics for theology as well as to critique the validity, consistency, and significance of those conclusions that are clearly metaphysical or theological in nature. This means that science must also avoid a protectionistic attitude that would imply that the metaphysical conclusions drawn from its data are beyond the critique of philosophy and theology. The physicist Richard Schlegel is correct when he suggests that what is needed for a fruitful dialogue is "a nature-respectful theology and a somewhat humbled we-do-not-know-it-all science."[13] The metaphysical and theological conclusions of contemporary physicists will therefore be analyzed on the basis of their correspondence with the scientific theories that they purport to be based on, their internal, logical coherence and consistency, and their comprehension of the metaphysical and theological ideas they address. This will be done with a view toward understanding their relevance for a Christian doctrine of God.

To accomplish this task, we begin with a brief historical overview intended to put the physics/theology dialogue in context. The major developments in physics and cosmology, especially in the twentieth century, are outlined for those who may be unfamiliar with them. In Chapter 2 we take up the question of God's existence. Specifically, we ask whether recent developments in physics make rational belief in the existence of God more or less difficult. We also take a look at what kind of God is "showing through" in these discussions. Chapter 3 addresses the questions of an original creation and, in more detail, of a creation out of nothing. Claims of physicists to have discovered an appearance or creation of the universe out of nothing are critically examined, and the implications for a Creator and the work of creation are brought into view. Chapter 4 deals with the question of God's present involvement in the physical universe. The focus is on difficult issues such as the possibility of miracles, the problem of evil, and God's ability to intervene providentially in the world, with a special emphasis on the implications of quantum theory.

Chapter 5 examines emerging "scientific eschatologies" and asks how or if these can be related to biblical-theological views of the end. Finally, we conclude our study with a summary of the influence of modern physics and cosmology on the Christian understanding of God and suggest guidelines for the ongoing dialogue between physics and theology.

Chapter One

Physics and Theology in Historical Perspective

The main motivating force behind the pursuit of natural knowledge from the time of Babylon and Greece in the East to the time of the Renaissance in the West was *theological* rather than *scientific*.
> —Harold P. Nebelsick

If the Church is largely ignored today it is not because science has finally won its age-old battle with religion, but because it has so radically reoriented our society that the biblical perspective of the world now seems largely irrelevant.
> —Paul Davies

If the God of the Bible is creator of the universe, then it is not possible to understand fully or even appropriately the processes of nature without any reference to that God.
> —Wolfhart Pannenberg

FROM THE DAWN OF MODERN SCIENCE TO KEPLER

The Origins of Modern Science in Antiquity

There is no fixed date, person, or era in which the undisputed, seminal beginnings of modern science can be seen. It seems certain, however, that the quest for knowledge of our physical world through observation and experimentation, and the effort to describe and harmonize these findings through theories and mathematical formulas, are to be found, in varying degrees of complexity and sophistication, in ancient cultures ranging from Babylon and Egypt in the Near East to Greece and Rome in the West. The origin of "modern" physics, within this milieu, is generally credited to the Greeks. The physicist S. M. Markus places the birth of physics as a science in the modern sense in third-century B.C.E. Greece with Euclid's geometry and Archimedes' discovery of hydrostatics and invention of the planetarium. Next to these developments, Markus places the astronomical theories of Ptolemy of Egypt that dominated Arab and Western astronomy with the geocentric planetary model for almost fifteen hundred years—in spite of the fact that Aristarchos had developed a heliocentric model already in the second century B.C.E.[1]

The ancients, in many regards, compiled an impressive record of scientific accomplishment, not only in physics, mathematics, and astronomy, but also in anatomy, medicine, botany, and other natural sciences. It will not do, however, to simply credit the ancients with a commendable anticipation of the methods of modern scientific research. Their intellectual world was not divided into neat categories such as physics, ethics, mathematics, theology, astronomy, and metaphysics. In antiquity the world was viewed as a unified and coherent whole. The ancients often mixed discussions of physics and metaphysics, mathematics and magic, geometry and theology, astronomy and astrology, all much to the chagrin of their modern successors.

Astronomy and astrology were so intertwined in antiquity, in fact, that it was often impossible to distinguish one from the other. It was not so much the desire to understand the workings of the physical reality we call the universe that often led the ancients to study the stars and the planets as it was the desire to be able to divine the future or understand the various astral divinities that the heavenly bodies were thought to represent. A cursory reading of almost any ancient or medieval book of "science" will show that this mixing of science, religion, philosophy, and even magic persisted up to the dawn of the modern age. Indeed, Harold P. Nebelsick argues that "the main motivating force behind the pursuit of natural knowledge from the time of Babylon and Greece in the East to the time of the Renaissance in the West was *theological* rather than *scientific*."[2]

The recognition of this relationship between religious and scientific epistemological systems in the ancient world up through the medieval period (and even, to a somewhat lesser extent, the Renaissance) is significant inasmuch as it sheds light on the conflict of the sixteenth and seventeenth centuries when science and theology split away from each other. Although reputable historians have long since abandoned the idea, it is still popular in some circles to conceive of the entire conflict as the misguided and perhaps even malevolent attempt of the church to hold a monopoly on all truth at the expense of intellectual freedom and much-needed progress in the realm of physical knowledge.

A recognition of the intertwining of religious and empirical approaches to knowledge in the ancient and medieval world calls for a long-overdue reassessment of popular views regarding this formative era in the modern relationship between science and religion. It would be beneficial for current discussions to recognize that however guilty the medieval and Reformation era church was in its attempts to have the final say in scientific matters, the "theological bondage" of science was at least partly self-imposed, and resistance to its "liberation from theology" was often as strong from scientists themselves as from theologians and church officials. What the sixteenth and seventeenth centuries witnessed was the dissolution of a unified worldview and epistemological system that had been accepted by philosophers, theologians, and scientists alike for at least two millennia.

Nicolaus Copernicus and the End of Geocentrism

Nicolaus Copernicus (1473–1543) stands at the headwaters of modern astronomy and physics. Often referred to erroneously as a "Polish priest,"[3] Copernicus, whose family seems to have originally come from Schlesien, was never ordained a priest, nor does he seem to have performed any specifically priestly or pastoral functions in the church.[4] Through the patronage of his uncle, Bishop Lukas Watzenrode, Copernicus was appointed a canon of the Chapter of Warmia in 1497. Thus he was provided with an income even though he did not return to Poland from his studies in Italy until 1503 to do administrative work for his uncle, and did not take up his canonry, for which he had been receiving a stipend, until after his uncle's death in 1512. Such examples of nepotism and monetary arrangements for well-connected students were common in the fifteenth and early sixteenth centuries and should not reflect negatively on Copernicus. In fact, he seems to be the exception in that he actually did work for the church in Warmia after his student days and eventually did take up the canonry to which he had been appointed.

The scientific revolution sparked by Copernicus was a result of a lifetime of astronomical observations and calculations that seem to have been motivated, at least in part, by a desire to help the church reform its calendar so that the dates of festivals such as Easter and Christmas could be calculated more accurately. Up to the time of Copernicus it was believed that the earth was the center of the universe and that the sun and the other planets revolved around a stationary earth. Incredibly elaborate geometric models existed to show how this was possible and could be harmonized with observable astronomical data.

Copernicus suggested a heliocentric model for the motion of the planets and developed geometric and mathematical proofs to demonstrate the feasibility of his theory. Copernicus set out his views in two works: the brief *Commentariolus,* the publication date of which is disputed, and the much fuller *De Revolutionibus Orbium Coelestium* (1543). Apart from the fact of his conviction that the planets must move in perfectly circular orbits (rather than elliptical ones), Copernicus had put together an essentially correct theory of the motion of the planets. Although it was apparently widely read among specialists, his theory did not cause much of a stir until more than seventy years later when it was condemned by the Roman church in 1616 at the so-called first trial of Galileo.

To be sure, the implications of Copernicus' theory contained all the ingredients for a theological conflict. The suggestion that the earth, the focal point of God's creative activity and the home of the pinnacle of God's creation—the human species—was not the center of the universe but just one of many planets, itself orbiting subserviently around the sun, did not sit well with a theologically construed, self-important view of humanity. Also, the then-common literalistic interpretation of the Bible, especially of those passages that speak of the sun rising or setting or of the earth remaining firm on its foundations, created additional problems.

Despite such potential for confrontation, however, the conflict did not come in Copernicus' lifetime, nor in the half century after his death in which *De Revolutionibus* was apparently widely circulated and used as an astronomy text.[5] The only evidence put forward in support of the view that Copernicus suffered real or potential persecution from the church for his view is the fact that he waited until the last year of his life to publish his magnum opus, ostensibly out of a fear of persecution from the church. In fact, however, the essence of his theory had already been made public through the earlier publication of his *Commentariolus,* and he had apparently not received any pressure from either local church officials or from Rome to keep silent. Not only close friends and members of the Lutheran University of Wittenberg, but also Cardinal Schönberg (in a letter dated November 1536), had urged him to publish so that his theory could be fully studied and discussed.

Why did Copernicus delay so long the publication of a work in which he had invested so many years? Fred Hoyle, the noted British astrophysicist, has observed that "the factors which deterred Copernicus [from publication] must either have been scientific or were personal to himself." Given the existence of some personal disputes in Warmia that had nothing to do with either science or religion, Hoyle further concludes that "Copernicus was immersed in a local world, not a world with modern ideas of freedom, not even the larger world of Rome, and in this small local world he was unwilling to be made to seem a fool. It is possible that his reluctance to publish arose at no deeper level than this."[6]

Copernicus did, however, eventually publish his revolutionary theory. Not only did it challenge prevailing cosmologies that were bound together with medieval theology, but it signaled a change in the way physics itself would be approached. Copernicus succeeded in raising mathematics to a new level of importance for physics, an importance that would eventually culminate in Newtonian physics and continues to dominate physics to this day. Yet for all the revolutionary scientific implications of Copernicus' theory, it was, in the end, the latent potential for theological conflict that placed *De Revolutionibus* and its author at the center of one of the most significant conflicts between science and religion—so significant, in fact, that nearly five hundred years later, most discussions of the often uneasy relationship between science and religion in the modern world begin with Copernicus.

Galileo Galilei and the Conflict with the Church

Galileo Galilei (1564–1642) was born near the Italian town of Pisa a year after the conclusion of the Council of Trent.[7] Galileo's training in mathematics and his remarkable comprehension of the principles of motion led him to make several early and important discoveries. In 1609 Galileo heard of the invention, a year earlier, of a magnifying device created by the Dutch spectacle-maker Johannes Lippershey that consisted of two convex lenses at separate ends of a tube. Galileo, intrigued, began experimenting with the construction of his own telescopes. In August of 1609 he had already improved on the Dutch model by using a convex and a concave lens (to avoid an inverted image), and produced a telescope of about 9×, which he demonstrated in Venice by showing that the sails of ships could be seen through the telescope from a tower before they could be detected by the naked eye.

By January of 1610 Galileo had produced a telescope with a magnification of 33× that he pointed, not at the sails of ships, but toward the heavens. The telescope proved so profitable that by March of the same year he published the results of his early observations. He found that the moon had a mountainous surface, that several new stars were now visible where previously none had appeared, that the Milky Way was composed of stars, and, significantly, that Jupiter had four satellites whose movements could be plotted. The latter discovery was especially significant in that it challenged directly the prevailing philosophy of Aristotle, who had claimed that the heavens were unchangeable, and lent credence to the views of Copernicus.[8]

Upon receipt in 1597 of Johannes Kepler's *Mysterium Cosmographicum*, Galileo wrote the author confessing that, "Many years ago, I became a convert to the opinions of Copernicus."[9] It was not until after the remarkable discoveries made with his telescope in 1510, however, that Galileo took up vigorously and publicly the defense of the Copernican theory. In his *Letters on the Sunspots* (March 1613) Galileo published for the first time his support of the Copernican theory. Reaction, needless to say, was mixed. Many theologians were still troubled by apparent contradictions with a literal interpretation of certain biblical texts, and some scientists remained skeptical of the new theory and of Galileo. At least one of Galileo's academic colleagues at the university in Padua (a fellow astronomer) was so skeptical, in fact, that he even refused to look through his telescopes![10] Yet there was also considerable support for Galileo's views. Among those enthusiastically welcoming the publication of *Letters on the Sunspots* was Cardinal Maffeo Barberini, the future Pope Urban VIII.[11]

A series of complicated events made Copernicanism and its chief defender, Galileo, the subject of a controversy that extended to Rome itself. Galileo, against the advice of his supporters, decided to go to Rome personally in late 1615 to defend Copernicanism, as well as his own reputation, before Pope Paul V. There he was confronted by Cardinal Bellarmine in the so-called first trial. Galileo argued that Scripture, essentially, is not a science text, and biblical statements such as those concerning the motion (or lack thereof) of the earth, sun, and planets should not be interpreted literally. He was also convinced of the correctness of the Copernican theory and wanted it recognized, perhaps too quickly, as more than a theory. Bellarmine, on the other hand, adopted an exegetical method that required a literal interpretation of the biblical passages in question and demanded that the Copernican theory be considered as just that, unless it could be proven.[12]

Pope Paul V pressed the Congregation of the Index for a quick decision. The result was that Copernicus' *De Revolutionibus* was placed on the Index "until corrected." One could still read Copernicus' book with permission, however, and his theory could still be discussed, but only as a hypothesis "false and contrary to Scripture" and not as fact.[13] Galileo was not forced to abjure his opinion at this hearing and even procured a letter to that effect from Cardinal Bellarmine in order to suppress rumors to the contrary. With Galileo's promise to comply with the ruling, the matter seems to have been dropped. Galileo's conflict with the church, however, was far from over.

In 1623 Pope Gregory XV died after a short reign of two years, and Maffeo Barberini, Galileo's friend and defender, became Pope Urban VIII. Not surprisingly, Galileo wasted no time in returning to Rome and seeking permission from his old friend to publish his long-anticipated book on the system of the world. After several discussions with the pope, Galileo obtained permission to discuss his theories hypothetically and impartially. Urban was unwilling, however, to revoke the decree of 1616, although Galileo, in long argumentation, attempted to persuade him to do so.[14] In conversation with Galileo, as Alfred North Whitehead relates the story, the pope

> made use of the irrefutable argument that, God being omnipotent, it was as easy for him to send the sun and the planets round the earth as to send the earth and the planets round the sun. . . . Galileo was annoyed—and very naturally so, for it was an irritating sort of argument with which to counter a great and saving formulation of scientific ideas. Unfortunately he

went away and put the pope's argument into the mouth of Simplicius, the man in the *Dialogues* who always advances the foolish objections.[15]

Galileo completed the *Dialogue Concerning the Two Chief World Systems* in 1630 and, after he received permission from church authorities in Florence to publish the work, it was finally printed there in March of 1632. Pope Urban VIII, after reading the book and recognizing his own arguments in the mouth of the fool Simplicius, was so personally offended that one visitor, writing to a friend of Galileo, commented that the pope could not "be in a worse frame of mind toward our poor Signor Galileo."[16] The perceived personal insult, combined with the challenges against the authority of the papacy from the Reformation and pressure from Spain to follow a political agenda favorable to its dynastic ambitions, put tremendous pressure on Urban to act. The fact that the Protestant armies, led by one of Galileo's former students, Gustavus Adolphus of Sweden, were turning the tide in the Thirty Years' War, and that Galileo's chief protector was the pro-Spanish Duke of Tuscany, certainly did nothing to help Galileo's position. As Ludovico Geymonat rightly observes, the condemnation of Galileo that took place on 22 June 1633 took on the character of a genuine political necessity for Pope Urban VIII.[17] The original harsh sentence of life imprisonment was quickly commuted to house arrest, which enabled Galileo, even though his writings were now forbidden, to complete a work on mechanics and strength of materials, *Two New Sciences*. Published in 1638 in Leyden, it is considered to be the "cornerstone of modern physics."[18] Galileo died on 8 January 1642, almost 78 years of age and still under house arrest. Only in 1992, 350 years after his death, was Galileo officially rehabilitated within the Roman Catholic Church.[19]

Johannes Kepler and Created Harmony

Johannes Kepler (1571–1630) shared many things in common with his contemporary Galileo Galilei. Both were devoted not only to astronomy but to understanding the system of the planets, both shared a halfhearted belief in the merits of astrology (though Kepler seems to have taken it more seriously than Galileo), and both suffered persecution at the hands of the Roman Catholic Church: Galileo for his scientific beliefs, Kepler for his religious beliefs. Kepler, a devout, if not always orthodox, Lutheran,[20] was expelled from Styria in Austria on 1 July 1600 on account of his refusal to convert to Catholicism.[21] The desperation of his situation was a boon for posterity, for it forced him back to Prague and further collaboration with the difficult and aging Danish astronomer Tycho de Brahe. Tycho, who died on 24 October 1601, left not only the post of imperial *mathematicus* vacant, to which Kepler was appointed on 6 November, but he also left behind more than thirty years' worth of the most detailed and precise astronomical observations ever carried out. The information provided by Tycho's immense collection of data was precisely what the young Kepler needed.

With Tycho's data Kepler was able to publish in 1609 his *Astronomia Nova,* in which he laid out the first two of his three planetary laws. His first law alone was sufficient to establish his place in history; it stated that the orbits of the planets around the sun are not circular, as Copernicus had thought, but elliptical, with the sun as one of the focal points of the orbits, thus removing the observational difficulties that hindered the full acceptance of the Copernican theory. His second law, though not as famous, was no less significant. It stated that planets do not orbit at uniform speeds but at the exact speed necessary so that an imaginary line drawn between them and the sun would travel across equal areas in equal times regardless of where the planet was in its orbit. Kepler's third law was revealed in his 1618 publication of *De Harmonice Mundi*. It stated that the squares of the periods of revolution (the time required to make a complete orbit) of any two planets are equal to the third power of their respective mean distances from the sun. Kepler even came intriguingly close to describing the forces of gravity and inertia as they affect the movements of the planets. He was convinced that there was "a force in the sun" that controlled the motion of the planets through some sort of attraction and that a counterbalancing force existed in the planets that resisted this attraction and accounted for their elliptical orbits. The precise solution to the problem, however, would have to wait another century for the genius of Isaac Newton.

It is worthy of note that Kepler, who seemed always the methodical scientist looking for physical laws that could be tested against observable phenomena, was often motivated (and limited) by his theological beliefs. He believed, for instance, that the sphere was not only the shape of the universe but the image of the divine, and was thus unwilling to abandon the sphere as the model of the universe. Concerning the trinitarian nature of the sphere, Kepler wrote: "in the sphere . . . there are three regions, symbols of the three persons of the Holy Trinity—the center, a symbol of the Father; the surface, of the Son; and the intermediate space, of the Holy Ghost."[22] Such a view allowed Kepler to go so far as to compute the respective densities of the three regions of the cosmic sphere based on the assumption that the matter in the universe must be divided equally among them—in correspondence to the equality of the three persons of the Trinity. Yet despite these quirks, his overall methodology and the significance of his planetary laws stand as a turning point in the development of modern science in general and of modern physics in particular.

Unfortunately, no one in Kepler's day seemed to understand the significance or implications of his work, including the great Galileo, who appears to have never read Kepler's works carefully, if at all.[23] Nevertheless, just as Galileo rightly deserves to be called the father of modern astronomy, so Kepler merits the title of father of modern astrophysics. Kepler's work, especially his three planetary laws, according to his biographer Arthur Koestler, "divorced astronomy from theology, and married astronomy to physics."[24] This is a somewhat ironic accomplishment for a man whose research was motivated by the resolute theological belief that an orderly Creator had certainly created a universe that operated harmoniously according to set laws of motion.

FROM THE BACONIAN COMPROMISE TO THE "WAR" BETWEEN SCIENCE AND RELIGION

Francis Bacon and René Descartes: Methodological Foundations
Sir Francis Bacon (1561–1626) and René Descartes (1596–1650) developed methodologies and philosophies of science that together determined the course of scientific development and its relationship with religion—especially Christianity—for almost four centuries. Bacon, as "a child of both the Renaissance and the Protestant Reformation," is said to have "demythologized the magical science of the Renaissance and brought its concepts down to earth by straining its concepts through the sieve of biblical doctrine." His concepts of the Christian faith played "no small part in his efforts to promote natural science."[25] It is somewhat ironic, therefore, that to whatever extent his theology may have influenced his scientific method, Bacon actually effected the separation of the natural and theological sciences. Apart from his well-known advocacy of an empirical philosophy and an inductive methodology, Bacon is perhaps most significant for the history of the relationship between scientific inquiry and religious faith because of his doctrine of the "two books," otherwise known as the Baconian compromise. Bacon suggested that two "books" existed: the book of God's word, that is, the Bible; and the book of God's works, the physical world. By sharply distinguishing between the knowledge gained by the study of Scripture and that gained through the study of the natural world, Bacon established the independence of science as an academic discipline while preserving the integrity of theology. In *The Advancement of Learning* Bacon wrote:

> Let no man upon a weak conceit of sobriety or an ill-applied moderation
> think or maintain, that a man can search too far, or be too well studied in
> the book of God's word, or in the book of God's works; divinity or philos-
> ophy: but rather let men endeavour an endless progress or proficience in
> both; only let men beware that they apply both to charity, and not to
> swelling; to use, and not to ostentation; and again, that they do not un-
> wisely mingle or confound these learnings together.[26]

Not only did Bacon argue against the unwise mixing of scientific and theological studies, but he also was insistent that the respective sources of the two
books not be mixed with or forced to conform to theories and presuppositions of our own invention. That is to say, the words of Scripture and the
works of nature must be allowed to speak for themselves and not be forced
to fit the preconceived molds of those pretending to objectively study either
of these two respective books.

The Baconian compromise, which was adhered to by such seventeenth-
century scientists as Robert Boyle and Isaac Newton, was, according to James
Moore, "a political compromise offering illustrations of the divine omnipotence, the true sense of the scriptures, and recovery from the noetic effects of
the Fall in exchange for the freedom of students of nature from harassment
by interpreters of biblical texts."[27] Likewise, theology was not only given
"illustrations of the divine omnipotence," but it too was given "freedom from
harassment" by interpreters of nature. Bacon made this clear when he wrote:

> We conclude that sacred theology is grounded only upon the word and
> oracle of God, and not upon the light of nature. . . . This holdeth not only
> in those points of faith which concern the mysteries of the Deity, of the
> Creation, of the Redemption, but likewise those which concern the moral
> law truly interpreted. . . . it is a voice beyond the light of nature. . . . So
> then the doctrine of religion, as well moral as mystical, is not to be attained
> but by inspiration and revelation from God.[28]

The Baconian compromise put aside for a time the debate over whether
theology or the budding natural sciences should be made to conform to the
other when the two appeared to contradict. The strict separation of the two
books, while giving equal freedom to both theology and science, was of
special significance to the advancement of science, becoming, especially in
England, "the basis of congenial relations between naturalists and exegetes,
and a chief sanction for the growth in volume and expertise of physical
research."[29]

On the Continent the philosophical and scientific work of the Frenchman
and Catholic René Descartes complemented that of Bacon and added to the
theoretical foundation that the seventeenth century was erecting for the fu-

ture development of the natural sciences. Descartes, in his *Meditations on First Philosophy* (1641), applied his skepticism (or as he would prefer, "systematic doubt") to every conceivable proposition—including that of his own existence. Everything had to be submitted to this systematic doubt in order to find a solid foundation on which a structure of knowledge could be rebuilt. What is remarkable here is that Descartes excluded the existence of God and "the realm of faith from the process of questioning."[30]

Descartes, despite the apparent inconsistencies within his own system at this point, apparently justified the exclusion of the realm of faith from the procedure of systematic doubt by treating revelation as a separate form of knowledge.[31] In doing this, Descartes, by example if not by clearly developed theory, added his weight to that of Bacon in establishing a sort of protective buffer between the fields of theology and natural science. Thus the stage was set, however unstable and temporary the arrangements ultimately proved to be, for a sort of truce between theology and science that allowed for, in principle at least, the separate and free development of each.

Apart from Descartes's philosophical contribution to the attitude toward the relationship between theology and science, he also made specific contributions to the way in which natural science was undertaken that surpassed even Bacon's championing of empiricism and inductive methodology in their significance. Descartes, in recognizing the importance of mathematics, developed a methodology that proved far more beneficial to the advancement of science than that proposed by Bacon.

Descartes was driven to erect an interlocking, unshakable foundation of knowledge that encompassed a physical reality that he saw as an interconnected whole. This led him to espouse a similarly unified methodology that included both intuition and deduction. As he wrote in his *Regulae ad Directionem Ingenii:*

> No knowledge can be acquired save by way either of intuition or of deduction. There can be no question of extending the method so as to show how these two operations ought to be performed, since they are the simplest of all mental operations and primary. If our understanding were not of itself qualified to perform them, it would be unable to comprehend any of the precepts prescribed by the method, however easy.[32]

While the concepts of Bacon and, to an even greater extent, those of Descartes are difficult to summarize, are filled with apparent internal contradictions, and are certainly incapable of being harmonized with one another, they nevertheless form an indispensable theoretical background for the work of future scientists—especially that of their near contemporary Sir Isaac Newton, who in his *Philosophiae Naturalis Principia Mathematica* of 1687 combined Baconian experimentation and empiricism with mathematical method and changed the course of modern science.

Isaac Newton: The Mechanistic Worldview and the Doctrine of God
In Sir Isaac Newton (1642–1727) we find the culmination of many streams of thought. Perhaps most significant for the development of modern science is his continuation of the work begun by Kepler in describing accurately the laws that regulate the motions of the planets. Of special note is Newton's well-known description of the gravitational attraction that exists between material bodies. Armed with this revolutionary new understanding of gravitational force, Newton was able to describe the "system of the world" for the first time in human intellectual history in a manner that could truly lay claim to being comprehensive and mathematically accurate. The scientific world would have to wait more than two centuries for the genius of Albert Einstein before any significant refinement of Newton's model took place. When we add to this monumental accomplishment Newton's work in such areas as optics, chemistry, and applied mathematics, the enormous weight of his contribution to scientific knowledge begins to come into perspective.

Newton's influence was felt not only in the physical sciences. The long struggle against Aristotelian natural philosophy with its categories of Forms and Ideas, which had dominated Western thought since the time of Aquinas, was put decisively to rest with the triumph of a mathematical analysis of reality as originally advocated by Plato and finally confirmed in the work of Newton. Yet this culmination of the rejection of Aristotelianism, as seen in Newton, was not a simple return to Platonism. Instead, we find in Newton the culmination of a movement that aimed to develop a mechanistic view of the natural world compatible with mathematical analysis and description. This mechanistic worldview provided for the dominance of Newtonian thought up to the dawn of the twentieth century.

The key to the mechanistic worldview is actually a rather simple concept; namely, that all matter is passive. Aristotle's concept of nature as an organic, self-developing being is rejected in favor of a model that views nature as a machine in which no part changes size, shape, or direction or speed of motion unless it is acted on by some other part of nature according to entirely predictable and rational laws—for example, inertia and gravity. Eliminated from this view were any mysterious internal forces that governed change; external laws accounted for the entire governance of material bodies. And, ironically, when one considers the strong theistic faith of Newton and many other early mechanists, this new view of the world inevitably placed serious restrictions on what role a Creator might have in the ongoing governance of the physical world.

Isaac Newton, a lifelong member of the Anglican church, was a committed theist with an active interest in theology and biblical studies. In fact, as Newton admits in a letter to the Reverend Richard Bentley, even his scientific *Treatise of the System of the World* was written with "an eye upon such principles as might work with considering men, for the belief of a Deity."[33] More than a passing interest, Newton's faith and the time he devoted to religious studies and writings have long been a curiosity to modern thinkers who, in the words of Richard Popkin, have explained Newton's religious views as "personal aberrations, infantile views, or premature signs of senility."[34] It is now beginning to be recognized, however, that Newton's religious views were integral to his overall view of reality, both physical and spiritual. That Newton, though always in good standing with the Anglican church, harbored anti-trinitarian and even Arian views,[35] is not of great significance to us here. What is significant is that Newton believed strongly in a Creator God who is active in human history, and how he correlates this belief with his mechanistic view of the physical world.

That Newton's theistic theology is also to some extent shaped by his scientific views and concerns is to be seen in his description of God and God's relationship to the physical world found at the end of his *Principia Mathematica* where he describes a God who is compatible with his mechanistic view of the world. Especially prominent in Newton's description of God is a Being who is utterly nonmaterial and transcends the physical world, a Being who cannot be acted upon by material bodies, yet who governs the whole of the material world as well as the course of human history. God, Newton writes, governs all things:

> not as the soul of the world, but as Lord over all. . . . He is Eternal and Infinite, Omnipotent and Omniscient; that is, his duration reaches from Eternity to Eternity; his presence from Infinity to Infinity; he governs all things, and knows all things that are or can be done. He is not Eternity or Infinity, but Eternal and Infinite; he is not Duration or space, but he endures and is present. He endures for ever, and is every where present; and by existing always and every where, he constitutes Duration and Space. Since every particle of Space is *always,* and every indivisible moment of Duration is *every where,* certainly the Maker and Lord of all things cannot be *never* and *no where.* . . . God is the same God, always and every where. He is omnipresent, not *virtually* only, but also *substantially;* for virtue cannot subsist without substance. In him are all things contained and moved; yet neither affects the other: God suffers nothing from the motion of bodies; bodies find no resistance from the omnipresence of God. . . . God exists necessarily; and by the same necessity he exists *always* and *every where* . . . but in a manner not at all human, in a manner not at all corporeal, in a

manner utterly unknown to us. . . . We know him only by his most wise and excellent contrivances of things, and final causes. We reverence and adore him on account of his dominion . . . [for] a God without dominion, providence, and final causes, is nothing else but Fate and Nature. . . . Thus much concerning God . . . does certainly belong to Natural Philosophy.[36]

Although one can see clearly the mind of Newton the physicist behind this careful description of God and God's relationship to the physical world—especially in Newton's care to distinguish the eternal Creator not only from the creation but also from eternity itself—one detects little trace of Deism in Newton. There is nothing remote or impersonal about the God in whom Newton believed. Yet the charge of Deism is often leveled against Newton because many of his successors, inspired by his mechanistic worldview, embraced such a concept of God during much of the eighteenth and early nineteenth centuries. The Deists believed that if the universe indeed functioned as a perfectly predictable machine, there was really no need to invoke the activity of God in the world except in the original creation. There developed, then, a "belief" in God that often never went beyond the recognition that some supernatural Being must have originally "wound up" the machinery of the world at the beginning of time. Although certainly unintended by Newton, this Deistic view of God became closely associated with Newtonian mechanism and in many ways continues to make its influence felt in the interplay between theology and physics in our own day.

Darwin and the "War" between Science and Religion

In a simple review of the development of modern physics, one might be able to jump from the work of Newton to the developments of the first half of the twentieth century without a great loss of continuity. Because we wish to trace the mutual development of theology and physics, however, such a transition is not possible. In order to understand something of the current relationship between theology and natural science, one must understand the developments of the nineteenth century.

Whatever one's opinion of the general state of the relationship between religion and science in the Western world in the middle of the nineteenth century, it is generally agreed that this relationship deteriorated significantly as a result of a revolutionary advance in the field of biology. Charles Darwin (1809–1882) changed our understanding of the natural world with his 1859 publication of the *Origin of Species*. The basic components of Darwin's theory are well known and need no review here. What is of interest to us is the impact, both perceived and real, of Darwinism on the theology of the day and on theology's relationship to the natural science of its day.

Contrary to popular perception, conservative theologians the world over did not immediately rise up in opposition to Darwin's theory of biological evolution. In fact, as David Livingstone thoroughly documents in his 1987 book, *Darwin's Forgotten Defenders,* many leading conservative theologians, including such notables as B. B. Warfield, William G. T. Shedd, A. H. Strong, A. A. Hodge, and James Orr, not only accepted but defended the essential points of Darwin's theory.[37] In fact, the landmark 1910 publication of *The Fundamentals,* widely cited as the beginning of the modern fundamentalist movement in the United States, are surprisingly free of polemics against the theory of biological evolution.

One of the few articles dealing with the question of evolution in *The Fundamentals* conceded not only that many elements of the theory of evolution were probably correct, but also that even if the Darwinian theory proved in all parts correct, it would not weaken the argument from design—in fact, quite the opposite. Professor George Frederick Wright, in his contribution to *The Fundamentals,* wrote that "by no stretch of legitimate reasoning can Darwinism be made to exclude design. Indeed, if it should be proved that species have developed from others of a lower order, as varieties are supposed to have done, it would strengthen rather than weaken the standard argument from design."[38] In the same series, in an article entitled "Science and the Christian Faith," the well-known Scottish theologian James Orr stated unequivocally that, "while it must be conceded that evolution is not yet proved, there seems a growing appreciation of the strength of evidence for the fact of some form of evolutionary origin of species—that is, of some genetic connection of higher with lower forms."[39] Orr even suggests revisions to the way evolution is understood in relation to humanity, which, he claims, would cause "most of the difficulties which beset the Darwinian theory to fall away."[40]

But what then of Bishop Wilberforce and "scientific creationism," of William Jennings Bryan and the Scopes trial? For reasons that are, to say the least, complex, a split developed in the Christian community over the theory of evolution in which those opposing the new theory eventually gained a vocal, if not actual, majority. The victory of the anti-Darwinians was probably the result of two basic factors, one having to do with the theological situation of the day, the other with the scientific.

For nineteenth-century theologians the doctrine of creation occupied a central place within the pervasive natural theology of the day. Because of this central place of creation and a corresponding Christian apologetic that, stemming largely from William Paley,[41] seemed to be especially dependent on arguments from design, any reinterpretation or change in the theology and symbolism of the doctrine of creation threatened to bring down the entire edifice of nineteenth-century orthodox theology. Charles Hodge, the most prominent theological opponent of Darwinism in America, concluded his 1874 book *What Is Darwinism?* with the assertion that "the denial of design in nature is virtually the denial of God."[42] In part by forcing such a connection between Darwinism and the question of God's existence, opponents of biological evolution, speaking to an audience already inclined toward a literal interpretation of the Bible, persuaded large segments of the Christian community that belief in Darwinian evolution and belief in God as Creator were incompatible.

The theological opponents of Darwinism had, however, much help from certain segments of the scientific community in forcing a choice between belief in Darwin's scientific theory and belief in a Creator God. Since the time of Newton many scientists had been Deists or nominal theists largely because options such as atheism lacked intellectual credibility and support. Darwin's theory presented an opportunity for many such scientists to begin to develop a theory of the origin of the earth and life, including the role and meaning of humanity, apart from any reference to a deity. A sort of Darwinism developed whose basic outlook was as much religious and philosophical as it was scientific. This, of course, presented a clear and visible threat to Christianity and made it difficult for Christian supporters of Darwin to separate his scientific theory from the philosophical Darwinism that was gaining ground rapidly in intellectual circles.

T. H. Huxley, an early and vocal supporter of Darwin, was one of the first to recognize the philosophical and theological implications of the Darwinian theory. It was Huxley, in fact, who coined the term *agnosticism* to describe the intellectual position that was neither theistic nor atheistic, which he was advocating based on his understanding of the implications of Darwin's theory of evolution. Huxley, who engaged various representatives of established religion such as Bishop Wilberforce in frequent and contentious debate, led many scientists away from a "Christian" Darwinism toward a purely scientific variety and readily replaced revelation with science as the only reliable source of truth. Huxley's position, as unsettling as it was to traditional churchmen, gained such wide influence that, "by 1900 the public stance of scientists in the English-speaking world have overwhelmingly come to resemble the views of Huxley."[43] Given Huxley's connections with Darwin, a defense of Darwinism by Christian theologians became all the more difficult. The cordial relations that had existed between science and theology from the time of the Baconian compromise seemed to be coming to an end.

The debate over Darwin influenced such writers as John William Draper (*History of the Conflict between Religion and Science,* 1875) and Andrew Dickson White (*A History of the Warfare of Science with Theology in Christendom,* 1896), who portrayed the entire history of scientific development as a war against a bigoted and narrow-minded establishment Christianity (Draper almost exclusively singles out the Roman Catholic Church) that feared science and was being engulfed by its advance. Draper, warning of an intensified conflict between science and religion, concludes his book with the admonition that "faith must render an account of herself to Reason. Mysteries must give place to facts. Religion must relinquish that . . . domineering position which she has so long maintained against Science. . . . The ecclesiastic must learn to keep himself within the domain he has chosen, and cease to tyrannize over the [natural] philosopher, who, conscious of his own strength and the purity of his motives, will bear such interference no longer." [44]

Even White, whose views were somewhat more moderate than those of Draper, painted the various conflicts between theology and science, both real and imagined, as one-sided affairs in which an aggressive and overbearing ecclesiastical structure continually seeks to suppress a pure and truth-seeking science and its unassuming practitioners. [45] Despite the sometimes poor documentation and obvious prejudice of the Draper-White thesis, as well as its eventual rejection by most respected historians of religion and science, it contained (unfortunately) a sufficient measure of truth to sustain its influence and to color the views of many in both the scientific and the religious communities. Its influence continues to this day.

THE RISE OF MODERN PHYSICS: FROM EINSTEIN TO THE BIG BANG

Albert Einstein: Relativity and the End of Newtonian Physics
Albert Einstein (1879–1955) is recognized as the greatest scientific mind of our century. Although his contributions to scientific theory are many, he is chiefly remembered for his pioneering theories of special and general relativity. Einstein's paper "Zur Elektrodynamik bewegter Körper," which appeared in September 1905 in the *Annalen der Physik,* was the most important of several papers appearing in 1905 in which the essential components of his theory of special relativity were expounded. [46] Essentially, Einstein's theory had the effect of demonstrating that physical laws are the same for all freely moving observers, regardless of their velocity. Thus, just as Newton had earlier laid to rest the idea of absolute position in space (though not the idea of absolute space itself), Einstein had now shown that there is not only no absolute space, but also no absolute time, because all of the laws of science are the same for (or relative to) each observer and it is possible for two separate observers to experience time in the same manner, relative to their own positions, yet differently in relation to each other. The most famous example of this

apparent paradox is the hypothetical "twins paradox" in which one twin lives his life at sea level, and the other on a mountaintop farther from the center of the earth's rotational spin and consequently moving at a faster speed relative to his sea-level twin. The twin on the mountaintop, because of the decreasing frequency of light waves the farther one is from the earth's center, would appear to age slightly slower than the twin at sea level. Thus each observer's personal measure of time is relative to his or her own position—and movement. Einstein's proposal that light travels at a constant speed, regardless of the motion of its source, and his demonstration that mass and energy are equivalent ($E = mc^2$), derived from papers in 1905 and 1907, have changed forever our understanding of the universe.

Einstein's remarkable contribution to our understanding of the universe was taken a decisive step further when, after eight years of thinking about gravitation, he published a series of papers (the most important being that of 25 November 1915) introducing his theory of general relativity, which predicted that even light should be subject to gravitational attraction.[47] The perihelion procession of the planet Mercury, already known to astronomers, was a first confirmation of Einstein's theory. The data gathered by a team of British scientists, led by Arthur Eddington and Frank Dyson, of the 29 May 1919 eclipse confirmed for most scientists the validity of Einstein's theory. The stir that Einstein was causing in the scientific world was mirrored, significantly, among philosophers and theologians.

The Irish playwright George Bernard Shaw, in his 1934 play *Too True to Be Good: A Political Extravaganza* gave expression to the broad impact of Einstein's theories when he wrote:

The universe of Isaac Newton, which has been an impregnable citadel of modern civilization for three hundred years, has crumbled like the walls of Jericho before the criticism of Einstein. Newton's universe was the stronghold of rational determinism: the stars in their orbits obeyed immutably fixed laws; and when we turned from surveying their vastness to study the infinite littleness of the atoms, there too we found the electrons in their orbits obeying the same universal laws. Every moment of time dictated and determined the following moment, and was itself dictated and determined by the moment that came before it. Everything was calculable: everything happened because it must: the commandments were erased from the tables of the law; and in their place came the cosmic algebra: the equations of the mathematicians. Here was my faith: here I found my dogma of infallibility. . . . And now—now—what is left of it? The orbit of the electron obeys no law: it chooses one path and rejects another: it is as capricious as the planet Mercury, who wanders from his road to warm his hands at the sun. All is caprice: the calculable world has become incalculable.[48]

Despite the fact that the unpredictability that Shaw's character is lamenting stems perhaps more from Werner Heisenberg than Einstein—or that precisely because of Einstein Mercury need no longer seem capricious—Shaw illustrates the potential of Einstein's ideas to disturb long-established worldviews. Even in Shaw's apparent misunderstanding of Einstein we gain an important insight into the philosophical and theological debate that he spurred. What Einstein was thought to have said, or what his theories, imperfectly understood, were thought to have implied, has often been more significant than strict scientific reality. Hans Reichenbach has rightly pointed out that "what has been called the philosophy of relativity represents, to a great extent, the fruit of misunderstandings of the theory rather than of its physical content."[49]

Einstein himself, in a postwar visit to England in 1921, was asked by the Archbishop of Canterbury what the implications of relativity theory were for theology. Einstein is reported to have replied, "None. Relativity is a purely scientific matter and has nothing to do with religion."[50] It was clear, however, that Einstein's theories were making a significant impact in the fields of philosophy and theology.

In the field of traditional philosophy, perhaps the most immediate impact of relativity theory was a strengthening—if not a revival—of the sort of idealism advanced by George Berkeley. For the idealist, reality and mentality are inseparable. Apart from thought, knowledge, or some form of mental cognition, no reality could exist. For Berkeley and other subjective idealists, only ideas, and not physical objects, are real. To say that a tree is real is to say no more than that our idea of a tree is real. Without someone having the idea of a specific tree, that tree would have no existence. Only by bringing an omnipresent, omniscient God into the picture was Berkeley able to elevate such phenomena to the status of reality. Such thinking had lost ground quickly in a world ever more influenced by a scientific realism that recognized the reality of matter in its own right, apart from mentality. Idealism received help from unexpected quarters, however, with the publication of Einstein's special theory of relativity. By demonstrating that space-time is not absolute but is relative to the individual observer, Einstein gave new life to an idealism that had long held that physical reality within space and time was only real insofar as it existed as an idea in the mind of an observer. Yet such an interpretation of relativity theory is essentially based on a misunderstanding that confused relativity with subjectivity.

While the belief that relativity theory lent scientific support to idealism may well have been misplaced, the legitimate, philosophical impact of Einstein's theories on our understandings of space-time and epistemology can hardly be doubted. In regard to time, relativity has made it impossible to think in terms of absolute time and, subsequently, in terms of simultaneous or sequential events as we did before. Whereas statements involving the simultaneous or sequential relationship of events were once considered demonstrably true or false, these are now seen as being definitions whose character is necessarily arbitrary.[51] As for epistemology, Reichenbach affirms the significance of the implications of relativity theory when he writes: "This discovery of a physicist has radical consequences for the theory of knowledge. It compels us to revise certain traditional conceptions that have played an important part in the history of philosophy, and it offers solutions for certain questions which are as old as the history of philosophy and which could not be answered earlier."[52]

Planck and Heisenberg: Quantum Theory and the Uncertainty Principle
The revolutionary impact of Einstein's theories of special and general relativity can hardly be underestimated in the role that they played in bringing to an end the Newtonian, mechanistic worldview. Yet there was another development in the first decades of the twentieth century whose contribution to the decline of Newtonian mechanism—and perhaps eventually to general relativity as well—has implications that surpass those of relativity theory not only for physics but also for philosophy and theology. We are speaking of quantum mechanics and the uncertainty principle that is derived from it. Paul Davies is not guilty of exaggeration when he says that "the theory contains some astonishing insights into the nature of the mind and the reality of the external world, and full account must be taken of the quantum revolution in the search for an understanding of God and existence."[53]

The Marquis de Laplace, the French scientist famous for allegedly telling Napoleon, when he inquired about the place of God in Laplace's theories, that he had "no need of that hypothesis,"[54] was a strict determinist. He felt that Newton's laws enabled us to predict every future event in the universe—provided we could determine with precision the complete state of the universe at any one time. Laplace believed that similar, yet-to-be-discovered laws determined other things in the universe, including human behavior. Needless to say, such scientific determinism was strongly resisted by theologians, who saw it as an infringement on God's freedom to act in the world. Yet scientific determinism remained "the standard assumption of science" up to our own century.[55] Einstein's relativity theories did nothing to undermine such determinism and its challenge to theistic views of the world. Rather, they simply refined our ability to predict future events in the universe, provided the state of the universe could be accurately known at any given time.

Scientific determinism's fate was signaled when the German physicist Max

Planck (1858–1947), as a result of his explanation of the laws of black body radiation, suggested in 1900 that waves from such sources were released in packets that he called quanta. The details of Planck's theory of quanta solved the mystery of heat emission by demonstrating that a body could lose energy only in finite, extremely small amounts (quanta), and was thus widely accepted as valid. It was not, however, until 1926 and the work of another German physicist, Werner Heisenberg (1901–1976), that the implications of quantum theory for determinism were realized. Heisenberg, using Planck's quantum theory to determine the feasibility of measuring the velocity and position of a given particle, found that the light quantum needed to measure the particle interfered with it in unpredictable ways so that the more accurately one attempted to measure a particle's velocity, the less accurately it was possible to measure its position, and vice versa. According to Hawking, "Heisenberg's uncertainty principle is a fundamental, inescapable property of the world, . . . [that] signaled an end to Laplace's dream of a theory of science, a model of the universe that would be completely deterministic."[56]

Heisenberg, along with Erwin Schrödinger and Paul Dirac, developed the theory known as quantum mechanics based on the uncertainty principle. Their theory predicted no specific observable events, but rather a number or range of possible results along with formulae for predicting statistically the chances of obtaining each possible result in any given instance. Despite Einstein's significant contributions to quantum theory, however, he remained unwaveringly opposed to the element of chance that it imposed.[57] In fact, it was this opposition to the element of chance included within what he referred to as "statistical quantum theory" that led Einstein, on several occasions, to make his oft-quoted remark, "Gott würfelt nicht" (God does not play dice).[58] Despite Einstein's opposition, however, the uncertainty principle had become an accepted, albeit diversely understood, fact of scientific life by midcentury.

The "Big Bang" and Theistic Creationism

In addition to Einstein's relativity theory and the uncertainty principle of quantum mechanics, only one other development of the twentieth century has had as much impact on modern physics or as many implications for philosophical and theological thought, namely the Big Bang theory of the origin of the universe. The history of the development of this seminal theory, unlike relativity theory and quantum mechanics, is not traced through the notebooks of theoretical physicists so much as through the observations of astronomers.

The American astronomer Edwin Hubble, after demonstrating conclusively in 1924 that our galaxy was not the only one in the universe, turned his attention to cataloging and calculating the speeds of the other galaxies. Previously it had been believed that all stars were stationary. But analysis of the light from stars showed that their light spectra were not even, but shifted toward one end of the spectrum or the other (either red or blue). Based on the Doppler effect and what it taught us about the effect of movement on the emission of waves, this shift indicated that the distant galaxies were moving. Most scientists expected that any movement of these distant galaxies was probably random. Given such expectations, Hubble's results were nothing less than a bombshell. When he published his famous 1929 report, he documented two remarkable facts: First, it appeared that every galaxy's light was red-shifted (meaning that they were all moving away from us); and second, the speed at which a galaxy was moving away from us was directly proportional to its distance from us.

Hubble's observations established that our universe is expanding, putting an end to the cherished scientific belief in a static universe.[59] In retrospect, Hubble's discovery seems so obvious that many have wondered why Newton himself had not deduced an expanding universe from his understanding of gravity, because without expansion the collective gravitational attraction of all matter in the universe would cause it to collapse.[60] Hubble's discovery raised an additional question, still awaiting a definitive answer: Is the universe expanding rapidly enough, in relation to its total mass, to prevent gravitation from slowing and eventually halting its expansion and causing an apocalyptic collapse?

The belief in a static universe was not the only cherished tenet that Hubble's discovery was to challenge. The belief that the universe was infinite, without beginning or end in space-time, was another scientific "given" at the time of Hubble's discovery. An expanding universe, however, seemed to lead to the inescapable conclusion of a beginning—which is precisely what Alexander Friedmann had predicted based on his understanding of relativity theory. The 1965 discovery by Arno Penzias and Robert Wilson of the uniform background radiation produced evidence of the very intense heat of the early universe and helped to confirm the view that an initial cosmic explosion (or Big Bang) brought our universe into existence. Today, therefore, it is generally accepted as a scientific reality that we live in a nonstatic, finite universe.[61] While many physicists, at least initially, seemed uncomfortable with such results, not a few theologians found in the emerging view of a nonstatic universe with a seemingly definite beginning a greater compatibility with the idea of a Creator God who providentially governs the world than the older, static model of the universe allowed.

CURRENT ATTITUDES AND RELATIONSHIP BETWEEN SCIENCE AND THEOLOGY

The tremendous changes that have taken place within the natural sciences, especially physics, as well as the corresponding upheavals in theology in the twentieth century, certainly complicate the analysis of the current relationship between the two disciplines. While the history of the relationship between theology and natural science is indispensable for an understanding of present attitudes, one must not forget that the science and the theology of today often bear little resemblance, either in outlook or content, to their respective predecessors of previous centuries. For the most part, the contents of past conflicts between theology and science—from Galileo to Darwin—are no longer disputed. Theologians concede as readily as their scientific counterparts that the earth rotates around the sun, and most now believe evolutionary theory to be an essentially correct explanation of the development of life on our planet. Scientists, while having to eat less crow in the last four centuries than theologians, have also been forced to abandon some cherished misconceptions. The nineteenth-century confidence in finding ultimate theories as well as the near-sacred illusion that scientists are unbiased seekers after truth who approach their studies without presuppositions or biased methodologies are seldom encountered today among leading scientists.

If the content at the heart of past conflicts between theology and science has largely fallen by the way, the residue they have left continues to cloud the relationship between the two disciplines. Theologians harbor a lingering suspicion that scientists view their methodologies as infallible and are overly resistant to allowing their findings to be called into question—even by other scientists. As for physicists themselves, theologians have paid scant attention to the implications of their work until recently. Also, the emerging position of theoretical physics as the unofficial "queen of the sciences" can only be viewed enviously by theologians, whose own discipline officially held that place of honor throughout the Middle Ages and up to the period of the Enlightenment. By contrast, theology finds itself today in a precarious situation in the secular universities, its inclusion resting on little more than tradition and its practitioners pressed to demonstrate in what sense theology can be considered a science at all.[62]

The scientific community seems to exhibit an inability (some would say a reluctance) to either forgive or forget the role that theology and the institutional church played in such notorious episodes as the Galileo affair or the Darwinian controversy. Many scientists have long predicted the demise of theology, as well as of religion in general, and seem somewhat bewildered by the role it continues to play in shaping the beliefs and ethical standards of society. The physicist Paul Davies confidently explains:

> . . . relevant to the decline of religion is the fact that science, through technology, has altered our lives so radically that the traditional religions may appear to lack the immediacy necessary to provide any real assistance in coping with contemporary personal or social problems. If the Church is largely ignored today it is not because science has finally won its age-old battle with religion, but because it has so radically reoriented our society that the biblical perspective of the world now seems largely irrelevant.[63]

Davies's short comment reveals a host of beliefs and attitudes that seem to persist among contemporary scientists. We see, as mentioned above, the belief that religion has already met its demise, or is at least tottering on the precipice. We note also the assumption that science has been at war with religion since before anything similar to modern science even existed. Such imagery of the ever-victorious battle against religion can also be seen when the sociobiologist E. O. Wilson writes, "Scientific materialism . . . presents the human mind with an alternative mythology that until now has always, point for point in zones of conflict, defeated traditional religion."[64] Perhaps even more troubling for theologians is the view that religion—and therefore theology—is irrelevant. Needless to say, to the extent that these attitudes continue to exist, genuine dialogue between scientists and theologians is difficult to achieve. Nonetheless, changing attitudes in both camps in recent years have led to an encouraging number of conversations between theologians and scientists.

Among theologians there are two essential attitudes regarding dialogue with the natural sciences. The most popular, largely by default, is the view that theology and the natural sciences are speaking about two completely different kinds of subject matter with very different methodologies and have little, if anything, to say to one another. Representatives of this view make virtually no attempt to undertake a genuine dialogue with modern science or to understand its implications for theology—and neither do they expect science to take heed of theological concerns.

Most notable among twentieth-century theologians who have taken such an approach to natural science is Karl Barth, who believed that theology and science operate in "two fundamentally distinct spheres," by which he means "heaven and earth," or the realms of the transcendent and the empirical. What this means for Barth in practice is that "exact science can furnish no means of an approach to an ontology of the cosmos," and "dogmatics has no business to broaden out into cosmology."[65] For Barth, theology "is fundamentally free in regard to all world-pictures, that is, to all attempts to regard what exists by the measure and with the means of the dominant science of the time."[66] It is therefore not surprising that Barth devotes more than two hundred pages to the nature and doctrine of time within the context of his treatment of the doctrine of creation without making reference to either Einstein or relativity theory.[67] Neither should it surprise us that in the entirety of Barth's *Church Dogmatics,* "there are references to Shakespeare, but none to Schrödinger; references to Hölderlin, but not to Heisenberg; references to Bach, but not to Bohr."[68]

More recently Langdon Gilkey has advocated a similar dichotomy between the realms of theology and science. The verdict of the scientific community following the Darwinian controversy has, in Gilkey's opinion, "effectively removed religious truth from the area of matters of fact" in such a radical sense that from this time on "no serious theologian . . . has claimed that . . . he could establish anything relevant to the data or conclusions of scientific inquiry." That is to say, theology must now be understood "to possess no legitimate ground to interfere with either scientific inquiry or scientific conclusions," because "theological truth no longer contains the sort of knowledge which entails particular factual propositions." The only legitimate aspects of theological language, in Gilkey's view, are "its transcending aspects pointing to ultimacy and sacrality." Theology, then, speaks rightly of symbol and myth, and science of facts, because the language of theology is "symbolic" and not "directly applicable to reality 'out there.'"[69]

The physicist Werner Heisenberg expressed his dissatisfaction with such an epistemological dichotomy when, commenting on the views of Max Planck, he wrote: "Planck considers science and religion compatible because, in his view, they refer to quite distinct facets of reality. . . . This view . . . associates the two realms with the objective and the subjective aspects of the world respectively. But I must confess that I myself do not feel altogether happy about this separation. I doubt whether human societies can live with so sharp a distinction between knowledge and faith."[70]

A second approach to dialogue between theology and natural science finds itself on the other end of the continuum from Barth. The proponents of this view believe that both science and theology are relevant for the other and must learn from each other. Theologians in this camp not only make it their business to familiarize themselves with what their colleagues in the natural and social sciences are saying, but they also insist that a scientific worldview is incomplete without the contributions of theology and that scientists must also, therefore, listen to theologians.

Wolfhart Pannenberg, whose dialogue with the natural sciences is considered a major contribution to modern theology, explains that although scientists could hardly be expected to seek the help of theologians in explaining the physical world, there is now a widespread awareness that science alone is not sufficient in order to cope with the consequences and side effects of scientific discoveries, especially in their technological application. Frightened first by the development of nuclear weapons and later on by the threat of ecological disaster and by the dangers involved in modern biochemical techniques, a sense of responsibility for the application of their work has led many scientists to look for moral resources that could be mustered in order to prevent or at least reduce the extent of fatal abuse of the possibilities provided by scientific discoveries. At this point, then, the churches are appreciated once more as moral agencies that should help the human society in responsibly dealing with the potential of science and technology.[71]

Pannenberg, going beyond a mere role for theology in the ethical questions raised by modern science, contends that without reference to God as Creator a complete understanding of the physical world is not possible. He writes: "If the God of the Bible is creator of the universe, then it is not possible to understand fully or even appropriately the processes of nature without any reference to that God. If, on the contrary, nature can be appropriately understood without reference to the God of the Bible, then that God cannot be the creator of the universe, and consequently he could not be truly God and could not be trusted as a source of moral teaching either." Therefore the abstract knowledge of physical processes gained through natural science should not "claim full and exclusive competence regarding the explanation of nature and, if it does so, the reality of God is thereby denied by implication."[72]

The approach to dialogue assumed by the present study is rooted firmly in this second major attitude toward dialogue with the natural sciences. We proceed based on the knowledge that developments in the natural sciences, including physics and cosmology, have had and will continue to have a decisive impact on the manner in which theologians are able to discuss God in the modern world. At a juncture in which more and more physicists are recognizing and attempting to deal with the metaphysical implications of their work, theology is called to the task of analyzing the theological impact of the changing world of modern physics. The failure of theology to take up this challenge would not only imply an unwillingness to listen to what our dialogue partners in the field of physics are saying, it would also indicate an abdication of the responsibility to participate in the development of a doctrine of God that is intelligible within the context of our modern, scientific world.

Chapter Two

Does God Exist?

Fools say in their hearts, "There is no God."
—Psalm 14:1

If it is fools who say in their heart, There is no God, those who try to prove his existence seem to me to be even more foolish.
—Johann Georg Hamann

If the universe is really self-contained, having no boundary or edge, it would have neither beginning nor end: it would simply be. What place, then, for a creator?
—Stephen Hawking

If one bases a proof of God's existence . . . on current physics, one runs the risk of having the proof falsified by later scientific developments. . . . If this happens the suspicion will grow that not only is the proof false, but also the conclusion is false: the proof fails not merely because the premises are false; it also fails because there is in fact no God.
—Frank Tipler

TRADITIONAL ARGUMENTS FOR THE EXISTENCE OF GOD: FROM ARISTOTLE TO THE PRESENT

Ontological, Cosmological and Design Arguments
The so-called God postulate—that is, the assertion that there is a supreme, supernatural Creator of the world—is as old as the records of human civilization and thought. In fact, the almost universal affirmation of belief in a Supreme Being found among all cultures up until recent times has itself been used as an argument or proof of God's existence. Ironically, it was within precisely such a context of presumed "universal belief" that the attempt to logically prove the existence of God originated. Already in the fourth century B.C.E. Aristotle, in his *Metaphysics*, put forth the essential form of what has

come to be known as the cosmological argument. Aristotle, looking at the world around him, observed that "there is something which always moves that which is moved, and the 'prime mover' is itself unmoved."[1] Not only did Aristotle originate the idea of an "unmoved mover," he also introduced the concept of a "first cause" in what may be the most concise statement of the cosmological argument: "It is obvious that there is some first principle, and that the causes of things are not infinitely many either in a direct sequence or in kind."[2]

Modern thinkers usually recognize five different categories of argument for the existence of God.[3] We will concern ourselves here only with the first three of these, the so-called traditional arguments for the existence of God, because they not only have the richest tradition in philosophical and theological thought but are also the arguments that, in one form or another, have been revived through recent developments in physics and cosmology.

First put forward by Saint Anselm, the eleventh- and twelfth-century archbishop of Canterbury in his now-famous *Proslogion,* the *ontological argument* contends that God exists necessarily. Anselm begins by presupposing the existence of God because his proof is intended for the "believer" seeking to understand what he or she already believes. Anselm defines God as "something-than-which-nothing-greater-can-be-thought," or in other words, as the most perfect being.[4] If things that exist in reality are greater or superior to things that do not exist in reality, then God must exist in reality if God is truly that than which nothing greater can be conceived. For Anselm, therefore, the existence of God is not only possible but necessary. As Anselm confesses, "You exist so truly, Lord my God, that You cannot be thought not to exist."[5] Although Anselm's ontological argument still attracts interest and has been taken up in more recent times by René Descartes as well as by Gottfried Wilhelm von Leibniz,[6] its inherent circularity has kept if from gaining wide support. Kant concluded his discussion of the argument with the cutting assessment that it "neither satisfies the healthy common sense of humanity, nor sustains the scientific examination of the philosopher."[7]

Originally put forward by Aristotle and expanded by Thomas Aquinas sixteen centuries later, the *cosmological argument* is built on our observations of the natural world. It is observed that everything in the world, whether matter or movement, is part of an unending series of contingency and causation. Nothing is caused or moved by its own self but by a preceding cause or mover. The various forms of the cosmological argument assert that there must be a "first cause" or an "unmoved mover" at the beginning of this chain of contingency and that this is God.[8] Modern expressions of the argument, going as far back as Aquinas, tend to focus on the idea of a "first principle" underlying the contingency of all matter rather than on a simple temporal succession of causes that seeks to establish a beginning of the universe in time.

The third traditional argument for the existence of God is the *teleological argument,* or the argument from design, and is essentially the fifth of Aquinas's five ways to prove the existence of God. The basic form of the argument can be seen already in the Hebrew Psalter where the psalmist writes: "The heavens are telling the glory of God; and the firmament proclaims his handiwork" (Ps. 19:1). Similar to the cosmological argument, it is based on the natural, observable world. The teleological argument, however, made famous by the eighteenth-century theologian William Paley in his 1802 work, *Natural Theology,* argues not from the beginning of the world process, but from its presumed culmination in the present world order. Overlooking or minimizing the chaos so often seen in the world, the argument is that there is so much beauty, order, harmony, and precision in the natural world that it must have been designed by a higher being who continues to govern the world.

The Kantian Critique

The German philosopher Immanuel Kant leveled what many consider a devastating critique of the traditional arguments for the existence of God. Kant observes that there are only three possible modes of proving the existence of God based on the grounds of speculative reason. "The first is the *physicotheological* [teleological] argument, the second the *cosmological,* the third the *ontological.* More there are not and more there cannot be."[9] For Kant it is clear that the conception of a necessary being is an idea, the reality of which cannot be established simply by demonstrating that it is a need of reason. Kant criticizes philosophers for speaking of an *absolutely necessary* being without taking the trouble to explain how such a being is cogitable—or why it is impossible to cogitate the nonexistence of such a being. These same philosophers, Kant reminds us, have long supposed that every geometrical proposition—for example, that a triangle has three angles—is absolutely necessary. Such logic, according to Kant, is hopelessly circular. It is true that a triangle necessarily has three angles (as well as three sides), and that these three angles must necessarily equal 180 degrees—but only on the condition that a triangle exists. The problem is that an *a priori* conception of a thing (for example, a triangle) is formed and its content made to embrace existence. If as an *a priori* conception it is truly necessary, then its denial would leave an inescapable contradiction. When the idea of God is annihilated in our conception, however, the internal properties of the idea, such as God's omnipotence or goodness, disappear along with the subject—thus leaving no contradiction and showing itself, as an *a priori* idea, to be unnecessary.[10]

As for Anselm's assumption that a thing which exists in reality is greater than that which exists only as a conception, Kant employs his famous example of a hundred thalers. Kant points out that a hundred real thalers contain no more than a hundred possible (or imagined) thalers. Yet in reckoning one's wealth it is clear that only the real thalers have value. The conception of imaginary thalers does not affect our real financial status in the least because the real thalers are not analytically contained in our conception but merely form a synthetic addition to our conception. Likewise, the statement "God exists," or the contrary statement "God does not exist," does not augment in the least the object of our conception.[11] Therefore our conception of God, even if we make it into a logical necessity, is neither a proof of God's existence, nor does it have any effect on God's existence or lack thereof in reality.

Although more appealing to common sense, Kant does not find it any more useful to reverse the process and argue in a supposed *a posteriori* manner from the realm of phenomenal experience to the existence of a Supreme Being in the realm of transcendence. The cosmological argument makes three basic assumptions about the physical world. First, everything in the physical world is contingent. Second, everything that is contingent must have a cause. And third, an infinite ascending series of causes in the world of sense experience is impossible. From these assumptions it is clear that a "first cause," which we may choose to call God, necessarily exists. Kant's criticism is that the assumptions themselves have not been critically examined. The first assumption is entirely valid and verifiable. Beginning with the second assumption, however, we have a problem. The principle that everything that is contingent must have a cause, as Kant observes, is "without significance, except in the sensuous world."[12] It is invalid, then, for such a principle to be "employed to help us beyond the limits" of the phenomenal sphere into that of the transcendent. As for the assumption that an eternal ascending series of causes is impossible, not only does this assumption have no meaning outside of the phenomenal world, but even within our world it is a conclusion that is not justified by the principles of reason. The assumptions, then, that everything contingent must have a cause—even in the realm of the transcendent—and that an eternal series of causes is impossible become in reality *a priori* presuppositions. Hence the cosmological argument's pretense of *a posteriori* reasoning is only that. It does not escape the essential weakness of the ontological argument.

If the ontological and cosmological proofs of the existence of a Supreme Being have failed, the only other possible alternative for such a proof would be that which is based "upon a determinate experience of the phenomena of the present world, their constitution and disposition."[13] This proof, termed by Kant the physico-theological argument, is what is usually known as the teleological argument. Although Kant recognizes this argument as worthy of respect because it is "the oldest, the clearest, and that most in conformity with the common reason of humanity," he maintains that it is "insufficient of itself to prove the existence of a Supreme Being, that it must entrust this to the ontological argument—to which it serves merely as an introduction." The teleological argument rests on the analogy with human art. A painting is evidence of an artist, a house is evidence of a carpenter, and a watch is evidence of a watchmaker. Such arguments, however, say nothing about the origin of the raw materials involved, that is, of their substance, but explain instead only their form. This argument can at most, therefore, in the words of Kant, "demonstrate the existence of an *architect of the world,* whose efforts are limited by the capabilities of the material with which he works, but not of a *creator of the world,* to whom all things are subject."

In order to prove the contingency of matter itself, and not just its form, the proponent of the teleological argument must turn to the cosmological argument, which is "merely the ontological argument in disguise." Thus Kant concludes: "The physico-theological is based upon the cosmological, and this upon the ontological proof of the existence of a Supreme Being; and as besides these three there is no other path open to speculative reason, the ontological proof, on the ground of pure conceptions of reason, is the only possible one, if any proof of a proposition so far transcending the empirical exercise of the understanding is possible at all."[14]

Current Status of the Arguments

Among theologians the impact of Kant's criticisms has been unmistakable. With few exceptions the traditional proofs of God's existence have become little more than footnotes in the history of theology. The Anglican priest and physicist John Polkinghorne has argued that the so-called proofs are useful today only as "pointers to the divine as the only totally adequate ground of intelligibility" because they "are not proofs but insights."[15] Significantly, no major theologian of our century has attempted to prove logically the existence of God after the manner of the three traditional arguments.[16] The German pietist Johann Georg Hamann, a contemporary of Kant, seems to have summarized the emerging view of the proofs of God's existence when he wrote in a 1786 letter, "For if it is fools who say in their heart, There is no God, those who try to prove his existence seem to me to be even more foolish."[17] Similarly, we think of Søren Kierkegaard's assessment a century later: "If God does not exist it would be impossible to prove it; and if he does exist it would be folly to attempt it."[18]

It is thus all the more surprising that the traditional arguments have witnessed a revival of sorts in recent years—not from theologians, but from physicists. An assortment of modern physicists, albeit for the most part inadvertently, have revived the logic of the traditional arguments for the existence of God, if not sometimes the arguments themselves. Moreover, the employment of such argumentation reveals significant discrepancies between the God being discussed by physicists and the God of most contemporary theologians.

THE DESIGN ARGUMENT AND CONTEMPORARY PHYSICS

The Design Argument among Physicists (Whittaker, Müller-Markus, Dyson)
Considering the reliance of the design or teleological argument on the observable data of our physical world, it is not surprising that it would attract the attention of scientists interested in demonstrating the probability (or at least possibility) of God's existence. The French biophysicist Pierre Lecomte du Noüy saw the process of evolution, an "epic of which Man is the crowning event," as "the logical basis of our belief in God."[19] Lecomte, looking at the world from his perspective as a scientist, maintained that "our entire organized, living universe becomes incomprehensible without the hypothesis of God." The unexplained tendency toward order in the development of the physical universe that the physicist Sir Arthur Eddington called "anti-chance," Lecomte preferred to give the name "God." For Lecomte, the fact that God could not be physically observed was no "proof of non-existence," considering that physicists who specialize in the study of electrons, protons, and neutrons do not doubt the existence of these particles even though they are unable to "visualize" them.[20]

Among physicists themselves the teleological argument has also found supporters. Sir Edmund Whittaker, for instance, made use of the argument in his 1946 Donnellan Lectures titled "Space and Spirit: Theories of the Universe and the Arguments for the Existence of God." Whittaker recognized the inherent weaknesses of the traditional form of the argument, noting that it did not "distinguish between a transcendent and an immanent mind, between theism and pantheism." He maintained, nevertheless, that modern cosmology makes possible a new form of the argument that is less vulnerable to this criticism because it "discloses an intramundane God, and then, by a second step . . . elevates Him to a supramundane status."[21]

Whittaker builds his argument on the modern scientific recognition that there is "order, system, adjustment, fitness in the nature of things and in their relations to other things." Indeed, Whittaker maintained that we are in a much better position than Aquinas to build an argument from design precisely because "our knowledge is vastly greater than it was in the thirteenth century, for we have attained the concept of a mathematical structure embracing the entire universe." This increased knowledge allows us to confirm that "the world is a system for which predictions can be made, a cosmos, not a chaos." The fact that the laws of mathematics are valid over the cosmos, showing that everything is interrelated and consistent, "leads to the inference that there is only a *single* mind involved in the whole creation," which fact excludes, on a scientific basis, polytheism. Hence according to Whittaker, "the proof from Order is to-day more complete, more comprehensive, and more majestic than in the form in which it was presented in the thirteenth century."[22]

Whittaker also feels that the argument can today be taken beyond Aquinas inasmuch as it can be demonstrated that God is transcendent and distinct from the world. Because we know, according to Whittaker, that "there must have been a Creation" and that there "must come a time when for physical reasons life will be impossible," then it would be "incredible to suppose that God is bound and conditioned by a world which has appointed times of birth and death." Whittaker concludes, therefore, that if we have "arrived at the conviction that God exists, modern cosmology points to the further conclusion that He must be, in one aspect at least, extramundane."[23] Yet these basic assumptions of a creation and a definite end to life in the universe would seem much more difficult to make today than when Whittaker wrote. Stephen Hawking's no-boundary-condition universe, for example, or Freeman Dyson's optimistic view of the possibility of intelligent life in an open universe demonstrate that these questions are today much more open than they appeared to be a generation ago.

The German physicist Siegfried Müller-Markus, in his 1960 book *Wen Sterne rufen,* sees unmistakable evidence of the "footprints of God" in the physical order of the world. "The world as a whole is the work of divine reason. Its order is the mirror of God's thoughts, its energy, the fire of billions of suns, is merely an image of *God's* creative power, and its architecture reveals the omnipotence of the Creator in the smallest particles as well as in the spiral of the Milky Way."[24] Müller-Markus concludes his remarks with the observation: "Nearly all the great physicists of the world reject materialism and many believe in God. . . . It is as if one cannot but help seeing the footprints of God with one's own eyes in the wonders of the universe and trembling under the breath of God's Spirit."[25] Müller-Markus, however, does not intend his design argument as a definitive proof but, in light of the Kantian critique, limits its force to uncovering "hints of the existence of God."[26] He concludes, therefore, that "the most that a rational theology can accomplish is a *hint* at the probable existence of God. A logical proof is not possible."[27]

More recently, the physicist Freeman Dyson has defended the use of a qualified "metascience" design argument leading to the existence of a sort of universal mind. Perhaps due in part to the fact that Dyson was addressing a committee of the U.S. Conference of Catholic Bishops, he suggests that one may even call this universal mind "God." Dyson proposes that "we allow the argument from design the same status as the anthropic principle, expelled from science but tolerated in metascience." With this qualification Dyson writes that he considers "the argument from design valid" when formulated in the following way:

> The universe shows evidence of the operations of mind on three levels. The first level is the level of elementary physical processes in quantum mechanics. An electron in quantum mechanics is an active agent, constantly making choices between alternative possibilities according to probabilistic laws. Every quantum experiment forces nature to make choices. It appears that mind, as manifested by the capacity to make choices, is to some extent inherent in every electron. The second level at which we detect the operations of mind is the level of direct human experience. Our brains appear to be devices for the amplification of the mental component of the quantum choices made by molecules inside our heads. . . . Now comes the argument from design. There is evidence from particular features of the laws of nature that the universe as a whole is hospitable to the growth of mind. The argument here is merely an extension of the anthropic principle up to a universal scale. Therefore, it is reasonable to believe in the existence of a third level of mind, a mental component of the universe. If we believe in this mental component and call it God, then we can say that we are small pieces of God's mental apparatus.[28]

According to Dyson the teleological argument, formulated in this way, makes it reasonable to believe in the existence of what he calls "a third level of mind" as mental component of the universe. He adds that if we "believe in this mental component and call it God, then we can say that we are small pieces of God's mental apparatus"—a description reminiscent of Newton's conception of space as the *sensorium* of God.

The scientists and physicists mentioned above have all made use of teleological arguments to argue for the reasonableness of belief in a creator or a higher being. The more complex and uncoincidental our universe appears to be, the more weight so-called arguments from design carry—even within the scientific community. Although by nature incapable of proving the existence of a creator, they can make belief in such a creator seem more reasonable. From a purely scientific perspective, the discovery of more randomness and less order in the universe would appear to counter such arguments. To these problems we now turn our attention.

The Problems of Disorder and Randomness

For proponents of the teleological or design arguments for the existence of a Supreme Being, evidence of disorder and randomness has always constituted a direct assault against the force of the argument. The order/disorder enigma has long posed a problem for natural theology. On the one hand, as Müller-Markus observes: "Every physicist and astronomer is overwhelmed by the mathematical order in the world. The greatest minds like Newton, Kepler, Planck and Einstein felt that by virtue of it they must believe in a supernatural intelligence." Yet on the other hand, "there is also a fundamental disorder in the world: There is probability in the elementary process of particles, there is the thermodynamic disorder in the concept of entropy," and, moving from the field of physics to that of human behavior, he adds, "there is [also] the chaos of unregulated relationships between living beings which are in continual warfare."[29]

Disorder, being somewhat difficult to define, has never constituted an insurmountable problem for natural theology. Natural catastrophes, human deformities, and other common examples raise the question of what constitutes disorder. Is it not possible, proponents of order would argue, that hurricanes, volcanic eruptions, and other such disasters are simply part of a large-scale order of the world that we only imperfectly understand? After all, it has only been in recent years that the largely beneficial function of fires for forest ecosystems has been fully understood. As for human deformities, it has never been easy to draw the distinction between what is truly an example of disorder within the human family and what is simply different from the norm. But even conceding that there appear to be inexplicable examples of disorder in the world, teleological arguments for the reasonableness of belief in a creator hold their appeal when weighed against the almost inconceivable order that is everywhere visible.

John Polkinghorne, former professor of mathematical physics at Cambridge, even finds evidence of design within indications of disorder and chance. Speaking of the "fruitful interrelation of randomness and orderliness" and the role of chance within such interrelation, Polkinghorne argues (contra Jacques Monod) that "the potentiality thereby exhibited as being inherent in the properties of matter—a potentiality which is explored through the shuffling operations of chance—is so remarkable as to constitute an insight of design present in the structure of the world."[30]

American physicist Charles Misner's advocacy of a "chaotic cosmology" in which the universe is believed to have begun at a random and therefore chaotic state, if true, would also seem to present difficulties for the idea of design.[31] As can be seen elsewhere in Misner's writings, however, this is far from the conclusion that he draws in regard to design.[32] Rather than an argument against design, the fact of a chaotic initial singularity would appear to indicate an even greater teleological tendency toward order that is necessary for the "dissipative processes" to have brought our universe to its present smooth state. Misner's view would also seem to correspond to the image of primordial chaos that can be seen in the "without form and void" condition of the world in Genesis 1:2 (cf. Ps. 24:1, 2). That process theology should find affinity with the idea of a "chaotic cosmology" is not surprising.[33] Seen from the perspective of traditional theology, however, a chaotic cosmology would not necessarily demand replacing a creation out of nothing with a creation out of chaos—it would merely suggest that the initial state of the universe, following an original *creatio ex nihilo*, would have been chaotic and in need of "design."

Of even greater significance than the problem of disorder is that of randomness, which does not necessarily imply disorder. This question was raised in earnest by the discovery of the uncertainty principle in quantum physics. Werner Heisenberg's 1926 formulation of the uncertainty principle has raised profound questions about the physical world in which we live. Since Laplace, classical physicists have tended to believe in a deterministic universe—that is, a universe in which, in theory, if the precise state of the universe could be known at any given time, then its state at any other time, past or future, could be calculated. Such a doctrine of scientific determinism was, quite naturally, opposed by those who believed it restricted too much God's freedom to intervene in the world.

Ironically, the uncertainty principle not only made room for "intervention," it also opened the way for potentially serious challenges not only to arguments from design but to the very notion of design itself. If the most elemental building blocks of our universe behave in an apparently random manner, then it becomes more difficult to credit the present order in the world to design—let alone build an argument from design on such data. Stephen Hawking has conceded, "If one likes, one could ascribe this randomness to the intervention of God, but it would be a very strange kind of intervention: there is no evidence that it is directed toward any purpose. Indeed, if it were, it would by definition not be random."[34] Polkinghorne indicates the implication of the uncertainty principle for the doctrine of God when he observes, "The old image of the divine Clockmaker presiding over a steadily ticking universe has been replaced by One responsible for a world at once more open to innovation in its process and more dangerously precarious in its possible outcome."[35]

Nevertheless, despite the uncertainty principle of quantum mechanics, our knowledge of the order of the large-scale universe has been increasing at such a rapid rate during the present century that proponents of teleological arguments have had little difficulty in finding evidence of design in the universe. Physicists, for instance, now know that the "fine-tuning" of the universe required precise initial conditions for a universe capable of sustaining life to develop. The so-called flatness problem, for instance, points out that our universe would have either recollapsed within a fraction of a second after the Big Bang or expanded so quickly that galaxy formation would have been impossible if the rate of initial expansion had varied more than perhaps one part in 10^{55} (or even as little as one part in 10^{60}) from the critical rate of expansion.[36]

Similarly, the smoothness problem involves the incredibly even dispersion of galaxies in our universe—to such an extent that our universe appears roughly the same in whatever direction we look. Since one could reasonably expect that the various regions coming out of the Big Bang would be causally uncoordinated (because light would not have had the time required to link them), a monstrous universe of black holes, turbulence, and a lack of organized galaxies should have resulted. The fact that our universe is quite different from such a scenario is considered a coincidence of incredible proportions. Even the electrical charge of the electron is so finely tuned, according to Hawking, that a slightly different charge would have meant that "stars either would have been unable to burn hydrogen and helium, or else they would not have exploded."[37] Just how finely tuned is our universe? The Oxford mathematician Roger Penrose has calculated that, "in order to produce a [low entropy] universe resembling the one in which we live, the Creator would have to aim for an absurdly tiny volume of the phase space of possible universes—about $1/(10^{10})^{123}$ of the entire volume" available.[38]

Such facts demonstrate why the design argument has continued to attract attention as well as why those not inclined to belief in God have been left with few satisfactory responses to it. With the coming of age of the anthropic principle, however, this situation has been radically altered.

The Anthropic Principle and Teleology (Barrow and Tipler)

The British astronomer and cosmologist John Barrow and the American physicist Frank Tipler produced a definitive summary of the current status of the anthropic principle in their 1986 book, *The Anthropic Cosmological Principle*. Barrow and Tipler date the appearance of the anthropic principle among modern scientists to a 1955 paper by G. Whitrow in the *British Journal for the Philosophy of Science*.[39] Whitrow, discussing the three-dimensionality of space, pointed out that mathematical physics, when formulated in terms of three dimensions, possesses certain properties prerequisite for the existence of rational observers. In other words, "only in three-dimensional spaces can the dimensionality of space be questioned."[40]

Such "common sense" observations led eventually to the formulation of what is known as the weak anthropic principle (WAP), which Barrow and Tipler explain as follows: "The observed values of all physical and cosmological quantities are not equally probable but they take on values restricted by the requirement that there exist sites where carbon-based life can evolve and by the requirement that the Universe be old enough for it to have already done so." To the question: Why is the universe the precise age that it now is? the WAP answers, Because it must be at least this age to allow enough time for the evolution of beings capable of asking such questions. For Barrow and Tipler the WAP is neither speculative nor controversial but is a given. "It expresses only the fact that those properties of the Universe we are able to discern are self-selected by the fact that they must be consistent with our own evolution and present existence."[41]

If the WAP constituted the extent of the anthropic principle, it would merit little attention in a discussion of teleology. There exist, however, several "strong" versions of the anthropic principle that introduce the element of necessity into the uncontroversial observations of the WAP. The strong anthropic principle (SAP) asserts that "the Universe must have those properties which allow life to develop within it at some stage in its history."[42]

Barrow and Tipler describe four major varieties of the strong anthropic principle:

(1) The view, which may or may not include the idea of a Creator, that "there exists one possible Universe 'designed' with the goal of generating and sustaining 'observers.'"[43] The British astrophysicist Fred Hoyle lends support to this view when he maintains that "the laws of nuclear physics have been deliberately designed with regard to the consequences they produce inside the stars" and that "apparently random quirks have become part of a deep-laid scheme."[44]

(2) The participatory anthropic principle (PAP), advocated by John Wheeler, affirms that "observers are necessary to bring the Universe into being," a view containing clear echoes of George Berkeley's radical idealism.[45]

(3) A third version, especially significant in light of current interest in the "many-worlds" interpretation of quantum mechanics, suggests that "an ensemble of other different universes is necessary for the existence of our universe."[46]

(4) Lastly, there is a "final" version of the anthropic principle (FAP), which holds that "intelligent information-processing must come into

existence in the Universe, and, once it comes into existence, it will never die out."[47] This is the version that Barrow and Tipler favor.

What all versions of the SAP have in common is their adoption of a teleological explanation of our universe. Carbon-based, information-processing observers, otherwise known as human beings, are either directly or indirectly responsible for the conditions of our present universe. The various forms of the SAP make use of many of the same arguments used in teleological proofs of God's existence. SAP proponents freely admit, and indeed depend on, evidence of design in the physical structure of the universe. The decisive difference is that God, in SAP arguments, is at best little more than an optional accessory and would probably prove ultimately counterproductive to the essentially anthropic orientation of any version of the SAP that attempted to make room for the existence of a Supreme Being.[48] Humanity, by contrast, is the undisputed teleological focal point of SAP arguments, thus making a decisive switch from theology to anthropology—and stealing much of the wind from the sails of proponents of traditional *theos*-oriented teleological arguments in the process.

The various versions of the SAP have encountered serious criticism from physicists on two major fronts. First, many physicists are uneasy with the uneconomic "many-worlds" theory that proponents of the SAP often seem to make an integral part of their cosmologies. Second, the SAP, as Hawking says, "runs against the tide of the whole history of science."[49] More a historical than a strictly scientific objection, there is a sense in which placing humanity at the center of a teleological explanation of our universe seems a return to a premodern worldview. As Hawking explains: "We have developed from the geocentric cosmologies of Ptolemy and his forebears . . . to the modern picture in which the earth is a medium-sized planet orbiting around an average star in the outer suburbs of an ordinary spiral galaxy, which is itself only one of about a million galaxies in the observable universe. Yet the strong anthropic principle would claim that this whole vast construction exists simply for our sake."[50]

The Possibility of Nontheistic Designers (Davies and Dawkins)

The strong anthropic principle, as we have seen, accounts for design in the universe by positing humanity, and not a Creator God, as the ultimate explanation for design. Yet humanity is not the only potential contender for the title Cosmic Designer. The teleological argument is limited by the fact, as Kant clearly saw, that it is at best able to argue for the existence of a cosmic architect of the world—but not for the existence of the Creator God of Christian faith. The physicist Paul Davies picks up acutely on this weakness when he argues that design in the universe might simply point to a "galactic architect." He writes:

> Those who invoke God as an explanation of cosmic organization usually have in mind a *supernatural* agency, acting on the world in defiance of natural laws. But it is perfectly possible for much, if not all of what we encounter in the universe to be the product of intelligent manipulation of a purely natural kind: within the laws of physics. For example, our galaxy could have been made by a powerful mind who rearranged the primeval gases using carefully placed gravitating bodies, controlled explosions and all the other paraphernalia of a space age astro-engineer.[51]

But could such a superintelligence be God? Davies argues that it could not, because "no being who is obliged to operate *within* the physical universe, employing only pre-existing laws, can be considered as a universal creator. . . . He would not be God if he could not actually create or destroy space and time." Such a natural God, or demiurge, would "not be omnipotent for he could not act outside the laws of nature," and "he would not be capable of creation out of nothing." It is clear that Davies does not actually believe that such an astro-designer exists. By demonstrating the possibility of a Platonic demiurge, however, he has shown that the existence of the Creator God of traditional theism is not the only possible conclusion to be drawn from the interpretation of the physical evidence supporting design.

The biologist Richard Dawkins, in his 1986 book *The Blind Watchmaker*,[52] turns the image once employed by Paley around and suggests, drawing on examples from the biological sciences, that the mechanisms of natural selection has a tremendous capacity for adaptation and adjustment. A certain degree of "fault tolerance" exists within living beings, and perhaps even within the structure of the universe itself, and is fully capable of producing the adaptation and adjustment that appear to us to be design. Thus, as John Houghton summarizes Dawkins's argument, "having found the mechanism, there is no need to invoke the existence of a designer; the mechanism of natural selection can be considered as the 'blind watchmaker.'"[53] The designer of the universe, then, becomes the physical universe itself. Roger Penrose seems to support a similar view when, explaining why he does not accept the SAP, he writes: "I cannot believe that the anthropic argument is the *real* reason (or the only reason) for the evolution of consciousness. There is enough evidence from other directions to convince me that consciousness *is* of powerful selective advantage, and I do not think that the anthropic argument is needed."[54]

If the design argument is able to withstand evidence of disorder and randomness in the universe, there is still no guarantee that the argument would lead inevitably to a Creator. A possible demiurge, as suggested by Davies, the universe itself (Dawkins), or one of several versions of the strong anthropic principle, as outlined by Barrow and Tipler, all take into account and accept, in principle, the evidence of design. That the "designer" of the universe must not necessarily be the Creator God of theism, however, neither constitutes a proof against the existence of such a Creator nor does it make design arguments irrelevant. It merely witnesses to the limitations of pure reason as an epistemological approach to God.

THE COSMOLOGICAL ARGUMENT AND CONTEMPORARY PHYSICS

The Cosmological Argument among Physicists (Whittaker and Misner)
The cosmological argument, like the teleological argument, has been of enduring interest within certain segments of the scientific community due to its presumed foundation on observable, physical data and its apparent openness to verification. Edmund Whittaker, writing shortly after the Second World War, believed that the cosmological argument had been strengthened by recent developments in physics and related fields. In regard to weaknesses in the traditional Thomistic second proof, Whittaker wrote: "Happily, the progress of science has made possible a restatement which not only restores the cogency of the general argument of the Second Proof, but may perhaps be regarded as strengthening it." Whittaker believed, and rightly so, that the proofs for the existence of God "are not merely metaphysical, but depend essentially on physics."[55] Thomas's second proof clearly depends on the existence of an indefinitely extended chain of causes and effects that cannot be reentrant—that is, circular—but must extend until some terminus is found, namely God. According to Whittaker, such an indefinitely extended chain cannot be demonstrated metaphysically, as Aquinas sought to do using an Aristotelian cosmology, but can only be demonstrated in light of modern physics.

Whittaker also contends that Aquinas's difficulty in demonstrating that the chain of causes and effects had its terminus in God and was not an infinite regress "now disappears automatically . . . since the chain cannot in any case be prolonged backwards beyond the Creation"—presumably a reference to the then new Big Bang theory. Thus we escape from "the order of the Newtonian cosmos, and, as in St. Thomas' original proof, the sequence of causes terminates in God."[56]

This reformulation of Aquinas's argument essentially represents the so-called *kalam*-type cosmological argument for a temporal first cause. Another significant version of the cosmological "proof" is the Leibnizian "sufficient reason" argument. Rather than arguing that the universe requires a first cause, the Leibniz-style argument focuses on the need of the universe for an explanation, that is, a sufficient reason for its existence. An example of the use of such an argument, albeit in a weak and not entirely coherent form, is found in the work of the American physicist Charles Misner.

Misner contends that it is "difficult to achieve an astrophysically comprehensive conception and explanation of a Big-Bang model," and this difficulty may suggest a certain need of creation as an explanation of its occurrence, thus making belief in a Creator reasonable.[57] Misner argues that "our Universe, . . . to the extent that it is currently intelligible, has a design that is distinct from its existence." The key thought is not that the universe has a design but that this design is distinct from its existence. This means that the universe does not contain the explanation of its own design or existence. Rather, it stands in need of a sufficient reason for its existence that lies outside itself. Misner illustrates how such a distinction between design and existence is possible with the example of a two-dimensional Minkowski space-time, which mathematicians can design but which eludes the ability of printers to illustrate outside of the context of a basic Euclidean two-dimensional space. Such an example, according to Misner, illustrates how it is possible for designs to be distinct from their existence.

The fact that the design of our universe exists, therefore, does not mean that our universe exists necessarily. It takes a special selection or creation by God to enact the design of our particular universe into reality. As Misner writes: "The entire spacetime fabric is . . . subject to God's creation, or the denial of it. . . . But it is not spacetime that is to be created, and then allowed to persist automatically, as one might think of a rock, it is the full spacetime fabric from beginning to end that needs to be saved from oblivion in a library of unused designs, and enacted into existence."[58] In arguing in this manner, Misner seems to be pitting the cosmological argument against the ontological argument in an either/or fashion. If the universe does not exist necessarily, then an original act of design (first cause) is required to explain its existence.

From considerations such as these Misner concludes that reinforcement is found "for the traditional teaching that God created the Universe." Misner finds that "physics does not even appear to be approaching an understanding of the Universe that would make its existence necessary." He concedes, however, that simply affirming that God created the universe explains neither God nor the universe. At this point he seems to back away from the standard conclusion of the Leibnizian argument. A belief in creation does, however, keep "our consciousness alive to mysteries of awesome majesty that we might otherwise ignore, and that deserve our respect." Misner concludes by suggesting that "the physicist, being asked, 'Why is the Universe built to follow certain physical laws, and not others?,' may well reply, 'God knows.'"[59]

Apart from Misner's mixing of design and cosmological argumentation, which in principle poses no problem other than a bit of incoherence in places, the main difficulty with his argument is his apparent invocation in several places of a God-of-the-gaps who is needed to explain, for example, why one formula may be chosen over another. He also seems to suggest that the fact that physics does not yet "appear to be approaching an understanding of the Universe that would make its existence necessary," is precisely the gap in scientific theory that allows us to speculate that a Creator God may provide such an explanation. To avoid the charge of invoking a God-of-the-gaps, Misner would need to build his argument on those things that are known about our universe rather than on those questions that remain scientifically open.

Quantum Mechanics and the Idea of Causation

Traditional cosmological arguments are based either on principles of causation or contingency. If traditional understandings of these principles are altered or called into question, there are inevitable consequences for the traditional forms of the cosmological argument. In the case of causation, as indicated earlier, the uncertainty principle of quantum mechanics has profound implications. In quantum theory particles are no longer seen as having distinct and well-defined positions and velocities that are observable. Rather, it is now known that they are in a quantum state that is interpreted in a statistical way with the result that position and velocity cannot be measured at the same time with unlimited precision. Simply put, this means that quantum mechanics does not predict the observation of any single definite result. Rather, quantum mechanics predicts a number of possible results and tells us statistically how likely each of these is.

Max Planck, one of the pioneers of quantum mechanics, explained the uncertainty principle's ramifications for traditional understandings of causality when he wrote that the concept of probability introduced into the interpretation of equations in quantum mechanics "seems to imply a surrender of the demands of strict causality in favor of a form of indeterminism. To-day, indeed, there are eminent physicists who under the compulsion of facts are inclined to sacrifice the principle of strict causality in the physical view of the world."[60] Planck himself, however, strongly preferred determinism (that is, strict causality) to indeterminism, stating that "so long as any choice remains, determinism is in all circumstances preferable to indeterminism, simply because a definite answer to a question is always preferable to an indefinite one."[61] Einstein's famous remark, "God does not play dice," was also made in resistance to the trend toward indeterminism resultant from the uncertainty principle of quantum mechanics. Later, realizing the essential validity of quantum physics, Einstein made the interesting suggestion, which is still worthy of attention, that causal factors not included within quantum theory exist, factors that are responsible for indeterminism.[62] In other words, indeterminism is causally determined!

Despite the qualms of Planck and Einstein, indeterminism seems to have won the day in the field of quantum mechanics, although the question has by no means been conclusively settled. As Polkinghorne points out, "the greatest paradox about quantum theory is that after more than fifty years of successful exploitation of its techniques its interpretation still remains a matter of dispute."[63] Nevertheless, Niels Bohr's principle of complementarity, "according to which it is not longer possible to admit the classical assumption that causal explanation is compatible with a spacetime description," has become the standard interpretation of quantum physics.[64]

If some form of indeterminism or noncausality continues to be the standard interpretation of quantum mechanics, then the first premise of the causal form of the cosmological argument (everything has a cause) would seem to be invalidated. If the behavior of individual electrons and other small particles is unpredictable, then the entire causal chain on which the cosmological argument rests appears to break down—despite its apparent validity within the large-scale world of classical physics. In a quantum physical world, therefore, the causal form of the cosmological argument for the existence of God is patently invalid. This in no way, however, addresses the question whether God actually exists. It simply implies that a conception of God as mere first cause is deficient and perhaps even inaccurate.

"Many-Worlds" Theory and Contingency (Barrow and Tipler)

A second form of the cosmological argument is based on the contingency of all matter. Already with David Hume's *Dialogues,* the idea of contingency, as used in cosmological arguments, was challenged as an illusion of our ignorance.[65] Until recent times Hume's objection to the argument from contingency has been relatively easily dismissed by defenders of the argument. With the advent of quantum mechanics and the possibility of "many worlds," however, proponents of the argument from contingency can no longer so easily dismiss objections to its major premise.

The so-called many-worlds interpretation (MWI), first proposed by Hugh Everett III in a 1957 summary of his Ph.D. thesis,[66] is considered an alternative to the standard Copenhagen interpretation in which "man, in his capacity as the observer of an experiment, is an essential and irreducible feature of physics."[67] The MWI is based on the "collapse of the wave-packet" in quantum theory. The problem is that this collapse "is an undetermined process, subject to probabilistic laws but not further explicable by anything in quantum theory."[68] The appearance of a particle at any particular point is essentially a chance occurrence; this has led many to the conclusion that an "ontological indeterminism" exists. In this context, Everett proposed that Erwin Schrödinger's equation of wave function is not, as it would seem, descriptive of an entirely deterministic universe, "but one in which a quantum-mechanical multiplicity (perhaps an infinity) of causal sequences 'split off' during a measurement or interaction."[69]

The many-worlds hypothesis has drawn much criticism for its violation of the principle of Occam's Razor, that is, the rule of thumb that whatever is nonessential to a theory, or to the explanation of a theory, should be trimmed away. The proposal of millions upon millions, and perhaps even an infinite number, of universes that are in principle unverifiable would seem an extravagance of immense proportions simply to explain the measurement of some subatomic, quantum phenomena. To counter this critique Barrow and Tipler propose a many-worlds interpretation in which "there is only one Universe, but small parts of it—measuring apparata—split into several pieces. They split—or more precisely, they undergo a drastic change—upon the act of measurement because they are designed to do so."[70] Thus, within our "single" universe many, or perhaps even all, possible worlds are realized as "measuring devices" continue to split.

This entire elaborate theory is an attempt to explain why quantum level activity cannot be measured or predicted with absolute accuracy. The Copenhagen interpretation suggests that the observer becomes inextricably a part of the measurement and produces the unpredictability. The version of the MWI proposed by Barrow and Tipler suggests that the object being measured is not affected by the observation but that the observer (or measuring device) splits into several possible "new worlds" with each observation. The possibility that the measuring apparatus (or observer) splits instead of the entire universe with each observation seems to have been suggested by Everret himself. When Einstein complained that he could not believe that "a mouse could bring about drastic changes in the Universe simply by looking at it," Everett replied, "It is not so much the system which is affected by the observation as the observer. . . . [Therefore,] the mouse does not affect the universe—only the mouse is affected."[71]

Before Everret, Alfred North Whitehead, the mathematical physicist turned philosopher, suggested that the problem of contingency could be solved if the universe realized all possibilities.[72] The result, if this were indeed the case, is that there would be no contingency in the large-scale universe.

Contingency-based cosmological arguments would then suffer the same fate as those based on causation.

Tipler is convinced that the many-worlds interpretation of quantum mechanics will replace the Copenhagen and hidden variable interpretations just as the Ptolemaic and the Tychonic systems were replaced by the Copernican.[73] Yet the many-worlds theory is far from being accepted as the standard interpretation of quantum mechanics. In fact, its scientific weaknesses are legion. Its main attraction seems to lie in the philosophical difficulties it eliminates for certain contemporary cosmologies and for most versions of the strong anthropic principle. As the physicist Richard Schlegel says, "The many-worlds hypothesis is rather outrageous; and yet within the structure of quantum theory it is logically impeccable."[74] Paul Davies puts it somewhat more bluntly when he writes that the many-worlds "interpretation of the quantum theory may be expensive in universes but it is extremely cheap in epistemology."[75]

The "No Boundary Condition" and the Cosmological Argument (Hawking)

The publication of Stephen Hawking's 1988 book *A Brief History of Time* has probably done as much to revive discussion of the cosmological argument as any recent work of theology or philosophy. The reason for this is twofold. First, Hawking suggests a radically new theory, based on a quantum theory of gravity, in which the universe is finite but without time or space boundaries, that is to say, without beginning or end. And second, Hawking boldly speculates as to the implications of his theory for the question of God.

Hawking first presented his suggestion of a "no boundary condition" of the universe at a 1981 conference at the Vatican. His basic contention was that time and space together form a surface that is finite in size but without boundary or edge. The implications of this proposal, however, "for the role of God in the creation of the universe were not generally recognized at the time."[76] The classical theory of gravity allows only a universe that has existed infinitely or one that began at a singularity. A quantum theory of gravity, however, by making use of Euclidean space-times, is able to put time and space on equal theoretical footing, hence allowing for the possibility "for space-time to be finite in extent and yet . . . have no singularities that form a boundary or edge."[77] Space-time, according to Hawking, can be compared to the earth, the surface of which is finite but has no boundary or edge off which one could fall. As Hawking further explains:

> The quantum theory of gravity has opened up a new possibility, in which there would be no boundary to space-time and so there would be no need to specify the behavior at the boundary. There would be no singularities at which the laws of science broke down and no edge of space-time at which

one would have to appeal to God or some new law to set the boundary conditions for space-time. One could say: "The boundary condition of the universe is that it has no boundary." The universe would be completely self-contained and not affected by anything outside itself. It would neither be created nor destroyed. It would just BE.[78]

If the universe has no boundaries and no initial singularity, it requires no first cause, essentially making the discussion over the cosmological argument a moot point. In case any have missed this seemingly obvious implication for the question of the existence of God, Hawking makes the point clear: "The idea that space and time may form a closed surface without boundary . . . has profound implications for the role of God in the affairs of the universe. . . . So long as the universe had a beginning, we could suppose it had a creator. But if the universe is really completely self-contained, having no boundary or edge, it would have neither beginning nor end: it would simply be. What place, then, for a creator?"[79]

As early as 1985 Hawking recognized that an edge to the universe would seem to beg the question of a Creator, if one truly sought a "complete theory" of the universe. When asked, therefore, why it was so important to him whether the universe had an edge, Hawking contended that "if there is an edge, somebody has to decide what should happen at the edge. You would really have to invoke God. . . . It would be a tautology. You could define God as the agent who was responsible for setting all this into motion. . . . If you want a complete theory, then we would have to know what happens at the edge. Otherwise we cannot solve the equations."[80] For Hawking, eliminating the edge (or beginning) of the universe eliminates at the same time the need for a God who fills the gaps of our knowledge because such a God would then be redundant. And, as Hawking implies in his 1988 book, a God who is not needed is a God who has no place.

The German philosopher of science Bernulf Kanitscheider sharpens Hawking's thesis when he claims that "a concept of creation is incompatible" with Hawking's model inasmuch as an original "creation can not occur in his model of quantum cosmology."[81] Similarly, the German physicist Johannes Knöppler has admitted rather bleakly that if the no-boundary condition is accepted by scientists as the best theory describing astrophysical observations, "then all talk about God as the creator of the world (in the sense of a *creatio originans*) can only take place in logical contradiction to prevailing scientific conviction."[82]

Hawking's proposal, however, does not necessarily imply the downfall of the cosmological argument and of rational belief in the existence of a Creator in the face of modern science. First of all, not all physicists and cosmologists are as optimistic about the possibilities of a no-boundary condition as

Hawking. The astrophysicist G. Börner reflected the feeling of many of Hawking's colleagues that his proposal is overly metaphysical and speculative when he commented that, "in regard to what may have happened before 10^{-20} seconds after the Big Bang, only the Dalai Lama, the Pope and Hawking know for certain."[83] Another, and for our purposes more important, point is that the suggested implications of a no-boundary condition for a Creator may be false. Thomas Becker, in his review of Hawking's *A Brief History of Time,* has insightfully commented:

> . . . even in a universe without a temporal beginning, the question of the existence of God has not simply become meaningless. On the contrary, it would appear that the question of God's existence has only become more urgent, now that the simple solutions, such as equating creation with the Big Bang, no longer work. The question as to why the universe exists at all and why it was created and constituted in precisely this way still cannot be answered by any theory of physics, no matter how grandly unified. There is also Stephen Hawking's admission that while he believes we have a good chance of discovering the laws which rule the entire universe, that still would not give us an answer to the question: Why does the universe exist?[84]

The British philosopher William L. Craig contends that Hawking does not, in fact, argue against the existence of God. To portray Hawking as if this is his intention is misleading. Craig argues that it is false to conclude that there is indeed no place for God in Hawking's system or even that God is absent. He concedes that Hawking "rejects God's role as Creator of the universe in the sense of an efficient cause producing an absolutely first temporal effect." Yet Craig believes that "Hawking appears to retain God's role as the Sufficient Reason for the existence of the universe, the final answer to the question, 'Why is there something rather than nothing?'"[85]

In maintaining this position Craig seems intent on taking statements of Hawking—such as, if we find the answer to the question why the universe exists, "it would be the ultimate triumph of human reason—for then we would know the mind of God"[86]—at face value, rather than as figures of speech.[87] His chief justification for doing this is a comment Hawking made in a letter to the editor of the *American Scientist* a few years before the appearance of *A Brief History of Time.* Hawking, in response to a reader who thought he seemed afraid to admit the existence of a Supreme Being, wrote: "I thought I had left the question of the existence of a Supreme Being completely open. . . . It would be perfectly consistent with all we know to say that there was a Being who was responsible for the laws of physics."[88]

Using an earlier statement, however, especially one from a letter to the editor, to form an interpretative basis of a later published work—especially in the case of someone like Hawking whose views on such matters seem to be continually evolving—is questionable. While one does indeed have the impression that Hawking is hesitant to close the door completely on the possibility of God, he must be interpreted on the basis of the direction and logic of what he actually said in *A Brief History,* which is the only place to date where he has attempted to interpret the metaphysical implications of his proposed "no boundary condition" universe.

On a more fruitful track, Craig suggests that Hawking's book should be read as "a discussion of two forms of the cosmological argument: the so-called *kalam* cosmological argument for a temporally [*sic*] First Cause of the universe, which he rejects, and the Leibnizian cosmological argument for a Sufficient Reason of the universe, which he prefers."[89] The claim that Hawking prefers a Leibniz-style sufficient-reason argument must be understood in light of Craig's interpretation of Hawking's use of God-language, as discussed above. What is significant, however, is that Craig has pointed out that Hawking is arguing against a specific form of the cosmological argument based on a temporal first cause, and thereby also against a specific understanding of God as Creator.

Indeed, it is creation more than the bare idea of a Supreme Being that is the key to Hawking's entire argument. If, as Hawking believes, his model leaves no place for a temporally understood first cause (that is to say, no creation), then his question, "What place, then, for a creator?" seems indeed to beg a negative response. Hawking overlooks the crucial fact, however, that the existence of God is not bound to a particular understanding of an original creation. That the existence of God can be maintained apart from an original creation can be seen already in Aquinas, who raised the cosmological argument to a new level yet admitted that we cannot prove demonstratively "that the world did not always exist. . . . The reason for this is that the newness of the world cannot be demonstrated from the world itself."[90] For Aquinas it was clear that rational belief in the existence of God was not contingent on our ability to demonstrate that the world had an absolute beginning in time.

In this regard, Craig rightly draws attention to the fact that Hawking's understanding of creation is theologically deficient inasmuch as it fails to distinguish between *creatio originans* (an original creation) and *creatio continuans* (continuing creation).[91] While Hawking seems to demonstrate that his model leaves no room for an original creation, he does not seem to recognize that a continuing creation "could involve a universe existing from everlasting to everlasting." Craig also notes that because "*creatio ex nihilo* does not, in Aquinas's view, entail a temporal beginning of the universe," neither *creatio continuans* nor *creatio ex nihilo* is incompatible with Hawking's proposed model. And where creation out of nothing and continuing creation remain meaningful concepts, the question, "What place, then, for a creator?" can be answered in the affirmative.

God in a Closed-Time, Hawking Universe: The Le Poidevin Critique

The British philosopher Robin Le Poidevin, taking a different approach than Craig, admits that "the conclusion of Hawking's argument is in direct contradiction with that of the cosmological argument," because "the possibility of a closed universe invalidates a crucial step in the cosmological argument."[92] Le Poidevin contends, however, that "Hawking's argument is itself invalid, ironically for the very same reason," and, throwing caution to the wind, adds that "the unexpected consequence is that the closed universe hypothesis is the basis of a new cosmological argument for creation."[93]

By way of critique of Hawking's "closed-time hypothesis," Le Poidevin points out that the view that time has a closed topological structure forces us to "revise our intuitions concerning the asymmetry of certain temporal relations." Specifically, this means that the relations of "earlier than" and "later than" are no longer usable in ordering events in closed time. And second, if we understand direction in time to simply be from earlier to later, "then closed time cannot have a direction," since earlier and later are symmetrical relations in closed time, meaning that any event A necessarily precedes and follows any event B.[94]

These considerations, however, do not automatically rule out a Hawking-type closed topological structure for time. As William Newton-Smith has pointed out, the fact that time has certain features simply as a matter of contingent fact and not necessity makes it invalid to rule out any model of time on *a priori* grounds. In fact, Newton-Smith argues that "time could have any one of a number of different topologies," and that it is even "possible to have evidence for the hypothesis of multiple time-streams."[95] Le Poidevin argues, somewhat unconvincingly, however, that because Hawking intends his model to apply to the actual world, "he does not want just to make the point that one can coherently posit a closed model for time. And the actual world, surely, is one where time has a direction. It is very hard to see how one could construct an *error theory* of our experience of time as having a direction, for it is an undisputed fact that we do not observe the immediate future, but we do observe, and have memories of, the immediate past."[96]

At this point, however, Le Poidevin seems to argue that the way things appear to us in our short-term experience of the world must correspond absolutely with the actual large-scale structure of space-time. Also problematic is that the supposed nondirectionality of time in a no-boundary-condition, closed-time universe is a deduction of Le Poidevin, not Hawking.

Hawking himself maintained the opposite in regard to the directionality of time in a no-boundary-condition universe. In fact, it was the proposal of a no-boundary condition that convinced Hawking that disorder would continue to increase in any contraction of the universe and that the thermodynamic and psychological arrows of time would not reverse.[97] Of course, even if they were to reverse, this is quite different from what Le Poidevin suggests in saying that Hawking's proposal leads to the unacceptable conclusion that the universe has no time directionality. Hawking, summarizing his view, writes: "I have shown that the psychological arrow [of time] is essentially the same as the thermodynamic arrow, so that the two would always point in the same direction. The no boundary proposal for the universe predicts the existence of a well-defined thermodynamic arrow of time because the universe must start off in a smooth and ordered state."[98]

If Le Poidevin fails, however, to invalidate the argument for a no-boundary, closed universe, he pursues another, more fruitful response to Hawking's proposal. Le Poidevin supposes, for the sake of argument, that Hawking's proposal accurately represents the cosmological space-time structure of our universe. In this case the crucial question is not, Does the cosmological argument still have any force? but, Is it still possible to posit a rational belief in a Creator over against such a view? One is led to infer from Hawking's own comments that the answer to this latter question would probably be no. It is in this regard that Hawking himself seems to make use of a cosmological (and perhaps even ontological) argument against the existence of God.

Traditional cosmological proofs are, as earlier noted, based on arguments either from causality or from contingency. A skeletal version of the traditional causality argument would run as follows:

a. Everything in our physical universe has a cause.
b. Nothing is its own cause.
c. An eternal series of causes is impossible.
d. Therefore there must be an uncaused first cause of all things.

Hawking's argument, on the contrary, would part company with the traditional argument with premise *c*. Hawking's argument against the existence of God might be stated as follows:

a. It is conceded that everything has a cause.
b. Nothing is its own cause.
c. In a closed universe without boundary conditions, an eternal series of causes is assumed.

d. If premise *c* proves to be an accurate picture of our universe, there is
no first cause that we might call God.

Such an argument, however, would appear weak in at least two points.
First, although premise *b* (nothing is its own cause) might seem unnecessary
in a Hawking-style argument (Hawking, in fact, does not mention it directly
in this context), it is a basic assumption not only of scholastic philosophy but
also of modern science. While it appears that premise *c* is Hawking's point of
departure from the traditional cosmological argument, a no-boundary condition applied to the topology of time would seem to indicate, as Le Poidevin
points out, that there is a sense in which things are indeed their own causes.[99]
Although in no way invalidating the proposal for a closed, no-boundary-
condition universe, it does raise certain explanatory problems and may require a complete rethinking of the principle of causation; within the scientific
community this may prove more difficult than dispensing with the role of
a Creator.

A second point, and this is perhaps most crucial, is that Hawking seems to
be arguing not only that in a closed, no-boundary-condition universe there
is no place for cosmological arguments, but also that there would be no place
for a Creator God. Here one finds echoes of the logic of the ontological
argument—namely, if God is not logically necessary for the explanation of
our universe, then there is no God. Simply because God does not seem to be
a necessary conclusion of a particular scientific cosmology does not mean,
however, if the cosmological model in question is correct, that God does not
exist. To prove this it would be necessary to demonstrate that a Creator could
not exist. To argue successfully to the contrary it would be necessary only to
demonstrate that a particular cosmological model does not necessarily exclude the possibility of a Creator.

In the case of Hawking's proposed model, Le Poidevin demonstrates that
the possibility of a Creator is not, in principle, excluded. While we cannot
go into the detail here of Le Poidevin's argument as well as his answers to
potential objections, he explains the possibility of a Creator using the model
of two circles, each with identical points. Both circles portray time in a
Hawking-type closed universe, the first without a Creator and the second
with a Creator.[100]

The first circle depicts what Le Poidevin terms "creation in a closed universe" so that any point *1* comes before and after any point *3*, and *4* comes
before and after *2*, making a temporal distinction between the points impossible. What we have in essence is a circular series of causes in which none
can be said to be the initial cause. In such a closed-time world it would seem

there is no place for a creation or a Creator. In the second circle, however, which is Le Poidevin's proposed variation of the Hawking model, we have the same cosmological model, only this time with an act of creation *C* depicted as lying outside the closed causal series—but not outside of time. A line connects *C* to a given point on the circle, for instance point *3*. There is nothing causally prior to *C*, yet the entire series is causally dependent on it. And *C*, in such a model, is not redundant because point *3* is not separately sufficient but is dependent on *C*. *C*, then, is not an intrusion into the series but the causal prerequisite for it.

Le Poidevin argues as follows that Hawking's model may even give rise to a new form of the cosmological argument for the existence of God:

> Since the closed universe is a finite series of causes, then . . . there must be a cause of that series. But . . . that cause cannot be a member of that series. Yet no cause lies outside that series, for the series contains all the causes that there are. In addition, there is no beginning to a closed causal series. So the simplest means of avoiding the traditional cosmological argument . . . still leads to the conclusion that there is a first cause of a universe that is causally closed.[101]

Unfortunately, as ironically pleasing as Le Poidevin's suggestion is, I find it unconvincing for several reasons. The chief reason is that a finite series of causes, as found in Hawking's closed-time universe, does not necessarily require a cause. If it did, it would mean that the universe does have a boundary condition. This would amount to a rejection of Hawking's model on unjustifiable, *a priori* grounds—and not in the creation of a new cosmological argument for the existence of God. Nevertheless, I believe that Le Poidevin has successfully made the case that Hawking's closed-universe hypothesis is compatible with the possibility of creation. There may indeed be other ways of demonstrating such compatibility of the idea of a Creator with the Hawking model universe. One such possibility suffices, however, to undermine the assumption that such a model, if correct, would disprove the existence of God.

Hawking is certainly correct when he states: "If the universe is completely self-contained, with no singularities or boundaries, and completely described by a unified theory, that has profound implications for the role of God as Creator."[102] We must point out, however, that a closed-time, no-boundary universe, if indeed our universe is such, cannot be presumed to leave no place for a Creator. The suggestion that it would, however, reveals much about the methodology and metaphysical presuppositions that necessarily lie behind such reasoning. In the end the use of cosmological and ontological argumentation to disprove the existence of a Creator God fails for precisely the same reason that the cosmological and ontological arguments are by nature unable to prove conclusively the existence of such a Being.

THE ONTOLOGICAL ARGUMENT AND CONTEMPORARY PHYSICS

The Ontological Argument among Physicists (Frank Tipler)
The ontological argument, having in principle the least connection to the physical universe of the traditional arguments for God's existence, is an unlikely candidate for utilization by physicists. It has, however, recently been employed by a leading physicist. To add to the irony, Frank Tipler, the physicist in question, is an avowed atheist. Tipler feels his credentials as an atheist add to the credibility of his ontological argument for the existence of God because they demonstrate that he is arguing from a theory based on "pure physics" and is not out to prove any presupposed notion of a divine being.[103] Tipler devotes a chapter to the ontological argument in his recent best-selling book, *The Physics of Immortality*.[104] The arguments contained here, however, were already found in their essential form in his decisive 1989 article, "The Omega Point as *Eschaton*." Tipler argues for an Omega Point theory, "which is a model for an omnipresent, omniscient, omnipotent, evolving, personal God who is both transcendent to spacetime and immanent in it, and who exists necessarily."[105]

Tipler argues from modern physics for the necessary existence of God despite his reservations about basing proofs of God's existence on science: "The trouble is, if one bases a proof of God's existence and an analysis of the divine nature on current physics, one runs the risk of having the proof falsified by later scientific developments. . . . If this happens the suspicion will grow that not only is the proof false, but also the conclusion is false: the proof fails not merely because the premises are false; it also fails because there is in fact no God."[106] Tipler nevertheless employs an ontological argument based on contemporary physics because he wishes to demonstrate that the God revealed by his "scientific" Omega Point theory is *the* God. As Tipler explains: "Elijah's challenge remains: Is this God of the Omega Point *the* God? It is generally felt that *the* God must be the uncreated creator of the physical universe, a being who not merely exists but who exists necessarily, in the strong logical sense of 'necessity'. . . . Furthermore, it is generally felt that only *the* God, the One who exists necessarily, is worthy of worship."[107]

Tipler's argument is based on his Omega Point theory. In brief, the Omega Point (a term he has borrowed from Pierre Teilhard de Chardin) is the point reached as the closed universe approaches final collapse and all things converge into one point that takes on the quality of personhood. Tipler names this point God. It might with some justification be suggested that Tipler is arguing for the necessary existence of the universe and not God. Yet because Tipler insists that his omega point is *the* personal, omniscient, and transcendent God, we shall treat his argument, at least provisionally, as an argument for the existence of God.

Tipler develops his ontological argument in the following way: "Suppose it were shown as a matter of physics that the Omega Point really exists. Then would it still be reasonable to assert the existence of a God over and above the Omega Point? Not if we could show that the Omega Point necessarily exists in the strong sense of logical necessity—that to deny its existence would be a logical contradiction." In this way he seeks to show that the Omega Point *is* God. But how does one prove the necessary existence of the Omega Point? First, Tipler needs to prove the necessary existence of the universe. Because the Omega Point is the necessary culmination of the physical universe within his theory, it is sufficient for him to prove that the universe exists necessarily. Thus he writes: "I think you can prove that the universe necessarily exists. The proof will be based on an analysis of what the word 'existence' means." [108]

Tipler's definition of existence is a mixture of Cartesian logic and anthropic principle assumptions. Tipler, explaining both what he understands by "existence" and why this leads to the conclusion that the universe exists necessarily, writes:

> Not all concepts exist physically. But some do. Which ones? The answer is provided by our . . . analysis of programs. The simulations which are sufficiently complex to contain observers—thinking, feeling beings—as subsimulations exist physically. And further, they exist physically by definition: for this is exactly what we mean by existence; namely, that thinking and feeling beings think and feel themselves to exist. . . . Thus the actual physical universe—the one in which we are now experiencing our own simulated thoughts and simulated feelings—exists necessarily, by definition of what is meant by existence. [109]

Based on this understanding of existence, which inherits the weaknesses and inherent circularity of both Descartes's "cogito ergo sum" and the strong anthropic principle, Tipler builds the following conclusion: "If it is logically possible for life to continue to exist forever in some universe, this universe will exist necessarily for all future time. In particular, if the Omega Point . . . is logically coherent, then the Omega Point exists necessarily."

One must finally ask, however, whether Tipler's use of the ontological argument, given his understanding of the deity, is, as we suggested earlier, simply an ontological argument for the necessary existence of the universe dressed in theological language. Consider for example the argument developed by Tipler and Barrow in *The Anthropic Cosmological Principle,* where they write:

> We are interested in the truly important implication of this notion of deity [as nontranscendent and pantheistic], which is that in the context of such a notion, the purpose of the ontological argument is to establish the existence of the Universe, or equivalently, the existence of something, as logically necessary. This is the caveat to the . . . refution of ontological [*sic*] argument which we wish to consider: granted that the existence of no single being is logically necessary, could it nevertheless be true that it would be a logical contradiction for the entire Universe, which is not *a* being, but all being considered as a whole, not to exist?[110]

This might also explain how Tipler, without noting any apparent inconsistency, can claim to be an avowed atheist while at the same time presenting an ontological argument for the existence of God. What we find in Tipler would seem to be a deification of the universe in which it is difficult to discern a distinction between Tipler's "God" and no God at all. Yet his specific use of ontological argumentation grounded on theories arising out of physics remains intriguing.

Accidental Ontology (Hawking)

Unlike the teleological and cosmological arguments, the physical sciences would seem to have no "natural" or direct interest in ontological argumentation. At two points, however, the ontological argument becomes potentially significant for contemporary physicists. First is the case in which, pursuing teleological or cosmological argumentation, a physicist attempts to conclusively demonstrate that God either exists or does not exist. In this event ontological argumentation is unavoidably engaged. The same result is arrived at, albeit more indirectly, when it is argued that because God is not necessary for the explanation of the universe, God therefore does not exist; that is to say, God is necessarily unnecessary. The second instance, which we will look at in the following section, is the possibility of arguing ontologically, not for the existence of God, but for the necessary existence of our particular universe.

  If William Craig is correct in his contention that Hawking accepts the force of the reasoning of "the Leibnizian cosmological argument for a Sufficient Reason of the universe" and is "inclined to accept it," then we would have in hand an example of the use of ontological argumentation.[111] This is so because the so-called argument from sufficient reason holds that the question why something exists rather than nothing can only be answered by postulating a metaphysically necessary being. Hence the boundary between a purely cosmological argument (if, indeed, such exists) and an ontological argument is clearly crossed. As we earlier pointed out, however, Craig's interpretation of Hawking on this point is questionable and further analysis along this line would not seem warranted.

If, however, we can take Hawking's language at face value when he suggests that a closed-time, no-boundary-condition universe leaves no place for a Creator, then he has indeed made use of an ontological argument of sorts but—in contrast to Craig's analysis—*against* the existence of God.[112] If Hawking had merely said that the role of a Creator must be redefined, or that his model does not need a Creator, there would be no use of ontological argumentation. The apparent suggestion, however, that a universe with no initial creation-singularity necessarily has no Creator God relies on the ontological assumption that since a Creator would seem redundant in such a universe, that Creator necessarily does not exist. Such argumentation might be called a weak, reverse ontological argument. It is reverse in the sense that it argues ontologically against rather than for the existence of a Creator God. And it can be considered weak in that it does not argue directly from the ontological necessity of no Supreme Being, but rather indirectly from the fact that such a Being would seem unnecessary—and only by implication necessarily unnecessary.

Willem Drees, without explicitly recognizing the ontological nature of such arguments, has pointed out that "no argument against God can be based upon completeness." That is to say, the simple fact that a scientific cosmology would seem complete in and of itself does not imply, as has often been claimed by "scientists and popularizers," that "the hypothesis 'God' is ruled out, or at least made superfluous."[113]

The Universe as Ontologically Necessary (Wheeler, Barrow, and Tipler)

If theologians can claim God exists necessarily and therefore contains the explanation of God's own existence, "why," asks physicist Paul Davies, "can't we use the same argument to explain the universe."[114] In other words, the universe itself becomes necessary being, containing within itself the explanation of its own existence. In fact, the theoretical physicist John Wheeler makes just such an ontological argument for the necessary existence of the universe. We find this argument in his theory of retroactive causation. In Wheeler's view the universe is necessary because intelligent life is necessary. Wheeler asks rhetorically: "Is the very mechanism for the universe to come into being meaningless or unworkable or both unless the universe is guaranteed to produce life, consciousness and observership somewhere and for some little of its history-to-be?"[115] Wheeler suggests that the mechanism that "causes" the universe to come into being is an anthropic guiding principle that culminates in an anthropic "Final Observer." This guiding principle enables the universe to come into being of its own accord. As Wheeler and C. M. Patton comment, "No guiding principle would seem more powerful than the requirement that it should provide the universe with a way to come into being."[116] Similarly, Wheeler asks:

> In what other way does an elementary quantum phenomenon become a phenomenon except through an elementary act of observer-participancy? To what other foundation then can the universe itself owe its existence except billions upon billions of such acts of registration [observation]? What other explanation is there than this for the central place of the quantum principle in the scheme of things, that it supplies the machinery by which the world comes into being?[117]

Barrow and Tipler suggest that an ontological argument for the necessary existence of the universe is a fairly straightforward conclusion. They believe that "if the speculations of some modern cosmologists are correct, there may be only one unique Universe that is logically possible, and the assumption of the Universe's existence is the only assumption we have to make."[118]

If our universe cannot, indeed, be conceived of as not existing, as many proponents of the strong anthropic principle argue, in that its being and the appearance of intelligent life are necessary, then we have in hand an ontological argument for the necessary existence of the universe. Such an argument, unlike the ontological argument for the existence of God, does not seek to establish that our universe does indeed exist—that is a given fact, which all but the most extreme idealists accept. The implication, rather, is that the universe not only exists, but that it *must* exist, its nonexistence involving an unacceptable scientific-logical contradiction. The question as to why our universe exists, as opposed to some other universe or no universe at all, could not, in such a case, lead to a cosmological-ontological sufficient-reason argument for the existence of God. The reason for our universe's existence would be contained within the very fact of its existence.

Theology, of course, could continue to posit the existence of a God who is the "sufficient reason" for God's own existence. God could not, however, be held to be the sufficient reason for the universe because the universe would be its own sufficient reason and this would produce a redundancy. If such cosmologies are correct, which remains to be seen, then theology would seem to be reduced to arguing for the existence of a God who is the sufficient reason for God's own existence alongside a universe that is also the sufficient reason for its own existence. This, of course, would amount to a dualism of such proportions as to require a radical redefinition of the traditional theistic concepts of creation and Creator and the relationship between the two.

The weakness of the ontological argument for the necessary existence of our particular universe is that it is subject to the same objection as the ontological argument for the necessary existence of God. The argument is based essentially on certain versions of the strong anthropic principle that hold that the appearance of intelligent life is inevitable and thereby necessary. This in turn implies that the existence of a suitable universe is also necessary, because the denial that such a universe must exist produces a contradiction when we consider the existence of intelligent life. A Kantian-style critique of such an argument might run as follows: If, for the sake of argument, we annihilate the idea of intelligent life from our thought (or theory), then a universe capable of supporting such life is not necessary and no contradiction would exist if there were indeed no such universe, since its apparent necessity disappears with the idea of intelligent life. Our universe, therefore, is not ontologically necessary as an *a priori* idea and contains no "sufficient reason" for its existence within itself.

Kant Revisited

As we have already seen, Immanuel Kant's critique of the traditional arguments for the existence of God essentially brought an end to the belief that logical proof of God's existence or nonexistence is possible. We have also seen, however, an apparent post-Kantian rebirth of the use of teleological, cosmological, and even ontological argumentation by some physicists and philosophers wishing to demonstrate either the existence or nonexistence of a Creator God. The crucial question, however, is whether modern physics and cosmology have in any way invalidated the Kantian critique of the traditional arguments. If not, discussions of the possible existence of a Creator God, whether by physicists, philosophers, or theologians, clearly must be limited to arguments of probability and avoid the appearance of conclusive proofs.

The Kantian critique can be summarized as resting on the following fundamental assumptions: First, there is nothing or no one, the denial of the existence of which/whom would constitute a logical contradiction (ontological argument). Second, because God is by definition transcendent, a series of causes (or a network of contingencies) cannot be shown conclusively to extend to such a Being (cosmological argument). Third, a "designed" universe could at best demonstrate the likely existence of an architect or designer, but not a Creator (teleological argument). Fourth, even if a cosmological or teleological argument were valid, it could not be argued that a Creator must indeed exist without reference to an ontological argument and the weaknesses that it entails.

Because these assumptions are philosophical in nature and in no way depend on a particular physical theory of cosmology, it would seem inconceivable that even the most radical developments in the physical sciences could invalidate them. This could be done only on philosophical grounds. The consensus among philosophers, however, seems to be that this has not been done, and so we must assume that the Kantian critique remains valid—even for physicists.

WHO IS THE GOD OF THE PHYSICISTS?

We have already seen, as in the case of Hawking, that physicists and theologians may understand something quite different when they speak of creation. It should come as no surprise, therefore, that physicists and theologians do not always understand the same thing when they refer to "God." To be sure, not all physicists have the same operational definition of God—as is also increasingly the case among theologians. In the context of the discussion about the existence of God by physicists, at least four different conceptions of God are to be noted.

The Deistic God

First is the assumption that if there is a God, this God's role would be limited to a possible *creatio originans,* or original act of creation. The possibility of such a God being involved with a continuing creation, implying an active and continuing sustenance of the physical world, does not usually merit serious consideration among physicists. There is more than a hint here of the God of Deism who, if existing at all, gave the universe its creative start and has since been conspicuous only by absence. Hawking expresses this view when, speaking of the laws of physics, he writes: "These laws may have originally been decreed by God, but it appears that he has since left the universe to evolve according to them and does not now intervene in it."[119] We would agree here with the physicist Steven Weinberg, who contends that if the word *God* is to retain any meaning at all—even for those who reject the idea of God's existence—"it should be taken to mean an interested God . . . who has established not only the laws of nature and the universe but also standards of good and evil, some personality that is concerned with our actions [and] . . . is appropriate for us to worship." Any other God becomes so "abstract and unengaged that He is hardly to be distinguished from the laws of nature."[120]

The God-of-the-Gaps

A second trend to be noted is the persistent assumption that the God being discussed is primarily, if not exclusively, a God-of-the-gaps. As early as Newton the tendency can be seen toward introducing the idea of God in order to fill the gaps in scientific theory. Newton believed that certain features of the physical processes of the universe could not be understood on the basis of scientific theory alone, and therefore constituted a sort of teleological argument for the existence of God. Newton's arguments, however, rested on the view that some aspect of our universe was, in principle, scientifically inexplicable and made sense only when a Creator-Sustainer God was introduced. As the gaps in scientific theory became increasingly smaller, the role of Newton's God-of-the-gaps diminished correspondingly. Indeed, the advance of scientific knowledge and the diminishing number and size of gaps in our knowledge of the universe that a God-of-the-gaps might be called on to fill or explain has become so pronounced in our time that physicist and Anglican priest John Polkinghorne has, with good justification, been moved to write an obituary: "The God of the Gaps is dead and with him has died the old-style natural theology of Paley. . . . No theologian need weep for them, for the God of the Gaps, hovering at the periphery of the known world, was far from being someone of whom it could be said that 'all understand that this is God.' He was . . . a sort of demiurge, a cause among the other competing causes of the world."[121]

Unfortunately, many physicists seem not to have taken note of the fact that theists, for the most part, have long abandoned the God-of-the-gaps. Perhaps it is too tempting to critique such a vulnerable God. Perhaps it is also a result of the fact that many physicists, eager to discuss the idea of God, simply are not sufficiently familiar with the conception of God within twentieth-century theology. Such a lingering view of God would seem to account for the idea that as science does away with the "need" for God, belief in God will also disappear. As Ted Peters has commented about the "theology" of Hawking: "The belief in God he is rejecting belongs in the 'God-of-the-gaps' category. He is rejecting the God affirmed by the kind of physico-theology that once sought to find a divine explanation wherever scientists failed to give us a natural explanation."[122]

The Pantheistic God

A third and more significant trend is the apparent assumption that if there is a God, then this God must exist within the confines of the physical universe, that is to say, must be nontranscendent. This view is becoming popular even among theologians. "If the Universe is by definition the totality of everything that exists," contend Barrow and Tipler, then "it is a logical impossibility for the entity 'God,' whatever He is, to be outside the Universe if in fact He exists. By definition, nothing which exists can be outside the Universe. This is a view-point which more and more twentieth-century theologians are coming to hold: they are beginning to adopt a notion of deity which insoyfar as questions of existence are concerned, is indistinguishable from pantheism."[123]

So-called pantheism undeniably holds a certain attraction today. Reacting to a period in which theologians emphasized God's transcendence, or God's wholly otherness to the exclusion of God's immanence, many theologians are understandably eager to show that God is not isolated from the world, existing "out there" somewhere far removed from our day-to-day problems and concerns. Yet rejecting God's otherness from the world carries the danger of no longer being able to distinguish clearly the world from God—or God from the world. This otherness from the world is precisely what distinguishes traditional theism from most forms of pantheism as well as panentheism. If God is reduced to a mystical synonym for the physical universe, one must question whether the word, from the point of view of traditional Christian theism, retains any meaningful content.

But is a pantheistic view of God, as Barrow and Tipler understand the term, unavoidable? If the universe is by definition everything that exists, and God also exists, then it would indeed seem reasonable to conclude that God cannot exist outside the universe. Whether such a syllogism leads inevitably to pantheism is questionable. It would seem, however, to exclude the possibility that God is other from the universe, that is, transcendent. From the perspective of theism, the assumption that God is a thing which/who must be counted with every other thing in the universe is unacceptable. Such a view of the relationship between God and the physical world precludes God's transcendence from the beginning. When the nontranscendence of God is presupposed, one should not marvel at the force of syllogistic reasoning that is able to arrive at the same conclusion with which it begins.

Although the view that God, if God indeed exists, must be nontranscendent seems to be the emerging dominant view of physicists and not a few theologians, it is by no means the only view being built on the collected data and theories of the physical sciences. Physicist and Anglican priest William Pollard seeks, for example, to refute "the scientific dogma of the unreality of the transcendent." Pollard demonstrates the importance of transcendence to Christian theology when he writes, "Viewed from within the prison of the modern scientific age, no transcendent domain of reality exists out of which the divine Word could come into space and time and be made flesh."[124] Pollard believes, however, that although the realm of the transcendent is by definition beyond the scope of natural science, there are hints within the natural sciences, and especially within physics, that such a reality exists. Specifically, Pollard cites the examples of the "miracle of the appropriateness of mathematics for the formulation of the laws of physics" and "the particular brand of transcendence represented by the waves in configuration space of quantum mechanics" as two examples from modern physics that bear testimony to "a reality which must ever lie beyond the means of physics to deal with," but yet "offer glimpses of a mystery which has had a potent fascination for man since time immemorial."[125]

Similarly, Arthur Peacocke provides another example of a close observer of the science-theology scene who reaches quite a different conclusion from that of Barrow and Tipler. Peacocke believes that the idea of God's transcendence is actually reinforced by "demonstration through physics and cosmology that vast tracts of matter-energy-space-time have existed, and probably will exist, without any human being to observe them—and this will be further compounded if it turns out to be the case that this 'present' observable universe is but one of a 'run' of possible universes."[126] Unfortunately, Peacocke does not explain precisely how this leads to a "sense of God's transcendence." It is almost certain that he does not wish to put forth the Berkelian, idealistic argument that because whole regions of the universe have existed and continue to exist "without any human being to observe them," they must therefore be observed by some transcendent Being. Perhaps he simply means to imply that the physical universe is very large and that humanity occupies a humblingly small place within it. How this might lead one to conclude that God must in some sense exist outside of or apart from the physical universe, however, is not clear. By whatever means Peacocke has reached his conclusion, however, it would seem to be a view not common among contemporary physicists and cosmologists.

The Limited Power God

A fourth and final conception of God to be found in the discussions of modern physicists is closely related to the idea that God, if God exists, is to be found only within the physical universe. If one accepts such a presupposition, then the laws that govern the universe are bound to place certain limitations on the nature and activity of such a God. In this regard the development of quantum physics has had and continues to have a profound impact on "definitions" of God. The American physicist Richard Schlegel summarized well the influence of quantum physics on the Christian doctrine of God in his 1979 article, "Quantum Physics and the Divine Postulate."

Schlegel believes that the change in method and epistemological assumptions that took place in physics in the change from classical to quantum physics is paralleled by, and has probably influenced, a similar change in theology.[127] He has here especially in mind definitions of God within process theology that identify God with the process of the physical universe.[128] Specifically, Schlegel believes that "if we accept the divine postulate the discoveries of this century in quantum physics surely must affect our conceptions of God. The independent, all-knowing deity of Christian orthodoxy is no longer within the possibilities allowed by the postulate. . . . [Instead, God] is limited in knowledge and power in accordance with the statistical, probabilistic properties that quantum theory finds for nature."[129] The implications for God's omnipotence might best be illustrated by a comparison with the dilemma posed by the old question: Can God create a rock so large that God cannot move it? Either way the question is answered would seem to limit God's power. This, of course, is a trick of logic that pits God against God (an impossible contradiction) and says little about God's actual power in relation, say, to rocks. The implications for God's omnipotence arising from recent theories of physics, however, might cause one to pose the question differently: Has God created rocks that God is not allowed to move? Or, Are there rocks whose location, mass, or velocity God cannot know—or can only know probabilistically?

In summary, we might say that the God being discussed more and more by physicists today is a God whose activity is limited to the original creation of the universe, and then often only to those aspects of creation that scientific theory cannot yet explain. This is a God who, in light of quantum physics, would appear to be neither omnipotent nor omniscient. This is also a God who is not wholly other from the universe but rather exists wholly within the physical universe, and therefore would seem, in principle at least, to be subject to empirical verification.

God: A Viable Hypothesis of Theoretical Physics?

If the natural sciences are not capable of either proving or disproving the existence of God, one might ask whether God is then completely irrelevant for physics. If the world indeed has a Creator, then one would think that it would be difficult to produce a comprehensive theory of the universe without reference to this Creator—unless of course the universe were *created* in such a manner that it were entirely comprehensible without reference to a Creator.

Even if this were the case, we might reasonably ask whether God could at least be introduced into natural science as a hypothesis. And if so, what function would such a hypothesis serve? Because God is by definition unavailable for experimentation, sense observation, or any other sort of objective verification, we must conclude that, in a strict scientific sense, God cannot be introduced as a hypothesis of physics. As the theologian J. F. Donceel correctly observes: "From a scientific hypothesis the scientist must be able to deduce certain consequences which can be experimentally verified. Nothing of the kind can be deduced from the existence of God. A scientific theory is a synthesis of many scientific laws and hypotheses. Hence it is evident that God, or an explanation of material phenomena through God, cannot be a scientific theory in the strict sense."[130]

Yet a conceptualization of God within scientific cosmologies—that is, as a sort of hypothesis to be incorporated into the worldview produced by modern physics—is not implausible if understood within the context of certain qualifying limitations. Willem Drees, for example, suggests that "the hypothesis 'God' might be seen as either one of the possible organizing principles, or a belief which is at a significant distance from, and therefore not too much constrained by, reality as understood through science."[131]

Similarly, Donceel suggests that a philosophy of nature, "which consists in an interpretation of the data of experience in the light of explicit or implicit metaphysical principles," can be considered a science in the broader sense of the word. If this view is taken, then we can certainly agree with Donceel that "the hypothesis of God's existence has some of the features of a scientific hypothesis or theory. It explains many facts and many laws of nature which without it remain unexplained. It is, in a certain sense, the best hypothesis, since it explains absolutely all facts and all laws."[132]

SUMMARY: THE DIVINE POSTULATE IN THE LIGHT OF CONTEMPORARY PHYSICS

We have seen a clear resurgence of interest in the question of the existence of a Creator God among physicists and among those philosophers and theologians who have been following recent developments in physics. There would seem to be no question, however, that it is not possible in principle to resolve conclusively the question of the existence of God on the basis of the results of scientific investigation or cosmological models. Whether the existence of God has become more or less probable, and belief in such a Being more or less rational, in light of the discussions spawned by modern physics is difficult to answer. Such a range of competing theories and cosmological models exists that one can be selective in choosing to give more weight to those that tend to reinforce (or at least present few serious problems for) one's own metaphysical presuppositions.

Additionally, the increasingly metaphysical direction of theoretical physics and modern cosmology would suggest that final verification or falsification of the relevant theories and cosmological models may prove illusive. At present, it would be difficult even to predict which theories and models may become standard among physicists. This has perhaps as much to do with the increasingly metaphysical direction of physics as with the complexity of the purely scientific aspects of the theories involved. As Richard Morris observed: "The boundaries between physics and metaphysics have become blurred. Questions that would have been considered metaphysical in another age enter into discussions of the origin of the universe. . . . Meanwhile, some all-embracing theories are proposed that yield unverifiable conclusions, and appear similar to the metaphysical systems constantly proposed by nineteenth century philosophers."[133] This does not mean, however, that theologians can simply ignore developments in physics, cosmology, and related fields. Yet a certain amount of caution is called for. As Mary Hesse has observed: "Some extrapolations from modern physical theory may undoubtedly constitute threats to central religious beliefs. . . . But theologians would be wise to treat such extrapolations with informed but healthy scepticism."[134]

Perhaps the most significant implication for the Christian doctrine of God to come out of recent discussions of the divine postulate among physicists is that God is seen more and more as nontranscendent within the world of the modern physicist. Whether God exists or not, God's existence (or nonexistence) is seen as being contained within our physical, measurable universe. Gone is the awareness of God's transcendence and the corresponding recognition that God's existence is beyond proof or disproof. In place of transcendence we find so much emphasis on the exclusive immanence of God within the confines of the physical universe, even among theologians, that various forms of pantheism and panentheism have become increasingly popular. The acceptance of such conceptions of God, however, is not only a questionable departure from traditional theism, it is also in no way necessitated by an objective reading of the results of modern physics.

Chapter Three

Did God Create the Universe out of Nothing?

In the beginning God created the heavens and the earth. The earth was without form and void, and darkness was upon the face of the deep; and the Spirit of God was moving over the face of the waters. And God said, "Let there be light"; and there was light.
—Genesis 1:1-3 (RSV)

Admitting that God created all things, the question arises whether He created them out of nothing or out of something. . . . If it were something uncreated, then this would have to be either God himself or a quantity independently co-existing with God from all eternity. Since this is impossible, there remains only the *creatio ex nihilo*.
—Karl Barth

In my model I assume that our Universe did indeed appear from nowhere about 10^{10} years ago. Contrary to widespread belief, such an event need not have violated any of the conventional laws of physics. The laws of physics merely imply that a Universe which appears from nowhere must have certain specific features.
—Edward Tryon

The quantum vacuum is a hive of activity, full of fluctuations, random comings-to-be and fadings away. . . . Suppose for a moment that such a fluctuation was the actual origin of our universe. It would certainly not have come from something which without great abuse of language could be called "nothing."
—John Polkinghorne

CREATION OUT OF NOTHING IN BIBLICAL AND THEOLOGICAL PERSPECTIVE

The canon of Scripture begins appropriately with a dual confession of creation and Creator: "In the beginning God created the heavens and the earth. The earth was without form and void, and darkness was upon the face of the deep; and the Spirit of God was moving over the face of the waters. And God said, 'Let there be light'; and there was light" (Gen. 1:1-3 rsv). Around this passage are built the Jewish and Christian doctrines of creation. More than a doctrine of creation, a fundamental and distinctive confession of the God of Judeo-Christian theism is also to be found here, a confession that has become inextricably bound with the concept of a creation out of nothing, or *creatio ex nihilo*.[1] The Old Testament scholar Gerhard von Rad tells us that the Hebrew verb *bara* (create) "contains the idea both of complete effortlessness and *creatio ex nihilo*, since it is never connected with any statement of the material." Von Rad explains the significance of this view of creation for an understanding of God when he writes:

> The hidden grandeur of this statement is that God is the Lord of the world. But not only in the sense that he subjected a pre-existing chaos to his ordering will! It is amazing to see how sharply little Israel demarcated herself from an apparently overpowering environment of cosmological and theogonic myths. Here the subject is not a primeval mystery of procreation from which the divinity arose, nor of a "creative" struggle of mythically personified powers from which the cosmos arose, but rather the one who is neither warrior nor procreator, who alone is worthy of the predicate, Creator.[2]

Von Rad is correct in distinguishing between a God who created "out of nothing" and one who simply subjected a preexisting chaos to God's ordering will. Although other exegetes downplay the significance of this passage for a doctrine of *creatio ex nihilo*, insisting that the question is not addressed in this text,[3] the theological implications of a creation out of nothing for our understanding of God and the world are undeniable—whether or not the author of Genesis 1:1ff. had in mind anything similar to a creation out of nothing.

Defining the Primal "Nothing"

Before proceeding further we must clarify what we mean by the "nothing" of *creatio ex nihilo*. Of late two streams of thought have arisen among theologians as to what constitutes "nothing." The traditional view has been that of a nondialectical, absolute nothingness with no relation to being (that is, an οὐκ ὄν, or a *nihil negativum*). Recently, however, a Platonic, dialectical view of nothing (a μὴ ὄν, or *nihil privativum*) has been advanced that sees nothingness or nonbeing as having a dialectical relation to being. The best known representative of this latter view is Karl Barth, who, dealing with the apparent scriptural conflict between a creation out of chaos and a creation out of nothing, reconciles the difficulty by identifying the original chaos as a *nihil pri-*

vativum, or a dialectical nothingness. Barth believes to have detected in the biblical accounts of creation "incontestable" reference to "a material used by God in the act of creation, which creates a theological problem for a doctrine of creation out of nothing. For Barth, "this difficulty was met by distinguishing between . . . a *nihil pure negativum* and a mere *nihil privativum.* Divine creation may well be effected on the assumption that a material already exists, but in this regard it should be noted that . . . the *creatio ex aliquo* is at least very near to the *creatio ex nihilo,* . . . since things were not real before they were created."[4]

Barth, however, remains in the minority in his elevation of "nothingness" to the status of a preexisting principle that stands in relation to being and out of which God called forth being. In such an interpretation the essential and historic meaning of a creation out of nothing would seem to be lost. From the perspective of Christian theology the judgment has always been that it is not enough simply to be "very near to the *creatio ex nihilo.*" Paul Tillich, who seldom found himself advocating a more traditional position than Barth, recognized the importance of this point. He noted that Christian theology "has rejected the concept of *me-ontic* matter on the basis of the doctrine of *creatio ex nihilo.* Matter is not a second principle in addition to God. The *nihil* out of which God creates is ουκ ον, the undialectical negation of being."[5] The maintenance of this view is essential, according to Tillich, if we are to "avoid positing a dialectical negativity in God himself."[6]

Yet this is not to say that the Christian doctrine of *creatio ex nihilo* is to be understood in the most radical sense of a creation from absolute nothingness. "Nothing" means simply no material substance or principle apart from the fullness of God's own being. Thus Democritus' ancient philosophical dictum, *ex nihilo nihil fit* (nothing comes out of nothing), is not in conflict with a correctly understood doctrine of *creatio ex nihilo* which asserts that God created out of nothing other than God's own "fullness of being." This position, significantly, is distinct from both a dialectical, Barthian concept of "nothingness," and God's own "substance." A creation out of *absolute* nothingness is an impossibility; a creation out of God's own "substance" leads to a pantheistic deification of the physical world. *Creatio ex nihilo,* therefore, signifies the theological recognition that God created a universe distinct from the divine being, not out of any preexisting matter or principle, but out of nothing other than the fullness of God's own being.

Biblical Roots of the Doctrine of Creation ex nihilo

The doctrine of a creation out of nothing is an interpretation only implicitly contained within the creation account of the first chapter of Genesis. Job 26:7 expresses an idea similar to *creatio ex nihilo* in Job's confession that God

"stretches the north over the empty place, and hangs the earth upon nothing."[7] The first explicit mention of the doctrine, however, is probably that
found in the apocryphal, first-century B.C.E. Second Book of Maccabees
7:28: "Look at the heaven and the earth and see everything that is in them,
and recognize that God did not make them out of things that existed."[8] Modern scholarship, however, has raised the question whether, because of the
ambiguity of the Greek terms used, even this passage contains an explicit
reference to *creatio ex nihilo* in the sense that the early church fathers used
the term.[9]

Evidence of a doctrine of *creatio ex nihilo* is also found in the New Testament in Paul's letter to the Romans 4:17 where the apostle writes that God
"gives life to the dead and calls into existence the things that do not exist."
C. E. B. Cranfield has expressed the opinion concerning this text that "there
is little doubt that the reference is to God's *creatio ex nihilo*."[10] Yet few other
commentators have been able to see such a clear expression of the *ex nihilo*
doctrine in this passage. Perhaps a more explicit reference is to be found in
Hebrews 11:3, where we read: "By faith we understand that the world was
created by the word of God, so that what is seen was made out of things
which do not appear" (RSV). In regard to this passage F. F. Bruce has observed
that, in contrast to Philo, "the writer to the Hebrews is more biblical in his
reasoning and affirms the doctrine of *creatio ex nihilo*," which doctrine he accepts based on "faith in divine revelation; the first chapter of Genesis is probably uppermost in his mind."[11] Also sometimes cited in support of a creation
ex nihilo has been Romans 11:36: "For from him and through him and to
him are all things [made]." Upon balance of judgment it would seem that the
idea of a creation out of nothing, whether explicitly contained in Genesis
1:1–3 or not, is a doctrine that can lay legitimate claim to being biblical in its
seminal form, if not indeed in its full expression.

Creation ex nihilo *in Theological Tradition*

If ambiguities have been found in the relevant biblical texts, there is little
doubt as to the teaching of the early fathers of the church concerning the *ex
nihilo* doctrine. The doctrine of a creation out of nothing seems, in fact, to
have been the universal consensus of the early fathers, including the author
of *Pastor Hermae* (*Mand.* I.1), Justin Martyr (*Apol.* 10), Tatian (*Oratio ad Graecos*
5), Theophilus of Antioch (*Ad. Autolykos* I.4), Irenaeus (*Adversus haereses*
I.22.1 and II.10.4), Tertullian (*Adversus Hermogenem* 8 and 16), and Origen
(*Commentary on John* I.17.103 and *De Principiis,* preface 4), all of whom made
explicit confession of a creation out of nothing.[12] Saint Augustine, in a classic
passage from his *Confessions,* expressed a developed doctrine of *creatio ex nihilo*
in which everything is created from God's own being but not out of God's

own substance. Augustine wrote: "You, O Lord . . . made something in the Beginning, which is of yourself, in your Wisdom, which is born of your own substance, and you created this something out of nothing. You created heaven and earth but you did not make them out of your own substance. . . . You . . . created them from nothing . . . for there is nothing that you cannot do. . . . You were, and besides you nothing was. From nothing, then, you created heaven and earth."[13] In fact, the doctrine of *creatio ex nihilo* was theologically so significant that "it became one of the firmest parts of the general teaching of the Church concerning creation."[14]

For Christian theology the doctrine of a creation out of nothing takes on the form of an inescapable conclusion. The possibility of a matter "existing with God from all eternity" is ruled out as constituting a radical spirit-matter dualism that Jewish and Christian theology has always rejected on biblical as well as philosophical grounds. As Wolfhart Pannenberg explains, "the uniqueness of the biblical conception of God's action in creation excludes every *dualistic* view of the origin of the world. The world is not the result of a cooperative effort between God and some other principle, as for example in Plato's Timaeus where it is portrayed as the formation of a shapeless material through a demiurge."[15]

Not only is *creatio ex nihilo* essential if a dualistic ontology is to be avoided, it is also a fundamental presupposition of a doctrine of divine transcendence and of the fundamental contingency (that is, absolute dependence) of the universe on God. Only a God who transcends the universe can be said to have created the universe out of nothing so that it is dependent in every moment on God for its existence. Philip Hefner insists, in fact, that *creatio ex nihilo* has primarily to do with contingency. Hefner explains that the doctrine of creation out of nothing "has less to do with origins than it does with dependence. . . . As a methodological strategy, it insists that everything that is depends for its being on God the creator."[16] Without an *ex nihilo* creation, therefore, the concept of the dependence of the creation on God is lost. As Friedrich Schleiermacher explained, "the expression 'out of nothing' excludes the idea that before the origin of the world anything existed outside God, which as 'matter' could enter into the formation of the world. And undoubtedly the admission of 'matter' could enter into the formation of the world. And undoubtedly the admission of 'matter' as existing independently of the divine activity would destroy the feeling of absolute dependence."[17]

That an inevitable linkage exists between a rejection of *creatio ex nihilo* and a radical alteration of the traditional Christian understanding of God is seen in the example of process theology. The process philosopher Alfred North Whitehead rejected the idea of a creation out of nothing, choosing instead to affirm a fundamental dualism between God and the world. Whitehead wrote in his 1926 book *Process and Reality,* "it is as true to say that God creates the World, as that the world creates God. . . . Opposed elements stand to each other in mutual requirement . . . God and the World stand to each other in this opposed requirement. . . . In every respect God and the world move conversely to each other in respect to their process." [18] Following the lead of Whitehead, contemporary process theology also rejects a *creatio ex nihilo,* seeing instead in Genesis 1:1ff. a dualism between God and the primordial chaos out of which God creates. [19] Thus John Cobb and David R. Griffin concede that "Process theology rejects the notion of *creatio ex nihilo,* if that means creation out of *absolute* nothingness. That doctrine is part and parcel of the doctrine of God as absolute controller. Process theology affirms instead a doctrine of creation out of chaos." [20]

Process theology not only accepts a fundamental ontological dualism between God and the world, it also associates God so intricately with the process of the physical world that the idea of divine transcendence must necessarily be radically restated if not, in fact, rejected. Thus for John Cobb "wholly other" means "numerically other" and applies essentially to our experience of God. When we think of the otherness of God, however, in terms of "the contrast of infinite with finite or eternal with temporal," and "when these contrasts are pressed radically for their strictest philosophical meanings, they prove misleading and display implications counter to the original religious intention." God, in Cobb's theology, has no beginning or end, yet God "exists within time and process." [21] Cobb admits that, "in an important sense God transcends space," but "in a spatial epoch he is characterized by spatiality." And also, because time is "metaphysically necessary" God's relation to time is not as "accidental" as to space. [22] For Cobb, therefore, God transcends space in a qualified sense (though in the present epoch God exists within space), but God would not seem to transcend time because time is metaphysically necessary.

The theological discussion of creation has, over the centuries, turned again and again to the doctrine of a creation out of nothing alongside of—and often superseding the idea of—an original creation. Traditionally, a creation out of nothing has often been viewed as containing the idea of an original creation. The bare fact of an original creation, on the other hand, does not necessarily imply a creation out of nothing. In fact, as can be seen as early as Aquinas, who admitted that it is not possible to prove an original creation (*Summa Theologica* I.46.2) yet sought independent proof of the existence of God (I.2.3) and seemingly also of a *creatio ex nihilo* (I.44.2 and 45.1), the two doctrines exercise a certain independence of each other and need to be treated, to a certain extent, separately. [23]

Although Aquinas did not doubt that there actually was an original creation, recent developments in physics may actually make it possible to maintain a rational belief in a *creatio ex nihilo* without accepting a *creatio originans* as its logical and necessary corollary. While such a development may prove ultimately advantageous for a doctrine of creation out of nothing, it means that theology can no longer speak simply of creation *ex nihilo* and assume that the question of an original creation has been addressed inclusively within the *ex nihilo* question. Therefore we will take up separately here the discussion of an original creation and that of a creation out of nothing.

DOES CONTEMPORARY PHYSICS POINT TO AN ORIGINAL CREATION?

The Second Law of Thermodynamics

Although the formulation of the famed second law of thermodynamics is by no means new to the twentieth century, the metaphysical questions that it raises and its implications for an original creation of the universe are as relevant as ever. The field of thermodynamics was developed during the course of efforts by various scientists in the nineteenth century to discover a maximally efficient conversion of heat into usable forms of work. The first law of thermodynamics has to do with the conservation of energy within closed systems. It tells us that decreases in energy in one part of the system are always matched by increases in another, and vice versa.

The second law of thermodynamics was formulated independently by R. E. Clausius in 1850 and W. Thomson (Lord Kelvin) in 1851 on the basis of discoveries made by Nicolas Carnot some three decades earlier. Essentially, the second law is the bad news part of a "good news, bad news" duo, the good news being the first law's observation that a closed system never loses energy. Yet there is an important distinction between simple energy and energy that is available for use. According to the second law, the amount of energy that is available for conversion into usable forms of work always decreases. Because of the connection between usable energy and order within closed systems, the second law can also be stated as: *entropy* always increases.[24] Because our earth is not a closed system but is constantly receiving new energy from the sun, we do not observe any increased entropy or loss of total usable energy in our world. Inasmuch as the universe, however, is by definition a closed system that receives no energy from sources outside itself, the second law would seem to imply an ever-increasing entropy and loss of usable energy within the total system of the universe.

Already in the nineteenth century physicists began debating whether entropy must indeed always increase. The German physicist Ludwig Boltzmann attempted to prove with his famous H-Theorem that entropy always increases and therefore was the only physical law that defines the direction of time.[25] Other physicists disagreed with Boltzmann's conclusion, however, including James Clerk Maxwell with his famous example of an intelligent, molecular-sized "demon" that could theoretically violate the second law and decrease the entropy in a system.[26]

Although the second law was shown not to be an absolute law of nature, but rather "a human artifact resulting from the relative size of Man to atom and of the Law of Large Numbers,"[27] physicists have tended to accept that it corresponds to, if not defines, the arrow of time.[28] In fact, the second law has held and continues to hold such sway in the world of science that Sir Arthur Eddington could write:

> The law that entropy always increases—the second law of thermodynam-ics—holds, I think, the supreme position among the laws of Nature. If someone points out to you that your pet theory of the universe is in dis-agreement with Maxwell's equations—then so much the worse for Max-well's equations. If it is found to be contradicted by observation—well, these experimentalists do bungle things sometimes. But if your theory is found to be against the second law of thermodynamics I can give you no hope; there is nothing for it but to collapse in deepest humiliation.[29]

The discussion as to what extent the second law actually defines the arrow of time seems to have begun in earnest when a student of Max Planck, E. Zermelo, pointed out in two *Annalen der Physik* articles of 1896 that a theorem developed by Jules Henri Poincaré actually demonstrated that almost any possible finite system (that is, any system limited in energy and space) must necessarily return to any previous state (the Poincaré recurrence).[30] The result was that, as John Barrow and Frank Tipler explain, "whatever the state of the Universe now, the entropy as defined by Boltzmann would almost certainly have to decrease in the future back to its present value."[31] Boltz-mann responded by showing, given Zermelo's demonstration of a possible future decrease of entropy, that "for the universe as a whole the two direc-tions of time are indistinguishable," and the second law is still valid in refer-ence to the direction of time, inasmuch as time would still be regarded as always going "from less probable to more probable states."[32]

This view was eventually confirmed by the acceptance of the statistical interpretation of the second law early in the twentieth century. In fact, the Oxford mathematician Roger Penrose points out that even in a collapsing universe "there are very good reasons for doubting that there could be such a turn-around of entropy."[33] The chief reason for this belief, and also the one that Stephen Hawking found convincing, has to do with the existence of black holes, which are essentially microcosms of a collapsing universe. If entropy (and the direction of time) would indeed reverse directions in a collapsing universe, then, since the same conditions govern black holes, a decrease of entropy ought also to exist in the vicinity of black holes. That is, the "reverse of entropy" theory would predict "observable gross violations of the second law." However, as Penrose states, "there is every reason to believe that, with black holes, the second law powerfully holds sway." [34]

A second point Boltzmann made was that there are two possible interpretations of the meaning of the second law for the question of the origin of the universe. The first, dubbed the creation interpretation, suggests the universe was at some point simply "given" or created "in a very improbable state." The second, dubbed the anthropic–fluctuation interpretation, suggests that at certain times and in relatively small regions of the universe certain fluctuations exist that allow enough order for life to develop; these would not violate the second law because vast regions of the universe would be "dead" (that is to say, in thermal equilibrium) and would offset the imbalance of order in the small living regions. [35]

Of Boltzmann's two possible interpretations of the second law, it is clear which would be the preference of creationists. As both pictures had their advantages and their advocates, however, it seemed unlikely that the creation interpretation of the second law could ever realistically represent anything more than the preference of creationists in scientific debate. The revelation in 1929 by Edwin Hubble that the universe is expanding, however, eliminated Zermelo's problem and the inevitability of the Poincaré recurrence by explaining the origin of the initial conditions of the universe via the beginning of the expansion, later known as the Big Bang. Roger Penrose summarized the implications of the second law within a Big Bang universe when he explained that "entropy is increasing now, and has been for a very long time. The question, then, is how far back one is entitled to extrapolate that trend. Well, physicists usually just assume the second law. They don't think that at a certain time the rules changed, and before that entropy was going the other way. . . . It looks, therefore, as though we might as well go right on back until we get to the beginning: time zero." [36]

Suddenly, with the possibility of such an extrapolation back to "time zero," the second law became an apparent proof of an original creation. The logic of the argument is actually quite sound. If entropy in the universe is continually increasing, and the universe is at present in a remarkably stable and well-ordered state, then the implied arrow of time would suggest that there must have been a point in the past when the universe would have been in an inexplicable state of minimum entropy (maximum order) from which our present universe devolved. This not only implies a beginning of the universe (because the thermodynamic arrow of time would stop [or begin] when it arrived back at the point of maximal order), but also an initial "perfect" state. As Eddington wrote: "Following time backwards we find more and more organization in the world. If we are not stopped earlier, we go back to a time when the matter and energy of the world had the maximum possible organization. To go back further is impossible. We have come to another end of space-time—an abrupt end—only according to our orientation we call it 'the beginning.'"[37] Such a view would appear to correspond particularly well with the biblical concepts of creation and fall.

Ted Peters, without attempting to prove too much, suggests the significance of the second law for a theology of creation. He argues that if the law of entropy is correct and the universe as a whole is moving steadily and irreversibly "from order to disorder, from hot to cold, from high energy to dissipative equilibrium, then . . . the universe must have had a point of origin. It has not always existed. It could not have existed with an infinite past, otherwise it would have suffered thermal death a long time ago. Such scientific speculations open up to intelligibility questions regarding an original creation."[38]

Indeed, the logic of the argument is essentially sound. The problem, however, is not with the logic of the argument but with the second law itself. Aside from the fact that it is still occasionally disputed whether entropy must in fact always increase, there is nothing inherent within the second law that would favor a creation interpretation. The development of the anthropic principle based on quantum cosmologies has, in fact, increased the attractiveness of Boltzmann's anthropic-fluctuation interpretation of the second law. This is despite Richard Feynman's 1965 objection that a fluctuation much smaller than the size of our present universe would be sufficient to explain life on a single planet and that the anthropic-fluctuation interpretation would therefore appear "ridiculous" in suggesting that our entire visible universe is in an improbable state.[39] For a time, then, the fluctuation interpretation of the second law was largely popular only among philosophers[40] and steady-state-theory physicists.[41] Supporters of the anthropic principle, however, have demonstrated that a large space is necessary for the appearance of intelligent life in the universe. The argument is based on the simple idea that a universe with significantly less mass than what our present, observable universe contains would have collapsed long before intelligent life had time to appear.[42] This answer to Feynman's objection would seem to breathe new life into the fluctuation interpretation and weaken the force of creation arguments based on the second law.

If the second law were indeed able to lead to a proof of an original creation and a Creator, we would have to ask what kind of Creator would be indicated. The bare fact of an inexplicable beginning in which an interventionist "jump start" from a Creator is called for seems to lead inevitably toward a deistic view of God since, taken by itself, it says nothing about the continuing relationship of the Creator with the low-entropy universe. In this way the "victory" of a demonstrable beginning of the universe for Christian theology is empty inasmuch as the God of Christian theism still has to be postulated on other grounds.

The bare idea of an original creation, without reference to what role it might imply for a Creator, seems compatible with the second law. Yet a proof of an original creation based on the second law is not possible. The second law does, however, provide us with an indication of the incredible precision required in the selection of the initial conditions of our universe that would seem to strengthen design arguments based on probability. Penrose has calculated, based on the second law, that in order to produce a low-entropy universe like the one in which we live, "the Creator would have to aim for an absurdly tiny volume of the phase of possible universes—about $1/(10^{10})^{123}$ of the entire volume" available.[43] In other words, the probability of the formation of a universe with an entropy as low as that of our present universe is in the neighborhood of 1 to $(10^{10})^{123}$, a number so large, that, in Penrose's words, "even if we were to write a 0 on each separate proton and on each separate neutron in the entire universe—and we could throw in all the other particles as well for good measure—we should fall far short of writing down the figure needed."[44] We must keep in mind, of course, that a nontheistic anthropic model (although Penrose does not favor such a model) reaches an entirely different, and philosophically no less valid conclusion based on the same remarkable precision involved in the "selecting" of our present universe.

While the second law, therefore, may not be the proof of an original creative act of God that it is sometimes portrayed to be, neither is it lacking in implications for a doctrine of God as Creator. For the theist, the very improbability of the low-entropy state of our universe is not only a witness to the incredible precision involved in the creative act, it is also testimony to the fact that the creation of our particular universe was a deliberate choice of the Creator. We think here of Charles Misner's design argument in which a cosmic "mind" is making certain choices about the universe. Rather than seeing the precise initial conditions required for a low-entropy universe such as our own as testimony to the narrow amount of leeway a Creator would have had, it seems instead a witness to the very freedom of the creative act. When we consider the unfathomable number of possible universes along with the fact that a Creator could have created intelligent life (not necessarily carbon-based) with a tremendous number of these (at least all of them that would be viable in their own terms), one cannot help, from the perspective of Christian theology, but recognize the creation of our universe as a deliberate and free act of God.

Additionally, what the second law tells us of the inherent propensity of physical matter (as contained within closed systems) toward increased entropy points not only to the transcendence of God but also to the dependence of the universe on God. If God is not transcendent (completely other) from the universe, then we would have to say that God, inasmuch as God would be contained within the closed system of our physical universe, is also subject to the increasing-entropy principle of the second law. That is to say, any theology that does not recognize the transcendence of God would, in light of what we know of thermodynamics and entropy, have a difficult time explaining how God could avoid necessarily "winding down" along with the universe— not to mention the problem of how a nontranscendent God could in any real sense be considered the Creator of space and time.

Concerning the dependence (or contingency) of the universe on the being of God, the second law offers a significant model. Everywhere we look in the observable world, the low-entropy state of everything from human beings to vegetation to the earth itself finds an explanation in the seeming dependence of all systems on other low-entropy systems.[45] People maintain their low-entropy state by eating low-entropy foods, which in turn (in the case of vegetation) maintain a low-entropy state through the various earth systems, which in turn are maintained by the energy input from the sun, which in turn is maintained by the low-entropy store produced by the gravitational attraction of diffuse gas that produced it and other stars. When we turn to the question of where this diffuse gas—or for that matter the law of gravitational attraction itself—came from and why it should be capable of producing such a tremendous store of low entropy, the answers become more theoretical and difficult. One could perhaps seek to build a cosmological argument for the existence of God upon the problem of the ultimate origin of low entropy, but that would seem pointless in light of the recent progress in developing cosmological theories capable of explaining this problem—not to mention the Kantian critique of cosmological arguments in general. Nevertheless, it is not invalid for theology to recognize within the second law and the "problem" of low entropy the contingency of all things physical. It is precisely in this fact of contingency that the dependence of the physical world on the continuing sustenance of a transcendent Creator is to be recognized—not in the sense of a proof for the existence of God but as a model for understanding what we mean by "divine sustenance," especially within the context of the singularity that theology confesses as *creatio originans*.

The Big Bang and an Original Creation

No other theory of modern science has corresponded more closely to (nor met so well the requirements of) a doctrine of creation than the theory of the Big Bang. If we follow the path of expansion from the Big Bang singularity back in time, we seem to be led to a point where one can speculate about the origin or creation of our universe—that is, a beginning of space and time. Indeed, the theory parallels so closely the idea of creation in Christian theology that Pope Pius XII took the virtually unprecedented step in 1951 of declaring the theory to be compatible with the Christian doctrine of creation.[46] For Pius XII this meant that the Big Bang represented a point beyond which human reason and science could not extend, a point beyond which one could only keep silent in face of the inscrutable mystery of God and God's creative act. In this assessment the pope was possibly influenced by the views of Edmund Whittaker, who nine years earlier had written in regard to what later became known as the Big Bang theory that it "is the ultimate point of physical science, the farthest glimpse that we can obtain of the material universe by our natural faculties."[47]

The Lutheran theologian Ted Peters recently expressed a similar view when he wrote that the Big Bang singularity "is the event at which space and time were created. Now this marks the end of the line for scientific research, because astrophysicists cannot within the framework of their discipline talk about the singularity, let alone what was going on before it."[48] This raises, however, two significant questions. First, from a scientific perspective, is the Big Bang actually the event at which space and time were created, and if so, does this original creation imply a creation *ex nihilo?* Second, does a Big Bang singularity necessarily mark "the end of the line for scientific research"?

As to the question of "the end of the line for scientific research," it must be noted that this idea sounds dangerously similar to a God-of-the-gaps argument that seeks to find room for God within those areas that at present seem beyond the reach of natural science.[49] One wonders how theologians who take such a position would react if someday high-energy-particle physicists would tell us that they believe they are able to go beyond the Planck time and suggest workable theories for the first fraction of a second of the universe's existence. Of course, it is also possible that the Big Bang theory in its present form may one day be replaced by a model that does not present such an apparently convenient "end of the line." When one thinks of the difficulty the Big Bang theory has had in making significant predictions[50] and the constant flow of scientific notices suggesting that the theory may need to be seriously revised[51]—or even abandoned—one cannot place too much confidence in theological models of creation built, even in part, on our apparent inability to get back to what is believed to be the absolute beginning of our universe. Yet there is also a sense in which Peters and others are correct in the recognition that natural science has reached the "end of the line" with the initial Big Bang singularity. Such an "end of the line," however, must be understood within the context of, and limited to current cosmologies that are based on, our present understanding of the initial singularity.

The other question that needs to be addressed is whether the Big Bang theory teaches or implies an actual beginning of space and time; that is, not only an original creation but also a creation out of nothing. Whittaker believed that not only a beginning of our universe was implied within the theory but that it also led to a doctrine of a divine *creatio ex nihilo*. Concerning what would eventually come to be known as the Big Bang, Whittaker wrote that "there is no ground for supposing that matter (or energy, which is the same as matter) existed before this in an inert condition, and was in some way galvanized into activity at a certain instant: For what could have determined this instant rather than all the other instants of past eternity? It is simpler to postulate a creation *ex nihilo,* an operation of the Divine Will to constitute Nature from nothingness."[52]

The oft-stated belief that our knowledge of the Big Bang singularity brings us back to the beginning of time ($t = 0$) and the beginning of space is, however, not quite accurate. We must remember that earlier than the Planck time (about 10^{-43} to 5.4×10^{-44} seconds ABB, that is, after the Big Bang), we have no precise theories of space and time, or for that matter, any real certainty of what "space" and "time" before 10^{-43} seconds might signify.[53] In fact, according to Bernulf Kanitscheider, the earliest threshold of our ability to begin to speculate as to what the physical conditions and laws of the early universe may have been is approximately 5.4×10^{-44} seconds ABB.[54] This would constitute, then, what seems to be the earliest threshold of the Planck time.

It may be helpful here, at the outset of our discussion, to offer a diagram of the history of the universe according to the Big Bang model.

The diagram opposite (not drawn to scale!) represents what physicists believe an expanding universe that began at an initial Big Bang singularity would look like. There is relative agreement on what must have transpired during the approximately 15 billion years between our present era and the beginning of the Plank time. What is controversial within Big Bang cosmologies is the first fraction of a second after the singularity. For the Planck time itself, which requires the application of special laws of physics, there are several competing but viable models. Present theories, however, do not even allow meaningful speculation as to what took place before the Planck time.

It is even possible that the absolute breakdown of all theories of gravity as we approach the initial singularity—providing, of course, there actually was

Space-Time Diagram from Big Bang Singularity to the Present[55]

e	Space	Event
5×10^{10} yrs	VVVVVVVVVVVVVVVVVVVVVVVVVVV	Today
$)^{10}$ yrs	VVVVVVVVVVVVVVVVVVVVVVVV	Planets Formed
$)^9$ yrs	VVVVVVVVVVVVVVVVVVVVV	Galaxies Formed
$)^6$ yrs	VVVVVVVVVVVVVVVVVV	Atoms Formed (2,000° K)
$)^5$ yrs	VVVVVVVVVVVVVVV	Atom Formation Begins
mins	VVVVVVVVVVVVV	Nuclei Formed ($10^{9°}$ K)
sec	VVVVVVVVVVV	Nucleosynthesis Continues
$)^{-4}$	VVVVVVVVV	Quarks>Protons & Neutrons
$)^{-10}$	VVVVVVV	Weak & Electromagnetic Forces Separate
$)^{-35}$	VVVVV	Strong Nuclear Force Separates
$)^{-43}$	VVVV	Planck Time ($10^{32°}$ K)
4×10^{-44}	VVV	Earliest Planck Time
	☉	Big Bang Singularity

an initial singularity—could mean that we never actually reach t = 0. That is to say, not only are we unable to discern what happened at t = 0 and immediately thereafter, but there may, indeed, have been no t = 0. This might explain why, from the standpoint of natural science, we seem to reach the end of the line as we approach this point. Against such a possibility we begin to see that any attempt to build a doctrine of *creatio ex nihilo* on the Big Bang singularity faces serious difficulties. Indeed, it seems somewhat incongruous to say that modern science is, and will remain, unable to get all the way back to t = 0, while at the same time contending that research in this direction supports a beginning of time. As we shall point out later in this study, t = 5.4 × 10⁻⁴⁴ seconds does not equal t = 0. The question, then, is whether t = 5.4 × 10⁻⁴⁴ necessarily implies the existence of t = 0.

As the Big Bang singularity is approached, what we know as matter begins to break down as the temperatures increase. The astrophysicist Sten Oden-wald describes the process of "simplification" as we get closer to the Big Bang:

> At sustained temperatures above 10,000° K, planets evaporate and compounds and molecules dissociate into atoms. Above 100,000° K, atoms are stripped of their electrons [ionization]. . . . Above temperatures of 10 billion degrees . . . all atomic nuclei dissolve into their constituent protons and neutrons, and matter loses its recognizable characteristics. . . . [And finally] at 1,000 trillion degrees, we expect that protons and neutrons will

dissolve into their constituent quarks, . . . which are what most physicists consider to be fundamental particles.[56]

Physicists do not anticipate any further "subquark" particles to emerge at even higher temperatures. From the 108 elements of the periodic table, then, we are left with perhaps as few as six subatomic quarks.

A reduction from the 108 elements of the periodic table to an electron, a muon, a tauon, and their respective neutrinos is certainly drastic. It is not, however, a reduction into oblivion. As we enter the time approaching t = 0 we retain at least six quark particles (and presumably their antiparticles as well), each with certain known qualities. Beyond this point, high-energy-particle physics has, at present, no functional theories. The Big Bang may well, then, demonstrate a beginning of our physical universe, which, if not actually indicating a creation singularity, certainly corresponds well with one. It by no means, however, witnesses to a *creatio ex nihilo*. But neither does it contradict a doctrine of *creatio ex nihilo* since, in terms of the present state of our knowledge of high-energy-particle physics, no one knows what happens before approximately t = 5.4×10^{-44} seconds ABB.

We have seen that our present knowledge of the presumed Big Bang singularity does not in itself lend support to a doctrine of *creatio ex nihilo*, that is, the appearance of fundamental particles out of nonmatter. But does it support the idea of a beginning of time? As was first pointed out by Saint Augustine, the concept of time is meaningless apart from the concept of space.[57] Without matter (or energy), there can be no time; with matter, time must also exist. If, therefore, particle physicists are unable to get beyond the six apparent fundamental particles mentioned above, we must assume that as long as they (or other even "smaller" fundamental particles) existed along with their various qualities, functions, and interactions, then time in some form must also have existed. For an actual t = 0 to be achieved, even these few fundamental particles would have to "disappear."

It would be difficult to imagine how we could get much closer to a creation out of nothing—to an absolute beginning of space and time—than current Big Bang cosmologies are able to take us. Yet for all the attractiveness of a correspondence between Big Bang cosmologies and a doctrine of creation out of nothing, we must once again stress that t = 5.4×10^{-44} seconds and perhaps as few as six different fundamental subatomic particles along with their antiparticles do not equal "nothing." The Big Bang singularity cannot, therefore, at our present state of knowledge, offer any hope of taking us back to t = 0, nor for that matter does it offer any conclusive scientific reasons for believing that there necessarily must have been a t = 0. The present scientific consensus, however, seems to assume that a t = 0 may have existed. Our inability to settle the question one way or the other, however, should serve as a caution to theologians eager to build a theology of a creation *ex nihilo* on science's apparent discovery of t = 0. As Stephen Weinberg writes: "We may have to get used to the idea of an absolute zero of time—a moment in the past beyond which it is in principle impossible to trace any chain of cause and effect. [However], the question is open, and may always remain open."[58]

We must ask, then, in light of these considerations, whether the Big Bang model of the origin of the universe has any value for the formulation of a doctrine of God as Creator. The answer would seem to be yes. If nothing else, the present state of research within Big Bang cosmologies demonstrates that neither a theological doctrine of *creatio originans* nor *creatio ex nihilo* is, from the standpoint of our knowledge of the physical universe itself, untenable. And, in light of the fact that the universe seems to have begun with an unfathomable explosion of energy and light (which is the same as energy), the language of the Genesis creation narrative: "In the beginning . . . God said, 'let there be light'; and there was light" (Gen. 1:1, 3), is certainly intriguing—although any attempt to read into such a passage an anticipation of the Big Bang theory would be foolish. To confess in the late twentieth century, however, our belief in the creative act of God using the ancient formula of Genesis 1:1ff. is admittedly less problematic than it has been in previous decades.

It must be emphasized, however, that we are drawing attention to an interesting correspondence between scientific and theological ideas—nothing more. Current Big Bang cosmologies do seem to create an atmosphere conducive to the discussion of an original creation. And those who believe in an original act of creation do seem to be favorably inclined toward most Big Bang cosmological models. Yet neither an original creation (and, we might add, a creation *ex nihilo* as well) nor the Big Bang theory can in any way be built on the other. This would be neither good theology nor good science. Ernan McMullin summarized the matter well when he wrote, "What one cannot say is, first, that the Christian doctrine of creation 'suppports' the Big Bang model, or second, that the Big Bang model 'supports' the Christian doctrine of creation."[59]

Beyond this, the Big Bang model, as was the case with the second law of thermodynamics, can be seen theologically as additional confirmation of the importance of confessing a Creator who transcends creation and on whose being the existence of creation is contingent. Yet at the same time the theological assertions of transcendence and contingency are independent of, though not irrelevant to or unaffected by, scientific theory.

t = 0, Imaginary Numbers, and Infinite Subjective Time

We have discussed the question of whether modern physics *implies* an original creation, and along with it, a creation out of nothing. A further question is whether contemporary physics *requires* or necessarily leads to an original creation. In the days when physicists believed in a static, eternal universe, the question of a beginning or creation of the physical universe was seldom dealt with outside of theological circles. Big Bang cosmologies, however, whether assuming a closed or an open universe, have seemed to lead to the inescapable conclusion of a beginning.[60] The fact that such an idea so closely parallels theological ideas seems to have played a large part in the extraordinary efforts of proponents of the steady-state theory such as Hermann Bondi and Fred Hoyle to find an acceptable alternative to the Big Bang model that would preserve the idea of an infinite universe—that is, a universe without beginning.

Apparent confirmation of the Big Bang model by the 1965 observation of the microwave background radiation of the universe seemed to signal not only an end of the steady-state theory but also the end of any hope of positing an eternal universe. Or did it? The question that now needs to be addressed is whether, in light of recent cosmological theories, it is possible to posit a universe that is eternal in time within the context of a Big Bang model of the universe. If this is the case then modern physics, while not necessarily ruling out a beginning, has shown that such an event, understood as a boundary condition of time, is not necessitated by an expanding universe.

Frank Tipler, in an intriguing article written in response to questions posed by Wolfhart Pannenberg to scientists, makes an interesting suggestion concerning the "end of time" in a closed universe. Tipler seeks to demonstrate how it might be possible for intelligent life to continue forever within an "infinite subjective time." After explaining, contra Freeman Dyson, why he believes life cannot continue forever in an open universe, Tipler indicates some special features of a closed universe that may allow such an infinite continuation of information-processing life. Closed universes, as Tipler explains, end in a "final singularity of infinite density, and the temperature diverges to infinity as this final singularity is approached."[61] These characteristics, it might be noted, are also shared by the initial singularity in Big Bang model universes.

Tipler believes that the "shear effect" produced by most closed universes as they collapse, contracting in different directions at different rates and even expanding in one spatial direction while collapsing in the other two, can produce a radiation temperature difference that is able "to provide sufficient free energy for an infinite amount of information processing between now and the final singularity, even though there is only a finite amount of proper time between now and the end of time in a closed universe." Tipler concludes, therefore, "that although a closed universe exists for only a finite proper time it nevertheless could exist for an infinite subjective time, which is the measure of time that is significant for living beings."[62]

Barrow and Tipler make a similar point in their 1986 book, *The Anthropic Cosmological Principle.* They explain that "there need be no correspondence between the duration of various measures of physical times such as proper time, and the number of bits processed in that time interval. It is quite possible for the universe to exist for only a finite proper time in the future . . . and yet for an infinite number of bits to be processed in that time interval."[63]

Tipler's proposal of an infinite subjective time, although made in reference to the end of the physical universe, is also significant for our discussion of the universe's beginning. Although the experience of the shear effect is lacking, the conditions at the very beginning of our universe are otherwise strikingly parallel to those expected at the end of a closed universe. Particularly significant is the fact that, as we go back to within a fraction of a second after the Big Bang singularity, we also expect infinite density and temperature. Given these conditions, which Tipler has already suggested would have an effect on time (but because no intelligent information-processing is postulated at the very beginning of the universe, this would need to be understood differently from Tipler), as well as the known connection between gravity and time, one wonders if something similar to Tipler's infinite subjective time might not be postulated for the very beginning of the universe.

Charles Misner, in his 1969 article "Absolute Zero of Time," seems to have already taken up this question. Misner wanted to address the question of whether a lower limit could be placed on time at the initial singularity that would make $t = 0$ seem "harmless." To do this Misner distinguished between a philosophical or psychological sense of time and a physical sense of time, which he calls proper time. In this way, Misner reached the following conclusion:

> . . . as we approach the singularity $\Omega \to \infty$, we see the Universe ticking away in Ω time quite actively. The Universe is meaningfully infinitely old because infinitely many things have happened since the beginning. . . . In the first second of its existence the Universe evolved slowly through infinite epochs, gradually speeding up toward an explosive expansion during the ten billion years of the most recent epochs. . . . [This] approach to the singularity shows a Universe which beats at a rather regular but gradually slowing rate in the infinite past.[64]

Interestingly, the theologian Wolfhart Pannenberg, in light of recent developments in physics, has inquired whether time might be seen as "stretching" as we approach the initial singularity. Pannenberg, after noting that our theories of time and space break down as we approach t = 0, suggests that "it is conceivable that the 'subjective time' in the vicinity of the beginning is stretched in correspondence with mass near the beginning, similar to what takes place in the vicinity of the 'event horizon' of black holes."[65]

The idea that time could be "lengthened," similar to space, near the event horizon of the Big Bang singularity is based primarily on Hawking's research on black holes. Because, according to relativity theory, there is no absolute time, each observer has his or her own measure of time. Hawking gives the example of an imaginary astronaut with a radio transmitting watch approaching 11:00 A.M. on the surface of a collapsing star. As the star begins to collapse his comrades in the spaceship would find the intervals between the signals getting longer and longer until the star shrank below the critical radius and the gravitational field would become so strong that no further signal could escape. His companions in the spaceship "would have to wait forever for the 11:00 signal," because "the light waves emitted from the surface of the star between 10:59:59 and 11:00, by the astronaut's watch, would be spread out over an infinite period of time, as seen from the spaceship."[66] When one considers the potential effect on a hypothetical observer's perception of time as one approaches the infinite gravitational attraction present near the Big Bang singularity, it is clear that a potential "stretching" or "curvature" of time may actually eliminate the necessity of a "beginning" of time within a Big Bang model of the universe. Hawking explains how this is made possible using "imaginary" time and "imaginary" numbers.

With the use of imaginary numbers, according to Hawking, "the distinction between time and space disappears completely." Gravitational fields, therefore, are represented by a curved space-time that appears to be bent as if by a gravitational field. In this way time, as represented by imaginary numbers, is subject to the same forces as space and can be curved or even stretched. As Hawking explains:

> In the classical theory of gravity, which is based on real space-time, there are only two possible ways the universe can behave: either it has existed for an infinite time, or else it had a beginning at a singularity at some finite time in the past. In the quantum theory of gravity, on the other hand, a third possibility arises. Because one is using Euclidean space-times, in which the time direction is on the same footing as directions in space, it is possible for space-time to be finite in extent and yet to have no singularities that formed a boundary or edge. Space-time would be like the surface of the earth. . . . [67]

We might legitimately ask, however, what point is there in speaking of an imaginary time using imaginary numbers? It would seem that if "real" and "imaginary" time are simply two alternative descriptions of the observed universe, it may not be that easy—or that meaningful—to say which is "real." As Hawking suggests, perhaps what we call real time "is just a figment of our imaginations. In real time, the universe has a beginning and an end at singularities that form a boundary to space-time. . . . But in imaginary time, there are no singularities or boundaries. So maybe what we call imaginary is really more basic, and what we call real is just an idea that we invent to help us describe what we think the universe is like."[68]

In such a model it is possible that "space-time stretches back to infinite imaginary time." If time, therefore, is understood from the subjective perspective of the potential observer (perhaps one could even posit God as this observer, in good Berkelian fashion, since no carbon-based life is present in the beginning), an infinite subjective time may also stand at the beginning of our universe. In other words, the gravitational attraction of the "infinite density" present in the first fraction of a second of the universe's existence may have stretched time to such an extent that, from the perspective of any hypothetical observer, the very conditions associated with a presumed Big Bang singularity would create a certain kind of infinity that would make it meaningless to speak of an initial singularity. Such a model demonstrates that Big Bang cosmologies do not necessarily lead to something resembling an original creation of the universe.

The Scientific Discovery of Creation out of Nothing

If theologians have been coming to the conclusion that the doctrines of an original creation and a creation out of nothing stand independently of one another, physicists seem to be moving in the opposite direction. If the universe had a beginning, they reason, this beginning must have been a true beginning with no previous time or space, and not simply a beginning out of a previous chaos or other unknown state. For the physicist seeking a comprehensive theory of the origin of the universe, there is something inherently unsatisfying with being left with simply another (albeit previous) unexplained state. If the universe is finite in time—and even perhaps if it is not (cf. the Hartle-Hawking proposal)—unless a beginning "out of nothing" is found, the search is never brought to a satisfying conclusion, however tentative that conclusion might be.

If the universe is truly finite in space and time, as many believe, then its beginning must have been *ex nihilo*. If a non–*ex nihilo* beginning is postulated, it is ultimately not an actual beginning of space-time but only the beginning of our particular space-time out of some prior reality. In such a case our present space-time arises out of some sort of infinite "physical" reality. The fact that such a reality may be in principle scientifically inaccessible to us would seem to make the issue somewhat irrelevant as seen from the perspective of potential practical applications of the theories of physical science. The philosophical and theological implications, in any event, are significant.

Ironically, the first serious *ex nihilo* model within modern physics was that of the steady-state theory proposed in 1948 by Hermann Bondi and Thomas Gold,[69] who were later joined by Fred Hoyle. As Michael Berry, among others, has observed, "the main empirical motivation for introducing the model was that it describes an infinitely old universe, and thus evades the problem posed by early observations which seemed to imply that H_o^{-1} [the Hubble constant] was smaller than the ages of the elements and stars."[70] Interestingly, in order to find an alternative explanation for the data of an expanding universe, a continuous creation out of nothing was proposed. Hermann Bondi wrote, "If we wish to remain true to our assumptions we have no choice but to postulate that there is going on everywhere and at all times a continual creation of matter, the appearance of atoms of hydrogen out of nothing."[71] Although not a true creation *ex nihilo,* because already existing matter is a necessary precondition of the proposed ongoing creation out of nothing, Bondi's proposal is an indication of the direction of future developments. It is not just the idea of an original creation but also a creation *ex nihilo* that models of an expanding universe seem to have difficulty avoiding—as can be seen in the fact that Bondi and Hoyle were forced to propose a pseudo–*ex nihilo* continuous creation in an effort to avoid the implication of a *creatio originans* within the Big Bang theory. The ultimate failure of the steady-state program can be seen in part in the fact that present discussion of *ex nihilo* models within contemporary physics and cosmology are set largely within the context of a presumed *creatio originans* or, in the case of the Hartle-Hawking model, something at least similar to it.

One must be careful to note that although theologians and physicists both make use of the concept and nomenclature of a creation out of nothing, they often assume entirely different meanings for the concept. Physicists, on joining the discussion of a possible absolute beginning of the universe, enter unavoidably into what was formerly a largely metaphysical question. That the language of metaphysics, and sometimes that of theology as well, should be borrowed by physicists is neither surprising nor inappropriate. Yet in the case of a creation of nothing, as we shall see, theologians and philosophers would have great difficulty identifying as *creatio ex nihilo* what many contemporary physicists have claimed to be precisely that. This does not, however, mean that science and theology speak necessarily two distinct languages and have no real basis for dialogue. The problem stems in part from the tendency of some physicists to use terms such as *creatio ex nihilo* loosely to describe anything that treats of an apparent absolute beginning of our universe in scientific terms. The fact, however, that metaphysical conclusions are often drawn from the claim to have found a workable *ex nihilo* theory demonstrates that physicists are in fact also addressing metaphysical and even theological issues. Dialogue therefore between physicists and theologians on the issue of a creation out of nothing is not only possible but necessary.

CREATION OUT OF NOTHING: EARLY MODELS

Matter/Antimatter Imbalance

In 1933 the American physicist Carl Anderson made a remarkable discovery. He produced in the lab a particle identical to the electron but opposite in charge—a particle that Paul Dirac had predicted in 1930. Unfortunately, Anderson's new subatomic particle, now known either as an antielectron or positron, does not have the prospect of a long life. As soon as it encounters an ordinary electron, both annihilate each other in a flash of energy that produces two photons (the so-called light particles). Particle physicists believe that for every particle, there exists potentially an antiparticle that corresponds in every way to the ordinary particle except that it carries an opposite charge. If ever the two meet they immediately annihilate each other in a burst of energy.

So why does our physical universe simply not annihilate itself in a big burst of light? It seems that the early universe should have done just that, except that there were a few more matter particles than antimatter particles. The matter/antimatter imbalance resulted in a minuscule percentage of the total material of the early universe being prevented from simply disappearing. This minuscule amount of matter is presumably what we now see as the physical, observable universe. The presumed efficiency of a perfectly symmetrical universe, however, allows for the existence of only a small amount of the matter (or antimatter) that we now observe in the universe, which suggests that the early universe was asymmetric.[72]

What has all this to do with a creation out of nothing? It sounds more like annihilation than creation. According to Einstein's famous theorem, $E = mc^2$, a natural conversion can take place between matter and energy. In the case of particle/antiparticle annihilation, energy is created as matter is destroyed. What is here crucial is that under very high temperatures—such as those encountered in the first fraction of a second after the Big Bang—the process can reverse itself, that is to say, photon particles can collide to produce matter and antimatter particles. The extreme energy of the initial singularity created a tremendous amount of such matter/antimatter pairs out of pure energy. Theoretically, the pairing should have been equal, but by some as yet unexplained fluke, the occasional production of an extra matter particle occurred. After the termination of the annihilation period in which the very early universe began to cool and the matter/antimatter particles collided with one another producing photons (the remnant of which is still detectable as the universal background radiation discovered by Arno Penzias and Robert Wilson in 1965), the remaining matter particles were left to develop into protons and neutrons, and eventually into atoms, galaxies, and planets.

It is precisely in the creation of matter (and antimatter) out of pure energy (photon particles are not considered matter) that some have seen a creation out of nothing.[73] From the standpoint of a purely materialistic worldview one could perhaps speak here of a creation *ex nihilo* in that the origin of the matter of the universe is explained as coming entirely from nonmatter. However, as Hawking writes, "in quantum theory, particles can be created out of energy in the form of particle/antiparticle pairs. But that just raises the question of where the energy came from."[74] Hawking's explanation is that a positive/negative energy balance means that the total energy of the universe is zero. This answer is not satisfying, for we must still ask where the zero energy balance came from. If, as Hawking suggests, the energy of the universe is all positive and it is all attracting itself by gravity (a negative force), then we still have something other than an *ex nihilo* origin of the universe.

Hawking is speaking here of the somewhat remarkable possibility that this matter/antimatter creation could have perhaps taken place from a state of zero energy. This possibility arises in that energy is essentially either positive or negative. The energy of motion or mass, for example, is always positive, while that of certain types of gravitational or electromagnetic fields is negative. If positive and negative energy exactly offset each other at the initial singularity, then we would have, from the perspective of mathematics, zero energy, from which matter and antimatter particles were created. That means that the "creation process" would have received a zero energy input.

Yet this is hardly descriptive of a *creatio ex nihilo*. We are left with the positive energy, the negative energy produced by its gravitational attraction, and the laws explaining gravitational attraction as well as the gravitational attraction itself, which must all be included within the "nothing" from which the universe sprang and which themselves stand in need of explanation. But what about the so-called zero energy? This energy, it would seem, must have been present in the form of photons for the creation of matter and antimatter to take place. Even this so-called zero energy is something. It is still energy— it is simply energy designated as "zero" because it is equally balanced between positive and negative forces. It is similar to say that $2 - 2 = 0$. While 2 minus 2 is certainly "zero," the numbers themselves cannot be said to be nothing; they simply cancel each other out mathematically.

From the perspective of theology the creation of matter/antimatter pairs cannot be considered a strict *creatio ex nihilo* inasmuch as the particles do not arise out of nothing but out of energy (even if we mean by that "zero energy"), which according to Einstein is essentially matter in another form. The theory does not explain where the energy contained within the explosion came from. What it does explain is a conversion process of energy into matter that is entirely comprehensible within the basic context of relativity theory. In other words, something comes out of something. If this, then, is the original creation, theology is left with an energy/God dualism, not a *creatio ex nihilo*.[75]

Initial Singularity in an Expanding Universe

Another early model of creation *ex nihilo* is built on the basic assumption of the existence of an initial Big Bang singularity within an expanding universe. Stephen Hawking, before he began working on the idea of a no-boundary-condition universe, did seminal work on the possibility and implications of initial singularities with his fellow Cambridge physicist G. Ellis. In their 1973 book, *The Large Scale Structure of Space-Time,* Hawking and Ellis argue that if gravity is always attractive, and if the universe is really expanding (which is today considered a given in modern astrophysics), then an initial singularity would seem unavoidable.[76] Barrow and Tipler have observed that "at this singularity, space and time came into existence; literally nothing existed before the singularity, so, if the Universe originated at such a singularity, we would truly have a creation *ex nihilo*. The singularity is to be regarded as being on the 'boundary' of space-time."[77]

But does an initial singularity really imply a creation out of nothing? There are at least two reasons why it does not. First, our inability to say what happens before the Planck time (10^{-43} to 5.4×10^{-44} ABB) as well as doubts as to whether an actual $t = 0$ point is ever reached, rule out the possibility of claiming that an initial singularity (the nature of which may be beyond our ability to ever understand) demonstrates a *creatio ex nihilo*. Hawking and Ellis wisely point this out at the conclusion of their book: "The creation of the Universe out of nothing has been argued, indecisively, from early times. . . . The results we have obtained support the idea that the universe began a finite time ago. However the actual point of creation, the singularity, is outside the scope of presently known laws of physics."[78]

The second reason a presumed initial singularity cannot be equated with a *creatio ex nihilo* has to do with the fact that we seem to end up with a conical model of the universe that begins from a single point within time. It is true that our "time" seems to begin with this singularity but, even if we rule out the possibility that $t = 0$ is never reached, hot Big Bang models assume some preexisting energy, infinitely dense matter, gravity, certain unknown physical laws, and/or some combination of these.[79] In such a scenario we must ask what $t = 0$ actually means. Chris Isham, who argues that such a singularity does not constitute a *creatio ex nihilo,* points out the difficulty of computing a single-point singularity model as opposed to "three-space" quantum models, which we will take up in our next section. Isham writes: "A singular point is not a smooth three-space, and the technique for computing $K(c_2, f_2; c_1, f_1)$

[the paths employed in the transition amplitude and state function of such a universe] breaks down, not least because the classical solution to Einstein's equations . . . is itself singular and ill-defined at this point." Isham concludes, therefore, that even if this procedure had worked, "it would have described the creation of the universe from an initial 'point'" and not a "creation from 'nothing.'"[80]

At the present state of research it would seem that cosmological models based on matter/antimatter and initial singularity theories are not capable of constructing a theoretical *ex nihilo* cosmogony. Theology would be wise, therefore, to avoid formulating theological conceptions of an *ex nihilo* creation on such models that are not themselves able to lay claim to describing an *ex nihilo* origin of the universe.

CREATION OUT OF NOTHING: QUANTUM WAVE-FLUCTUATION MODELS

Early Wave-Fluctuation Models: Tryon and Vilenkin
To date, no complete theory of quantum gravity exists; nevertheless, several *creatio ex nihilo* models have been built specifically on the components that it is believed such a theory must contain. All such models of an origin of the universe "out of nothing" have been based on theoies of quantum wave fluctuation. The first proposal of an *ex nihilo* model using the idea of a quantum vacuum wave fluctuation was made by Edward Tryon in a brief article appearing in *Nature* in December 1973. Tryon believed that "in any big bang model, one must deal with the problem of 'creation.'" Unhappy with oscillating universe models and the idea that "the conservation laws of physics forbid the creation of something from nothing," Tryon proposed a Big Bang model in which the "Universe is a fluctuation of the vacuum" of quantum field theory. He wrote that in his model he assumes "that our Universe did indeed appear from nowhere about 10^{10} years ago. Contrary to widespread belief, such an event need not have violated any of the conventional laws of physics. The laws of physics merely imply that a Universe which appears from nowhere must have certain specific properties. In particular, such a Universe must have a zero net value for all concerned quantities."[81]

Tryon begins with the phenomenon of "the spontaneous, temporary emergence of particles from a vacuum." This is known as a vacuum fluctuation and is common in quantum field theory. Tryon takes this phenomenon and applies it on a much larger scale to suggest that our universe "may simply be a fluctuation of the vacuum, the vacuum of some larger space in which our Universe is embedded."[82] Odenwald observes that in Tryon's model, "characteristics of our universe would be analogous to those ghostlike quantum particles that flash in and out of existence within the atom and disturb electronic energy levels." [83] In answer to the question of how "such a creation may have come about," Tryon refers to quantum field theory in which "every phenomenon that could happen in principle actually does happen occasionally in practice, on a statistically random basis." This leads Tryon, on the basis of quantum statistical probability, to suggest an answer to the question of why the universe came into being. For those who ponder such questions as the purpose or reason for our existence and that of our universe, Tryon's answer is deeply unsatisfying. He suggests that "our Universe is simply one of those things which happen from time to time." [84]

Tryon's speculation as to why the universe exists, however, does not interest us so much as does his claim that in his model the universe "appears from nowhere." What precisely Tryon means by "nowhere," however, is not clear. Setting aside for the moment the question of whether a quantum vacuum fluctuation can really be considered "nothing," the idea that the vacuum arises out of "some larger space in which our Universe is embedded" would seem by itself a direct contradiction of the claim that the universe arises out of "nowhere." As Odenwald remarks, Tryon is describing "the creation of the entire universe out of the 'empty' vacuum—a small patch of space, perhaps 10^{-33} cm across, that suddenly inflated to enormous size." [85] In Tryon's theory the question of origins is simply pushed back—in this case to a larger space, the existence of which must also be explained. Tryon's proposal, however, was merely a first attempt at a model creation out of nothing built on the idea of a quantum vacuum fluctuation. [86]

The next decisive step in the development of the theory of an *ex nihilo* origin of the universe out of a quantum fluctuation was taken by Alexander Vilenkin in a series of papers appearing between 1982 and 1986. Vilenkin proposes a "cosmological scenario in which the universe is spontaneously created from literally nothing." Similar to Tryon, he suggests that "this scenario does not require any changes in the fundamental equations of physics; it only gives a new interpretation to a well-known cosmological solution." [87] Unlike Tryon's model, however, Vilenkin's "goes further in that it gives a mathematical description of the tunneling process and determines the initial conditions at the moment of nucleation." [88]

Vilenkin explains: "We know that in quantum mechanics particles can tunnel through potential barriers. This suggests that the birth of the universe might be a quantum tunneling effect" of the bounce solution type. "Normally, bounce solutions are used to describe the decay of a quasistable state. If the decaying state is at the bottom of a potential well at $x = x_1$, then the bounce solution starts with $x = x_1$ at $t \to -\infty$, bounces off the classical turning point at the end of the barrier, and returns to $x = x_1$ at $t \to +\infty$." [89] Essentially, when there is no classical path between a certain point and a time (e.g., point 1 at time 1) and another point and time (point 2 at time 2), the transition from p_1,t_1 to p_2,t_2 can arise at the quantum level and is known, therefore, as quantum tunneling.

Crucial to Vilenkin's tunneling origin of the universe is a formula known as the de Sitter instanton, $a(t) = H^{-1}\cos(Ht)$, which Vilenkin claims "can be interpreted as describing the tunneling to de Sitter space from *nothing,* where by nothing I mean a state with no classical space-time."[90] Based on this calculation Vilenkin writes: "The only relevant question seems to be whether or not the spontaneous creation of universes is possible. The existence of the instanton suggests that it is." "Possible" does not mean "probable," however. Given the fact that an instanton with the smallest value corresponds "to most probable universes, then most of the universes never heat up to temperatures greater than 100 GeV and have practically vanishing baryon numbers." This leads Vilenkin to conclude that, "we must live in one of the rare universes which tunneled to the symmetric vacuum state."[91] Additionally, Vilenkin anticipates Hartle and Hawking by claiming that an advantage of his theory is that it provides "a cosmological model which does not have a singularity at the big bang . . . and does not require any initial or boundary conditions."[92]

Vilenkin claims his model represents a creation out of nothing inasmuch as "the wave function can be thought of as describing the state . . . called 'nothing.'"[93] Again, we will defer the discussion of whether a quantum wave fluctuation itself can truly be considered "nothing" in a strict sense of the word until our next section. Vilenkin's model would seem to be disqualified as a creation *ex nihilo* model on other grounds, namely the tunneling phenomenon. The quantum tunneling that allows the universe to emerge out of nothing is itself something—a something that presupposes the existence of certain quantum physical laws that govern its process. Because this model eliminates initial boundary conditions, the precise meaning of "time" within the process is unclear. Nevertheless, the image of a tunneling process would seem to assume that the universe has come from some prior position/ state/time from which it appears "out of nothing" as our time and space. More specifically, Vilenkin supposes that the universe tunnels from a point at $t \to -\infty$. Although we can ascertain nothing about the nature or quality of any $t \to -\infty$ occurrence, we have no scientific or philosophical justification for equating it with "nothing." That is to say, the fact that our universe "tunneled to a symmetric vacuum space" does not answer the question from whence (or from what previous state) it tunneled.

The Hartle-Hawking Proposal

Among reputed *creatio ex nihilo* models that are built on concepts of quantum gravity, the Hartle-Hawking proposal is perhaps the best example. In their now-famous 1983 paper titled "Wave Function of the Universe," James

Hartle and Stephen Hawking, making use of "imaginary" numbers,[94] propose a definition of a ground-state, quantum vacuum wave function for closed universes that extends to gravity "the Euclidean-functional-integral construction of nonrelativistic quantum mechanics and field theory."[95] They also incorporate the "quantum tunneling" mechanism employed by Vilenkin, although it does not play as central a role in their model as in his. In the Hartle-Hawking model the emphasis is on the wave fluctuation itself within a three-dimensional space. The Hartle-Hawking proposal is essentially the "no-boundary condition" for the universe that Hawking popularized in his 1988 book, *A Brief History of Time*. The relevance of the Hartle-Hawking proposal for a creation out of nothing can be seen when they explain that their proposal "means that the universe does not have any boundaries in space or time. . . . There is thus no problem of boundary conditions. One can interpret the functional integral over all compact four-geometries bounded by a given three-geometry as giving the amplitude for the three-geometry to arise from a zero three-geometry, i.e., a single point. In other words, the ground state is the amplitude for the Universe to appear from nothing."[96]

It is precisely because Hartle and Hawking demonstrate the possibility of a universe without boundary in space or time that one can speak here of a *creatio ex nihilo*. It is also crucial that within their model the matter wave function does not oscillate. An oscillating wave function would mean an eternally oscillating universe, a concept Hartle and Harking wish to avoid.[97] Thus we are left with a nonoscillating wave function that essentially contains within itself the creation of a space and time without boundaries. This sounds like a contradiction, that a space-time without boundary conditions could be spoken of as being "created," but within the Hartle-Hawking model it makes sense because the wave fluctuation itself becomes the nonspatial and nontemporal "point" of origin of the physical universe. Actually, this remaining nonspatial, nontemporal boundary is better described as a single three-dimensional space that forms the boundary for a four-dimensional space, because the image of a three-dimensional conical structure beginning at a single point is precisely what the Hartle-Hawking proposal seeks to avoid and what gives merit to its claim to portray a creation out of nothing.[98]

By eliminating, through the use of imaginary numbers, the initial boundary condition (point in time), the Hartle-Hawking universe can be represented to look something like an inverted cone that is rounded rather than beginning at a specific point, with the three-dimensional wave fluctuation forming the only boundary. Time, in such a model, is not eliminated but simply incorporated into the topological structure of three-dimensional space—therefore a four-dimensional space-time is depicted as a three-dimensional space. This would be classified, therefore, as a "time indifferent" model of the universe. Because it is "indifferent" to time, recognizing no initial (or final) time boundary, it cannot be said to represent a creation arising out of a point in time. While it is an extremely speculative model with little chance of observational verification given our present state of knowledge, the Hartle-Hawking model is one of the most promising to come out of quantum cosmology. Chris Isham, in fact, believes that a Hartle-Hawking universe "is what we need to describe creation 'from nothing.'"[99] Similarly, John Barrow has written that this model "admits of an interpretation of the translation probability as creation out of 'nothing' because no initial state exists: there is a single boundary."[100] The question we must ask then is: What is the *nothing* from which the Hartle-Hawking universe is "created"?

"Nothing," within the context of the Hartle-Hawking proposal, would seem to mean nothing other than the boundary condition of the quantum wave fluctuation itself along with the various laws of physics presupposed by such a fluctuation.[101] In a sense, therefore, the universe does have a boundary condition, namely that of the quantum wave fluctuation.[102] While this makes the model comprehensible within a Big Bang cosmology, it would also seem to rule out any claims that we have here a strict *creatio ex nihilo* in either a theological or philosophical sense. As Willem Drees comments, "The 'nothing' which has a precise meaning in the context of this proposal is not an absolute 'nothing' in a more philosophical sense."[103] Similarly, John Barrow notes in regard to the Hartle-Hawking proposal that we "must still grant the existence of quite a body of preexisting laws of Nature in order to get away with this trick."[104] Heinz Pagels, in an attempt to define the "nothingness" assumed in the Vilenkin and Hartle-Hawking models, also runs into the problem of necessarily preexisting laws. He writes: "The nothingness 'before' the creation of the universe is the most complete void that we can imagine— no space, time or matter existed. It is a world without place, without duration or eternity, without number. . . . Yet this unthinkable void converts itself into the plenum of existence—a necessary consequence of physical laws. Where are these laws written into the void? It would seem that even the void is subject to law, a logic that existed prior to time and space."[105]

It would appear, therefore, despite all the talk of the Hartle-Hawking and similar models representing a creation *ex nihilo,* that the *nihil* from which such quantum universes spring is far from being "nothing" in either a theological or philosophical sense of the word. Yet this does not mean that the Hartle-Hawking model is without theological significance. Although it is not a true *ex nihilo* model in the strict theological sense, its near lack of dependence on boundary conditions may be a useful model in illustrating the dependence/contingency of the universe on God alone for its being. And this, of course, is really the point of the theological assertion of a creation out of nothing.

The Barrow-Tipler Model

Another example of an *ex nihilo* model based on quantum gravity is that proposed by Barrow and Tipler. Barrow and Tipler claim that they have developed "a model quantum universe in which the wave function does depend on a time parameter explicitly, and in which the Universe originates out of the point $R(t) = 0$—that is, out of nothing—at a finite time in the past as measured by this time-parameter."[106] The Barrow-Tipler model is, like that of Hartle and Hawking, built on the idea of a wave fluctuation arising out of a quantum vacuum. Unlike the Hartle-Hawking model, however, it is not time indifferent. This means that it entails an actual beginning of the universe in time.[107] Not only does the Barrow-Tipler model differ from that of Hartle and Hawking in that it contains an initial singularity, or initial time boundary; it is also, in light of the needs of the anthropic principle, compatible with the many-worlds theory. As Barrow and Tipler point out, "whatever the wave function of the Universe, the MWI implies that it should represent a collection of many universes." For Barrow and Tipler the initial wave fluctuation sets off a series of universes, to which they refer as a "collection of branch universes."[108]

Interestingly, this model includes not only an initial but also a final singularity, which seems to be required by the strong anthropic principle.[109] Yet our primary interest here is with the model's postulate of an initial singularity that lies on the boundary of time. Barrow and Tipler explain that the universe has no radius "before the first interaction occurs that can encode a scale measurement. . . . After the first two scaled interactions have occurred, the Universe has been split by the interactions into a large number of branches, in each of which an essentially classical evolution is seen. . . . In the quantum Universe, all the classical universes are present, one classical universe defining a single branch. The classical universes are equally probable."[110]

The Barrow-Tipler model, which would essentially seem to be an adaptation of the Hartle-Hawking model to the needs of the strong anthropic principle and the many-worlds theory, claims to represent a creation out of nothing. In this regard, however, it suffers the same liability as the Hartle-Hawking model in that the quantum wave fluctuation itself and the laws that it presupposes could only with great juggling of language be called "nothing." The initial boundary condition in such a model has certainly become very "small," but it has hardly disappeared into a quantum *nihil*.

Perhaps the best evaluation of all quantum wave fluctuation models (including the Barrow-Tipler and Hartle-Hawking models) in regard to a Christian understanding of *creatio ex nihilo* is that given by physicist and theologian John Polkinghorne. He writes:

> It is not true in that theory [that is, quantum wave fluctuation arising out of a vacuum] that if there is nothing there then nothing is happening. Quite the contrary, for the quantum vacuum is a hive of activity, full of fluctuations, random comings-to-be and fadings-away. . . . There are no particles present, no permanent excitations, but there is a continual chaos of transient blips, rising and falling away again. If one of these excitations were particularly big, it might get blown up by the effects of inflation to cosmic proportions! On this view we would be living in a grotesquely swollen quantum fluctuation. . . . The notion is speculative to the highest degree. . . . However, suppose for a moment that such a fluctuation was the actual origin of our universe. It would certainly not have come from something which without great abuse of language could be called "nothing." There has to be a quantum field [or fields] given as the source of the fluctuation. The price of the "free lunch" is the provision of those quantum fields. On a Christian understanding that provision would be the continuing act of the Creator.[111]

CREATIO EX NIHILO WITHOUT GOD?

The classical Christian doctrine of *creatio ex nihilo* may no longer be scientifically unintelligible, but the scientific models of an *ex nihilo* beginning of our universe can and have been used as arguments against the existence of a Creator. As Isham explains, "these theories . . . have been billed by anti-theists as further evidence of science's ability to explain 'everything.'"[112] It is easy to see how this takes place. None of the *ex nihilo* models we examined makes reference to God. Theology has always defined *creatio ex nihilo* as creation out of nothing other than the fullness of God's own being. Obviously, a *creatio ex nihilo* model built on purely physical explanation (if that is not itself a contradiction) eliminates the "fullness of God's own being" from the *ex nihilo* formula.[113] It is precisely such a possibility that prompted Hawking to ask his now-famous question, "What place, then, for a Creator?" The implication of the Hartle-Hawking proposal (and other *ex nihilo* models) for the divine postulate has been put sharply by Bernulf Kanitscheider, who writes: "If the Hartle-Hawking model stands up to the critical review of other specialists then it will without doubt have enormous implications for metaphysics and natural theology. . . . Hawking himself recognizes this and contends that his model excludes a creation."[114]

The discovery of a true *ex nihilo* cosmogony, if such is possible, would cut both ways for theology. On the one hand, the scientific discovery of an "event" long-maintained by theology (even when it seemed scientifically laughable) would certainly add fodder to the popularized apologies for theistic belief. It could probably be used as a metaphor, if not a sort of proof, for the traditional Christian doctrine of creation out of nothing. On the other hand, a purely scientific model of an *ex nihilo* origin of the universe would not only seem to make a Creator redundant within such a model, it would also threaten the continued existence of the various forms of cosmological arguments—even in their reduced role as witnesses to the reasonableness of theistic belief. Such a scenario, however, may never arise.

When the question is examined seriously, and "nothing" is not loosely defined, it would seem that there can be no true creation *ex nihilo* without God. From the perspective of theology, which defines *ex nihilo* as "out of nothing but the fullness of God's own being," an *ex nihilo* creation without God is ruled out *a priori*. From the perspective of philosophy, when the postulate of a divine Creator is removed, we would seem to be left with the unanswered naked dictum: *ex nihilo nihil fit* (nothing comes out of nothing). Even from the perspective of physics it is questionable whether a functional theory containing a true *creatio ex nihilo* is within the realm of possibility.

As we have seen, some set of quantum laws, some form of energy, quantum fields, mathematical logic, wave fluctuations, or, as is most often the case, some combination of these, is always the "nothing" out of which the universe is said to have originated. We should not expect the case to be otherwise. Natural science deals with matter, physical laws, and the relationships that exist between and within the physical realities of the universe. But most of all, natural science deals with explanations. For a true *creatio ex nihilo* there can be no explanation. The moment one claims to have a theory explaining *how* the universe could have originated out of nothing, one enters into an unavoidable contradiction. Any theory explaining how something has come from nothing must assume some preexisting laws or energy or quantum activity in order to be a credible theory. It could be claimed, naturally, that there was nothing and then suddenly there was, without apparent physical cause or ground, something. But this would be more a statement of philosophical or theological belief than a genuine scientific theory. With some caution we might even say that the claim that science has "reached the end of the line" could be applied with better justification to the search for a theory describing a creation out of nothing than to the general idea of an initial Big Bang singularity, which does not necessarily require an *ex nihilo* beginning of the universe.

Polkinghorne has rightly observed that there is always a price to the "free lunch" that some physicists have sought to find for the explanation of the existence of the universe. This price, as we have seen, is the provision of quantum fields or of some other reality that in turn needs an explanation. Polkinghorne believes that from the perspective of Christian theology this provision "would be the continuing act of the Creator."[115] But by bringing in a Creator in this fashion, has Polkinghorne introduced a God-of-the-gaps in a fashion similar to bringing in a Creator at the Big Bang singularity, which seems an impenetrable wall to contemporary physics? I believe he has not, but the distinction is a fine one. There is no claim here that God can be introduced because of an acknowledged limit or based on the material content of any particular scientific theory. There is no claim in Polkinghorne's statement that science has reached its appointed limit and beyond this point God is to be found. Polkinghorne makes a theological observation rather than a pseudoscientific one. When we understand this as a theological affirmation of God's role as Creator, made independent of any presumed limitation of scientific knowledge, then we can agree with Polkinghorne: Without a Creator there is no *creatio ex nihilo*.

SUMMARY: GOD AS CREATOR IN THE LIGHT OF CONTEMPORARY PHYSICS

We have treated the subject of an *ex nihilo* creation largely within the context of an original creation, taking our cue in part from the discussion of an *ex nihilo* beginning of the universe within modern physics and cosmology. This does not mean, however, that the doctrine of creation out of nothing within Christian theology is primarily intended to support the concept of an original creation. The true significance of the *creatio ex nihilo* axiom is not as a theory of origins but rather first and foremost as a statement about God and God's relationship to the physical, contingent universe. The contingency and dependence upon God of each aspect of the physical universe in each moment of its existence is, therefore, the central message of a creation out of nothing.

The confession of an *ex nihilo* creation enables Christians to say what impact their understanding of God has on their understanding of the physical world in which they live. The *ex nihilo* axiom also makes it possible for us to state what difference our understanding of the world makes for our understanding of God. Not that God is contained within the world or is in any way to be equated with it—nothing could be further from the idea of an *ex nihilo* creation. Rather, because the universe finds its sole source of being in God, the nature of the universe is relevant for our understanding and confession of God as Creator. This does not mean, however, that theology must rewrite its doctrine of God as Creator every time a theory or model within physics rises or falls. The actual impact of developments within physics and cosmology on Christian theology in general, and the doctrines of God and creation in particular, may not be that dramatic. As the physicist Chris Isham admits: "What then can these new scientific ideas on creation contribute to the theological archive of metaphysical wisdom? I suspect that the honest answer is 'not very much,' although some attention should surely be paid to the shifting forms in which the archetypes of space and time are impinging on the scientific world." [116]

The natural sciences neither determine the content nor set alone the agenda for theological reflection. Yet in the modern world they do determine much of the context in which theology takes place. Christian theology and Christian apologetics cannot hope to speak seriously of the nature of God as Creator if the information being gathered by the natural sciences about the nature of the creation itself is ignored as being irrelevant to the task of theology. The challenge to theology is essentially this: If we confess a God who is beyond space and time yet created space and time, can we neglect to listen to what contemporary physicists are saying about the nature of space and time?

One specific question posed by modern physics that is especially significant for the doctrine of God is simply: How free could a Creator have been in choosing the initial conditions of the universe? Roger Penrose has spoken of the pinpoint accuracy that would have been required of a Creator. The scientific discovery of such fine-tuning has often led to the question of how much freedom a Creator would have had in creating the universe. The response, we would suggest, is that the evidence is being looked at from the wrong perspective—from that of a time after the event. Seen from the perspective of a Creator facing a universe of options, the evidence of fine-tuning points to the incredible freedom a Creator would have had in choosing from an incomprehensible number of possible universes. Hawking recognizes this as well when he writes: "At the big bang and other singularities, all the laws would have broken down, so God would still have had complete freedom to choose what happened and how the universe began." [117] Theology, which has always confessed the essential freedom of God in the creative act, has no difficulty with such a viewpoint.

The freedom of God in the creative act is not, however, to be taken for granted. Einstein, for instance, seems to have questioned the extent of freedom a Creator would have had when he wrote: "What I'm really interested in is whether God could have made the world in a different way; that is, whether the necessity of logical simplicity leaves any freedom at all!" [118] Similarly, in light of the no-boundary condition and the possibility of a unified theory, Hawking writes: "'How much choice did God have in constructing the universe?' If the no boundary proposal is correct, he had no freedom at all to choose initial conditions. He would, of course, still have had the freedom to choose the laws that the universe obeyed. This, however, may not really have been all that much of a choice; there may well be only one, or a small number, of complete unified theories . . . that are self-consistent and allow the existence of structures as complicated as human beings."[119]

We can only begin to formulate a response to this challenge. One avenue may be to explore the nonspatial, nontemporal three-space boundary that a no-boundary-condition universe is left with. Would a Creator who is beyond space and time have had freedom in determining the nature of space-time at this "no-boundary" boundary? And if only one possible unified theory exists that makes our universe comprehensible, could we not say that God exercised a certain creative freedom in "finding" or creating this theory? In light of a genuine *ex nihilo* creation it would seem that a Creator would have had considerable freedom in creating a universe of such a nature that there would be only one comprehensive theory capable of explaining it. Indeed, physicist James Trefil has confessed that he feels "much more comfortable with the concept of a God who is clever enough to devise the laws of physics that make the existence of our marvelous universe inevitable than . . . with the old-fashioned God who had to make it all, laboriously, piece by piece."[120]

Also, modern physics and cosmology, in their search for an *ex nihilo* origin of the universe, have provided theology with a potent reminder of the importance of this doctrine. Modern science would like to find (and sometimes tells itself it has found) a "creation" or origin out of nothing, as this would settle the question of whether the universe is ultimately contingent in its existence. At present, the most promising models seem to contain an array of laws, principles, and quantum fluctuations that themselves require explanation. The Christian affirmation of a creation out of nothing is a recognition that the universe in the entirety of its space-time existence is dependent on God. Hence the *ex nihilo* affirmation corresponds with the confession of a Creator who transcends creation. Without the traditional doctrine of the transcendence of God, modern physics, as it moves closer and closer to an initial singularity, $t = 0$, or a *creatio ex nihilo*, brings the existence of God increasingly into question. If God does not transcend the physical universe, what place is left for God within it? We would either be forced to adopt a God-of-the-gaps and hope that some ultimate gap will remain, or go in the direction of a crass pantheism and rename the physical universe, inclusive of its laws and processes, "God." Neither of these paths is a particularly attractive option for Christian theology. Thus we are left with the creation *ex nihilo,* which alone does justice to the Christian understanding of God as Creator.

Even though much of the discussion about a creation out of nothing remains bound to the concept of an original creation, the former is not dependent on the latter. Although this insight is not new, developments in modern physics have shed much light on it. Ian Barbour, one of the best known contemporary advocates of this view, explains that "the contingency of boundary conditions . . . expresses the message of *ex nihilo* without requiring an absolute beginning. If it turns out that . . . time were infinite, we would still have contingent boundary conditions."[121] The creation *ex nihilo* axiom and an original creation fit quite naturally and beautifully together. Yet the awareness is significant that the *ex nihilo* assertion and its corresponding doctrine of the dependence of the world on God is not dependent on an absolute beginning of time. This recognition liberates not only the *ex nihilo* doctrine but also the doctrine of God as Creator from the uncertainty of the outcome of present discussions among physicists and cosmologists.

In analyzing the various *ex nihilo* models of modern cosmogony, we have been rigorously strict with our definition of "nothing" with regard to the instrumentality of claimed *ex nihilo* origins. In fact, in every case we have seen that the instrumentality itself (on which the models are built) stands necessarily in contradiction to the claim of a creation or origin of the universe out of nothing. In fairness we must approach the Christian doctrine of *creatio ex nihilo* with the same degree of critical rigorism. Does theology go beyond a mere affirmation of an *ex nihilo* creation and speak of the instrumentality of such an act; that is to say, does it address the "how" of a *creatio ex nihilo?* The answer would seem to be yes, although not in the strict scientific sense. Traditionally, theology has always spoken of creation as taking place through the spoken word of God in connection with the *ex nihilo* doctrine. That is to say, God spoke the world into existence—which would indeed seem to address the question of instrumentality. Martin Luther gave classic expression to this idea in his *Commentary on Genesis* when he wrote: "Through His speaking God makes something out of nothing. . . . [The 'word' is] the means and the instrument God used during His work."[122]

Theology runs into difficulty here if it attempts to interpret the Genesis account of God's speaking the world into existence in any sort of a literal sense. If there was simply God and then God spoke, we might ask what kind of words were spoken. The very idea of the spoken word presupposes a whole set of physical laws governing sound waves, not to mention the fact that these sound waves need something to travel through. It has been claimed, therefore, that Christian theology contradicts itself in the expression of its doctrine of *creatio ex nihilo*.

Taken at face value, the objection is entirely valid. Yet we must not overlook the fact that God's speaking the world into existence has almost universally been interpreted in a metaphorical or symbolic sense within the Christian theological tradition. Seen as a metaphor, the image of God's speaking the world into existence addresses the question of instrumentality only in the

sense that it confesses that whatever process may have occurred, it was entirely contingent on the being of God. This, of course, has always been the
essential point of the *ex nihilo* confession. Thus interpreted, God alone is
presupposed. If it is objected that this, too, is not an *ex nihilo* creation in the
strictest sense, that is certainly true. Nothing comes out of nothing—but out
of nothing other than the fullness of God's own being was created a life-
producing universe that is contingent on God in each moment and each
aspect of its existence.

Chapter Four

Is God Still Active in the Universe?

O Lord, how manifold are your works! In wisdom you have made them all; the earth is full of your creatures. . . . When you hide your face, they are dismayed; when you take away their breath, they die and return to their dust.
—Psalm 104:24, 29

[The Lord] covers the heavens with clouds, prepares rain for the earth, makes grass grow on the hills. He gives to the animals their food, and to the young ravens when they cry.
—Psalm 147:8-9

Today, thanks to the relentless advance of the science which Newton pioneered, God's immanence has been pushed to somewhere below the subatomic particles or beyond the farthest visible galaxy.
—E. O. Wilson

The processes revealed by the sciences are in themselves God acting as Creator and God is not to be found as some kind of additional factor added on to the processes of the world. God, to use the language usually applied to sacramental theology, is "in, with and under" all-that-is and all-that-goes-on.
—Arthur Peacocke

WHAT IS CONTINUING CREATION?

We have already seen the significance of affirming God's transcendence in the light of modern physics. Not only the divine postulate itself but also the doctrines of an original creation and a creation *ex nihilo* point to a Creator who transcends the physical universe. The results of recent research programs in physics and cosmology, though incapable of addressing the nature of a transcendent reality directly, have nevertheless helped to demonstrate the importance of the traditional Christian emphasis on the transcendence of God. In this chapter we turn our attention to the question of God's immanence. In contrast to some recent streams of theological thought, we do not consider transcendence and immanence mutually exclusive affirmations about God. The idea that we must choose between affirming God's immanence and God's transcendence is as false as the notion that an original creation out of nothing and a continuing creation (*creatio continua*) are competing models of God's creative activity.

Theology has traditionally held the doctrines of creation out of nothing and continuing creation to be interrelated on the view that they are complementary aspects of God's creative involvement with the physical universe. This has not, however, been a universal consensus among theologians. In recent times many have sought to portray an *ex nihilo* creation and a *creatio continua* as competing descriptions of God's creative activity. Because the *ex nihilo* concept was formulated and defined at a time when the universe was believed to be static, many have felt that it is not flexible enough to describe God's creative activity in the dynamic universe in which we live. There has been an attempt, therefore, to adapt theology to the ideas of modern science by rejecting a static creation out of nothing in favor of a dynamic continuing creation. Ian Barbour, representing this viewpoint, argues that "today the world as known to science is dynamic and incomplete. Ours is an unfinished universe that is still in the process of appearing. Surely the coming-to-be of life from matter can represent divine creativity as suitably as any postulated primeval production of matter 'out of nothing.' Creation occurs throughout time."[1]

Regarding the merging of creation into providence, Barbour contends that "if creation is continuing, the [temporal and ontological distinctions between creation and providence] . . . vanish. If time is infinite, there was no initial act, no state of '*nihilo*,' and God has always been working along with other causes. Even if time is finite creation occurs throughout its span and in the midst of other entities."[2] Similarly, Langdon Gilkey seems to prefer a concept of continuing creation over that of an original *ex nihilo* creation. He argues that "creation is seen now to take place throughout the unfolding temporal process, for new forms of life and institutions . . . continually appear during that process. If God creates at all, therefore, he/she creates over time; thus, creation and providential rule seem to melt into one another. . . . The symbol of God's creation of the world points not to an event at the beginning."[3]

This separation of continuing creation and an original creation out of nothing is especially to be noticed among process theologians who reject a creation out of nothing precisely because it seems bound with the concepts of God as absolute controller over a static universe.[4] The idea that an original static creation *ex nihilo* needs to be replaced by a dynamic *creatio continua* represents, I believe, a profound misunderstanding of the original intention of both the *ex nihilo* and *continua* aspects of the doctrine of creation. Correctly understood, "these two concepts are complementary and . . . we need not substitute one for the other. Christian theology needs both."[5] Wolfhart Pannenberg is correct in his observation that "the *creatio continuata* formula presupposes the strict conception of creation as *creatio ex nihilo* inasmuch as it characterizes God's preserving activity as the continuation of the creation out of nothing. For this reason alone the idea of a continuing creation cannot be set in opposition to the *creatio ex nihilo* formula."[6] The idea that an original creation out of nothing must preclude dynamic change within the creation is largely an intellectual "discovery" of our modern era. Traditional theology, although lacking the understanding provided by modern science of the full extent of the evolutionary process of the world, always maintained the continuing activity of the Creator in the physical cosmos.

What exactly do we mean, then, by continuing creation? The definition is admittedly broad. It encompasses not only the idea that the act of creation is a continuing process, but also the continuing sustenance and involvement of the Creator in regard to the physical world. We would not agree with the restrictive view that continuing creation is limited to "the constant process of bringing *de novo* into existence things that hitherto had not existed, i.e., ongoing *creatio ex nihilo*" and that "it does not mean changing things that already exist."[7] Continuing creation has instead to do with God's multi-faceted immanence in the world. Just as it is false to choose between an original creation *ex nihilo* and a continuing creation, so it is also wrong to choose between affirming God's transcendence and God's immanence. The God who creates "out of nothing" necessarily transcends the physical reality thus created. Yet God's transcendence does not prevent God from being present in every moment and every aspect of creation as God sustains the physical universe and the life within it in its continuous processes of dynamic flux and becoming.

Like the *ex nihilo* doctrine, aspects of the affirmation of a *creatio continua* are to be found already in the Scriptures of the Old and New Testaments. The dependence of living creatures on the continuing sustenance of God is confessed by the psalmist in what has been called a summary statement of God's providence.[8] "O LORD, how manifold are your works! In wisdom you have made them all; the earth is full of your creatures. . . . When you hide your face, they are dismayed; when you take away their breath, they die and return to their dust" (Ps. 104:24, 29). Similarly, the psalmist affirms the activity of the Creator in the ongoing process of our physical world when he writes:

"[The LORD] covers the heavens with clouds, prepares rain for the earth, makes grass grow on the hills. He gives to the animals their food, and to the young ravens when they cry" (Ps. 147:8-9). The fact that the biblical writers believed God to be free to intervene in creation is apparent from the many miracle accounts in the Scriptures. While many such miraculous events have been explained as entirely consistent with natural law, others would seem to defy any such explanation.[9] What seems to be absent from the biblical account, however, is testimony to any sort of ongoing creation out of nothing. The closest the Scriptures come to such a confession is in God's activity in the continual creation of new human life, as in Psalm 139:13. "For it was you who formed my inward parts; you knit me together in my mother's womb." However, unless one accepts the view of Karl Barth that each human being is created out of the dialectical nothingness of nonbeing,[10] this text hardly speaks of the sort of ongoing *creatio ex nihilo* that some modern theologians seem to have in mind. In fact, Wolfhart Pannenberg cites Psalm 139:13 as supporting the idea of a continuing work of God in which the presupposition of an original act of *creatio ex nihilo* is found that is not to be identified with the idea of a continuing creation out of nothing.[11]

Perhaps the most frequently cited biblical text relating to continuing creation is Colossians 1:16, 17, in which God's creative and sustaining activity through Jesus Christ is confessed in the form of an early Christian hymn: "In him [Christ] all things in heaven and on earth were created, things visible and invisible, . . . all things have been created through him and for him. He himself is before all things, and in him all things hold together." Concerning this text the New Testament scholar Ralph Martin has pointed out that "it is unlikely that Paul had 'some quasi-scientific world-view in mind' . . . more probably he is at pains here to assert that Christ is the sole and rightful Lord of creation who not only set the universe in motion at the beginning of time but is responsible for all that appears since then."[12] Peter O'Brien is even bolder in his assertion that a doctrine of divine sustenance is to be found in this text. He writes that we see here that Christ "is the sustainer of the universe and the unifying principle of its life. Apart from his *continuous* sustaining activity all would disintegrate."[13]

What is difficult to substantiate is the claim that, "although less developed than the *ex nihilo* tradition in church history, continuous creation theology is the older tradition."[14] This claim is apparently based on the assumption that the *ex nihilo* doctrine is found only in seminal form in the Scriptures and is not fully developed until Augustine. The *continua* tradition, however, is likewise only to be found in seminal form in the Scriptures and, in the sense of an ongoing creation out of nothing as some intend it, is absent from the biblical witness altogether. Pannenberg certainly assesses the situation more accurately when he writes: "As far as formulas are concerned the *creatio contin-uata* formula comes from a much later time than that of the *creatio ex nihilo,* namely from the European Middle Ages." [15]

There is a great deal of disagreement today as to the precise meaning of continuing creation. As has been noted, some would have it apply only to an ongoing creation *ex nihilo.* Others view it as an alternative to an original *ex nihilo* creation. In our discussion, continuing creation is to be understood as complementary to a doctrine of *creatio ex nihilo.* Under continuing creation we understand primarily divine sustenance and conservation (including change), providence, and the possibility of divine intervention/activity in the physical universe. What all of these various facets of a continuing creation have in common is that they point to the immanence of God in the physical cosmos. The sociobiologist E. O. Wilson, in regard to the question of God's immanence in the light of modern physics, has written, "Today, thanks to the relentless advance of the science which Newton pioneered, God's imma-nence has been pushed to somewhere below the subatomic particles or be-yond the farthest visible galaxy." [16] Whether this is an accurate assessment of the status of the doctrine of God's immanence, as expressed in the many facets of a *creatio continua,* will be the primary focus of the present chapter.

CONTINUING CREATION AS DIVINE SUSTENANCE

Continuous "Creation out of Nothing" and Change in a Dynamic Universe
Philip Hefner, who identifies continuing creation primarily with God's suste-nance of the world, affirms that "creation . . . is not limited by what happened at the beginning when time was first created. Creation also refers to God's ongoing sustaining of the world. Every moment of the world's existence de-pends upon the ongoing grace of God." [17] The insight that God sustains the world in every moment of its existence is crucial. Sustenance does not have to do with a static maintenance of the world as originally created but rather with its being sustained in each moment of its existence. If modern scientific investigation of the physical universe tells us that the cosmos exists as a dy-namic process, then we must confess that it is precisely in this nonstatic pro-cess that God sustains the universe.

The Christian confession of divine sustenance contains no *a priori* predis-position toward either a static or dynamic universe. It is, rather, a statement about God's *relationship* to the cosmos. At this point theology must listen to the physical sciences to learn what kind of physical reality it is that God is sustaining. Both the ideas of change within already existing matter and the possibility of a continuous *de novo creatio ex nihilo* are to be classified as belong-ing to the broader understanding of God's sustenance of the physical cosmos.

Whether any biblical or scientific justification actually exists for a continuous *de novo* creation out of nothing, however, is questionable.

Does the process of the cosmos contain any kind of ongoing creation out of nothing? Only one serious theory of such a continuous *creatio ex nihilo* has been put forward in recent times, namely the steady-state theory.[18] As a major alternative to the standard Big Bang interpretation of the expanding universe, Hermann Bondi and Thomas Gold, joined shortly thereafter by Fred Hoyle, proposed in 1948 a model that would allow the universe to be understood as static and without beginning. The theory required the postulation that "there is going on everywhere and at all times a continual creation of matter, the appearance of atoms of hydrogen out of nothing."[19] The rejection of the steady-state theory has been previously discussed and does not need to be taken up here. What is of interest, however, is how Christian theology would have or could have responded had the steady-state theory rather than the Big Bang model become the standard cosmological model.

Could theology have accepted or incorporated the steady-state model of continuous creation—even if it cast doubt on an original creation? John Polkinghorne believes the answer to be yes, based on a correct understanding of the affirmation of a continuing creation. He believes it erroneous to assume that "big bang cosmology, with its dateable point of departure for the universe as we know it, has a superior value for theology over the steady-state theory, which essentially supposed the universe to have been everlasting." Polkinghorne explains that although the steady-state theory has been discredited since the 1965 discovery of the cosmic background radiation, "theology could have lived with either physical theory, for the assertion that God is Creator is not a statement that at a particular time he did something, but rather that at all times he keeps the world in being. The doctrine of creation is a doctrine of ontological origin."[20]

That theology could have lived with either theory is certainly correct. Most theologians, however, were probably cheering for the Big Bang theory for precisely the reason that the doctrine of creation has traditionally been understood as more than simply a doctrine of ontological origin. If in 1965 the creation of hydrogen atoms "out of nothing" had been discovered instead of the uniform microwave background radiation of the universe, the question of the eternity of the universe would likely have remained an open one from the standpoint of philosophy and theology. Verification of the steady-state model would have eliminated the scientific need of speaking of a "beginning," but it would not have been a proof of the eternality of the universe. Theology could have postulated an original creation of the universe in such a steady-state form. In doing so, however, it would have isolated itself from dialogue with scientific cosmology. Most important, however, a continuous creation out of nothing could have been reconciled with Christian theology as a part of God's keeping the world in being at all times, that is to say, as an aspect of God's divine sustenance. The steady-state theory has become little more than a footnote in the history of mid-twentieth-century physics. Yet new theories and cosmological models are constantly arising and no one can guarantee that a similar theory may not one day become the "standard" operating theory within physics and cosmology. For this reason, if no other, the lessons of the steady-state theory deserve continued theological reflection.

The steady-state theory should also serve as a reminder of the danger of using any specific scientific theory as confirmation of a theological position. As Robert John Russell has observed, "The fact that a scientifically acceptable alternative cosmology was possible should make us at the very least cautious of using cosmology (Big Bang or steady state) to give direct support to any theological position whether that position be theistic or . . . atheistic."[21]

While it appears that theology need not make room for an ongoing creation out of nothing within its understanding of God's sustenance of the physical universe, we are nevertheless far removed from the old view of a static universe that is simply maintained by God. Modern science has dispelled forever the idea that we live in a static, unchanging universe. We live undeniably in a dynamic, changing universe. Whether seen from the perspective of the "positive" evolutionary advance of biological life forms on our planet or from that of the "negative" increase of entropy in the universe as a whole, our universe is in process, or flux. Hence a theology engaged in dialogue with the natural sciences must affirm a God who sustains the universe—not in some static, originally created form, but in its dynamic process of change.

Field Theory, Divine Contingency, and the Preservation of Creation

The seminal form of modern field theories can be traced back to the Stoic doctrine of the divine *pneuma* (spirit), which has been identified as the "direct predecessor of the field concept" in modern physics.[22] The history of the modern concept of field theory, however, begins with the experimental and theoretical work of the nineteenth-century British chemist Michael Faraday on electricity and magnetism. Faraday, unhappy with the concept of "action at a distance" in which force was seen simply to leap across space, developed a concept of force in which forces themselves were "the sole physical substance"[23] and were all interconnected to such an extent that the "mutual relation and conversion of forces would surpass the human intellect."[24] The concepts of force and fields of force were known long before Faraday, "but the prevailing viewpoint was not to regard such 'fields' as constituting, in themselves, actual physical substance. . . . However, Faraday's profound experimental findings led him to believe that electric and magnetic fields are *real* physical 'stuff.'" In this way Faraday may be said to have been "the first scientist to have made a serious challenge to the 'Newtonian' picture."[25]

Although considered the founder of modern field theory, Faraday himself never spoke of fields of force but used the phrase "physical lines of force" to describe his concept of field theory. Although there has been some controversy as to what precisely Faraday's field concept was, its essential features would seem to be "that force is a substance, that it is the only substance and that all forces are interconvertible through various motions of the lines of force."[26] Although most of these features were not adopted in successive concepts of field theory, the essential idea of a field theory itself was developed further by James Clerk Maxwell and Heinrich Hertz and, within classical physics, culminated in the relativity theory of Albert Einstein. The concept of field theory has also been carried over into quantum theory, which through the application of quantum mechanics to the behavior of fields (for example, electromagnetic fields) overcomes the paradox of the wave-particle duality.[27] This achievement was first accomplished by Paul Dirac, who applied quantum mechanics to Maxwell's theory of the electromagnetic field and produced the first example of a quantum field theory, leading physicists to conceive of light as both wave and particle. Quantum fields demonstrate a certain interconnectedness on the micro-level that corresponds to that already observed on the macro-level. The concept of quantum fields, however, must be viewed with some caution in regard to its metaphysical significance.

Quantum field theories, which arise from the combination of concepts taken from special relativity and quantum mechanics, have been helpful in overcoming the tension of the wave-particle dualism. The best example of a quantum field theory—that of quantum electrodynamics—has had a great deal of success in making accurate predictions about the precise value of the magnetic moment (or strength) of the electron.[28] Yet even as the most successful example of a quantum field theory, quantum electromagnetism has problems. As Roger Penrose points out, "It is a rather untidy theory—and a not altogether consistent one—because it initially gives nonsensical 'infinite' answers," which must be "removed by a process known as 'renormalization.'" Unfortunately, "not all quantum field theories are amenable to renormalization, and they are difficult to calculate with even when they are."[29] To assume that quantum field theories are a complete and final description of the nature of quantum "reality" is a mistake. Such theories may turn out to be nothing more than provisional descriptions of quantum relationships. Even if this does not prove to be the case, the analogical character of the field concept, especially within quantum physics, must not be overlooked.

In quantum theory the concept of force, and of fields of force, takes on a sort of double analogical character. First, the concept of force in classical physics is essentially "a device for the economy of thought, based upon analogy with human experience."[30] In quantum mechanics the concepts of force and fields of force become a sort of double analogy inasmuch as they rely on analogy with classical physics. As Max Jammer has written, in quantum mechanics "the concept of force . . . is introduced in complete analogy to macroscopic dynamics and is consequently, strictly speaking, an analogy of an analogy." The analogical character of the concepts of force and fields of force is significant for the discussion of the implications of such concepts for theology. Words such as *field* and *force* are analogies that help us comprehend physical reality; they are not themselves reality—unless perhaps they be understood as mathematical reality. Caution should be exercised in drawing philosophical and theological conclusions from such ideas, especially in light of the theoretical and practical problems that continue to plague many field theories.

Nevertheless, despite the essentially analogical nature and sometimes provisional character of field theories, they hold a rich possibility for metaphors that can be explored by theology. In fact, it is precisely because of the theological reflection generated by the concept of field theory that we take up the topic here. The concept of field theory has, for example, been employed by theologians as a model for understanding God's sustenance of the creation through the Holy Spirit. Thomas F. Torrance seems to have been the first to make use of field theory in this capacity in his 1969 book, *Space, Time and Incarnation*. Torrance suggested that we must allow the incarnation to create a field of "organic connections" within which we can speak and think about the incarnation. This field, contended Torrance, "is surely the interaction of God with history understood from the axis of Creation-Incarnation. . . . Our understanding of this field will be determined by the force or energy that constitutes it, the Holy and Creator Spirit of God."[31]

Similarly, Wolfhart Pannenberg has given a great deal of attention to the relationship between field theory and the doctrine of the Holy Spirit. Pannenberg believes that, "since the field concept as such corresponds to the old concept of *pneuma* . . . theologians should consider it obvious to relate the field concept of modern physics to the Christian doctrine of the dynamic presence of the divine Spirit in all of creation."[32] What is of specific interest to us here, therefore, is to determine to what extent contemporary concepts of field, especially those emerging within quantum physics, may be of use in illustrating the contingency of all matter and consequently suitable as a model for our understanding of God's sustaining presence in the physical cosmos.

The physicist James Jeans long ago pointed out that field theory, which many have seen as a metaphor for understanding God's sustaining presence in the cosmos, is itself only a metaphor of reality. Wrote Jeans: "Energy can be transferred from place to place, but waves, electrical and magnetic fields do not belong to the transfer mechanism; they belong simply to our efforts to understand and visualize this mechanism. Before man appeared on the scene there were neither waves nor electrical nor magnetic forces; these were not created by God, but by Huyghens, Fresnel, Faraday and Maxwell."[33] Similarly, John Polkinghorne has warned against going beyond the use of fields of force as analogical models and identifying them with God or God's activity. Polkinghorne specifically cautions against regarding "quantum fields as the 'sensorium of God' (in the way that Newton was emboldened to talk about absolute space), a panentheistic idea which does not commend itself [since,] . . . when all is said and done, quantum fields are simply creatures."[34]

Wolfhart Pannenberg and Field Theory
The chief advocate of the use of field theory models for understanding the sustaining work of God's Spirit in the creation has been Wolfhart Pannenberg. Pannenberg takes as his starting point the fact that "the theological affirmation that the world of nature proceeds from an act of divine creation implies the claim that the existence of the world as a whole and of all its parts is contingent."[35] We have already discussed the contingency of the cosmos as a whole and of all its parts upon God as a result of *creatio ex nihilo*. But how is such contingency to be understood as a continuing activity of the Creator under the category of a *creatio conservata*, that is, of God's continued sustaining of the physical universe? Pannenberg suggests that the field theories of modern physics provide insight into how this is to be understood:

> The turn toward the field concept in the development of modern physics has theological significance. This is suggested not only by its opposition to the tendency to reduce the concept of force to bodies or masses but also because field theories from Faraday to Albert Einstein claim a priority for the whole over the parts. This is of theological significance because God has to be conceived as the unifying ground of the whole universe if God is to be conceived as creator and redeemer of the world. The field concept could be used in theology to make the effective presence of God in every single phenomenon intelligible.[36]

Pannenberg cautions, however, that he is proposing only a model and does not intend to equate the activity of the Holy Spirit with the field theories of physics. He writes: "To be sure, even a cosmic field conceived along the lines of Faraday's thought as a field of force would not be identified immediately with the dynamic activity of the divine Spirit in creation. In every case the different models of science remain approximations. . . . Therefore, theological assertions of field structure of the cosmic activity of the divine Spirit will remain different from field theories in physics."[37] Here we encounter a problem that has led to some confusion in understanding Pannenberg's use of the field concept, namely his differentiation between physical, philosophical, and theological uses of the term. Pannenberg insists that the theological understanding and application of the concept will be different from those in the natural sciences. For Pannenberg the fact that scientific models of field are only approximations and that the use of the concept of field necessarily will be different in physics and theology provides justification for theology to break out of the conceptual mode of physics and explore new, theologically based applications of the field model. Yet because he makes great effort to show the connections to the use of field theory in physics, it is not always easy to distinguish whether he means a field in the theological or physical sense. Pannenberg seeks to develop new conceptual models for the Trinity, the Holy Spirit, and angels in light of the concept of field theory. At some points, however, as in his doctrine of angels, he seems to identify these messengers of God with specific physical forces and fields and thus confuse the theological and physical concepts of field. This difficulty can also be seen in his doctrine of God.

Pannenberg justifies the introduction of the concept of field theory into our understanding of the doctrine of God on the ground that God is spoken of biblically as "spirit." This is significant because *pneuma,* the Greek word for spirit, eventually became associated with the concept of fields of force in physics.[38] In regard to the relation of the Holy Spirit to the Father and the Son, Pannenberg develops his own "theological" field theory. He writes:

> The criticism of the traditional conception of God's spiritual character (*Geistigkeit*) as rational subjectivity has led to the insight that it corresponds better with the biblical testimony about God's spirit and God as spirit to conceptualize what is thereby meant as dynamic field which has a trinitarian structure in which the *person* of the Holy Spirit is conceived as one of the personal concretizations of the essence of the one God as Spirit in relation to the Father and the Son. The person of the Holy Spirit is not itself to be understood as field but rather as a unique manifestation (singularity) of the field of the divine essence. But because the person of the Holy Spirit is only revealed in relation to the Son (and thus also the Father), its action in the creation has more the character of the dynamic working of a field.[39]

Despite the distinction he makes between theological and scientific concepts of field, Pannenberg seems to link his conceptual model of God as Spirit to a specific scientific viewpoint when he makes the unification of space and time as contained in relativity theory a precondition for a theological interpretation of the "dynamic presence of the Holy Spirit." He claims that the "reduction of space to time is a prerequisite for the theological interpretation of God's presence in space as the dynamic working of the divine Spirit."[40] In making this claim Pannenberg seeks to incorporate Einstein's field theory of an integrated space-time into his understanding of God's continuing dynamic sustenance of the world through the Holy Spirit—which is a part of the larger trinitarian field that Pannenberg identifies as God. What Pannenberg does not explain is, if the Einsteinian view of space-time is a prerequisite for a theological interpretation of the presence of God as seen in the dynamic work of the Holy Spirit, then in what way can pre-Einsteinian theological reflection on this theme be considered valid? Did Christian theology really have to wait nearly two millennia for the appearance of a specific scientific viewpoint before it could appropriately address the presence of God through the dynamic working of the Spirit? Let us assume for a moment that a correct scientific view of space-time is not just an aid but an actual precondition for theological reflection, as Pannenberg seems to imply. How then can we be certain that the Einsteinian view is really the correct or complete view and that a thousand years hence someone else, in light of scientific insights that we cannot now anticipate, will rule our current theological reflection on the topic invalid on the basis of an inaccurate or incomplete understanding of space-time?

An intriguing part of Pannenberg's larger understanding of God's continuing sustenance of the physical cosmos is the place he assigns to angels, which he also integrates into his understanding of "field." Pannenberg suggests, "From the point of view of the field structure of spiritual dynamics one could consider identifying the subject matter intended in the conception of angels with the emergence of relatively independent parts of the cosmic field."[41] And if one keeps in mind that the idea that angels are personal spirits can be explained by "the fact that the concept of person in phenomenology of religion is related to the impact of more or less incomprehensible 'powers,'" then the problem of person in the doctrine of angels can be overcome. Thus, "if one considers this background of the biblical language about angels as personal realities, they may very well be related to fields of forces or dynamic spheres, the activity of which may be experienced as good or bad."[42] Pannenberg identifies some of the particular forces and dynamic spheres he feels can be identified with angels (and demons) in his *Systematic Theology:* "If such forces as Wind, Fire, and Stars are identified as angels of God then they would be (explained) thematically in their relationship to God as creatures and likewise in view of the mixed experiences of them by human beings who experience them either as servants of God or as demonic powers which strive against the will of God."[43]

From the viewpoint of the natural sciences, Pannenberg's work with the field concept presents some special difficulties. In the first place, as has already been seen, for Pannenberg field theory seems to become more than simply a model or paradigm for theological reflection inasmuch as he seems to make an actual identification between various physical fields of force and angels. Is there ultimately a qualitative distinction between Pannenberg's proposal to understand angels as physical force fields and identifying God with the sum total of physical laws or forces in the universe? That is to say, is there a danger in Pannenberg's program that angels, the Holy Spirit, and ultimately God could be reduced to metaphors for physical realities? John Polkinghorne points to a similar difficulty when he suggests that Pannenberg's use of field theory is "dangerously close to Newton's equation of absolute space with the sensorium of God."[44]

Also, there are a number of field theories in the natural sciences, biological as well as physical. Within physics alone there are classical and quantum field theories of different types. Pannenberg does not distinguish between any of these. He builds his theological field model on the general idea of fields of force, borrowing ideas from various and sometimes unrelated field theories. But which field theory (or theories) does Pannenberg rely on most in formulating this general concept? The essential idea of lines of force (or fields of force) developed by Faraday in the middle of the nineteenth century seems to provide Pannenberg with his basic paradigm. This leads to other problems. First, Faraday, for all his brilliance, is hardly a contemporary physicist and his ideas concerning fields of force have been greatly altered, diversified, and advanced in the last 130 years. Some of his concepts regarding fields of force have never been verified or have been proven inaccurate—for example, the idea of the conservation of force in which force depleted in one field must be replaced in another, and the connection he drew between gravity and electromagnetism. Pannenberg seems to rely particularly on Faraday's vision "to reduce all the different forces to a single field of force that determines all the changes in the natural universe."[45] Modern physics, however, while seeking a unified field *theory* that would combine classical and quantum field theories, has long ago abandoned the idea that a single unified *field* exists. By relying on pre-Einsteinian, pre–quantum theory concepts of field, Pannenberg would seem to neglect his goal of relating "the field concept of modern physics to the Christian doctrine of the dynamic presence of the divine Spirit."[46]

This would account, perhaps, for some of the strong criticism Pannenberg has received from contemporary scientists who have accused him of misunderstanding and/or misusing the concept of field theory. Jeffrey Wicken, for instance, commenting on Pannenberg's use of field theory, writes:

> If we want to use the word *energy* or *field* in science-theology discourse, let us do so in some way commensurate with their understandings in physics. Talking about "spirit" as "energy" and granting it by implication the status of physical law runs dangerously close to usurping the hard-won denotative language of science for physicalizing theology. This serves neither enterprise. . . . *Field* has been used in a spectrum of senses in science ranging from the specifically denotative to the connotative to the metaphorical. Pannenberg uses them all in pursuing a theology of wholeness in evolutionary process. . . . [The specifics of his argument] . . . are overly bound to physical science, and they misconstrue much of that science.[47]

Wicken concludes that, "although as metaphor this notion [of field] is rich for theology, taken literally it binds God needlessly to physics. Is God conceived here as a *field in physics?* If so, why the need for God at all?"[48]

This does not imply that field theories are irrelevant for understanding God's sustaining presence in the world. In fact, Pannenberg is certainly correct in his assessment of their importance in this regard. Likewise, as models of the contingency of all matter they are very fruitful. Field theory certainly has value as a metaphor for God's continuing sustenance of the universe and may well influence the way in which theology confesses this continuing "creative" presence of God. It would be a mistake, however, to build any part of our theology on a specific physical theory in such a way that the theory provides more than metaphors of meaning but becomes necessary for our theological formulations.

Bell's Theorem, Nonlocality, and David Bohm's Implicate Order

Another development in modern physics that has significant metaphysical implications for the doctrine of God's continuing sustenance of the universe is Bell's theorem. In order to understand Bell's theorem we must turn to the thought experiment proposed by Albert Einstein, Boris Podolsky, and Nathan Rosen in 1935.[49] The purpose of the thought experiment was to demonstrate a paradox within quantum theory. The EPR experiment (named for Einstein, Podolsky, and Rosen) made two fundamental assumptions (1) *classical realism,* which states that individual particles possess definite properties even when no one is observing them; and (2) *locality,* which states that no causal influence can be transmitted between two isolated systems at a speed faster than the speed of light.[50] If quantum theory is correct, then it would seem that one of these fundamental assumptions would have to be given up, at least at the quantum level. As Einstein, Podolsky, and Rosen originally put the dilemma, "Either the quantum-mechanical description of reality given by the wave function is not complete or when the operators corresponding to two physical quantities do not commute the two quantities cannot have simultaneous reality."[51]

The experiment assumed that a two-proton particle with zero spin splits into proton *A* and proton *B* with one proton going in each direction. Proton *A* has an equal probability, according to quantum theory, of having a spin oriented in either direction. Proton B, however, must have a spin of the opposite direction in order to equal the zero spin of the original two-proton system. Also, according to the uncertainty principle of quantum theory, *A* and *B* have an equal probability of having either a left- or a right-oriented spin, and this spin (for both particles) is not determined until such time as it is observed or measured. If *A* and *B* go in opposite directions for a great distance until one or the other is "measured," there is no possibility of instantaneous "communication" between the two—yet quantum theory tells us that somehow *B* must "know" in which direction it must spin to balance the spin of *A*. Given the assumption of classical realism, Einstein, Podolsky, and Rosen argued that such instantaneous communication between the two systems could not possibly take place in the sense that a measurement of one system could affect the other. They contended that because "at the time of measurement the two systems no longer interact, no real change can take place in the second system in consequence of anything done to the first system." To argue otherwise, they maintained, "makes the reality of P and Q [the two noncommuting operators of the two systems in question] depend upon the process of measurement carried out on the first system, which does not disturb the second system in any way. No reasonable definition of reality could be expected to permit this."[52]

Niels Bohr responded to the EPR challenge in the same year with a paper of the same title. Bohr, commenting on the EPR paper, wrote: "The trend of their argumentation . . . does not seem to me adequately to meet the actual situation with which we are faced in atomic physics." Bohr argued, in contrast, that "quantum mechanics within its scope would appear as a completely rational description of physical phenomena."[53] Bohr maintained, on the basis of the Copenhagen interpretation of quantum mechanics, which he championed, that even though no signal could travel instantaneously between the two separate particles, they nevertheless form a quantum system and measurements taken of particle *A* cannot be ignored when discussing the state of particle *B*.[54] In conclusion, Bohr pointed to the wider implications of quantum theory, maintaining that "it means a radical revision of our attitude as regards physical reality, which may be paralleled with the fundamental modification of all ideas regarding the absolute character of physical phenomena, brought about by the general theory of relativity."[55]

Einstein, however, in opposition to Bohr, found the idea of two separated particles conspiring somehow to give coordinated results of seemingly independent measurements performed on each too incredible for belief, deriding it as "ghostly action at a distance." Many of Einstein's followers, such as David Bohm, maintained that there must be hidden variables in each of the traveling particles that determined a particular outcome. Essentially, this is a classical viewpoint which maintains that there is some hidden variable that we have not yet discovered within the particles when they split and that explains the phenomenon.

Yet it seems that support of the "hidden variable" solution is falsely attributed to Einstein himself. The historian of science Max Jammer has pointed out that while Einstein seemed sympathetically inclined toward such ideas, he never himself endorsed a hidden variable theory.[56] In fact, Einstein commented concerning Bohm's theory of hidden variables that he did not believe "that this theory can hold up."[57] According to Jammer, the false attribution of support of this idea to Einstein can be traced to John Bell's influential 1964 paper on the EPR paradox, in which he says that the original 1935 paper on the EPR paradox "was advanced as an argument that quantum mechanics could not be a complete theory but should be supplemented by additional variables."[58] Most subsequent discussions of the EPR paradox that have taken Bell's theorem into account have simply repeated this statement as fact. Nevertheless, there remains no doubt that Einstein believed his thought experiment indicated that quantum theory was inconsistent and was only a provisional theory until the deeper, causal relationships could be understood.

A "delayed decision" version of the EPR experiment, in which the decision as to which direction A spins is not made until after the particles are well separated, has prompted most contemporary physicists to reject hidden-variable solutions.[59] As Roger Penrose comments, the hidden-variable "viewpoint just won't work as an explanation for all the puzzling apparently nonlocal probabilities that arise in quantum theory."[60] From the perspective of Christian theology there is no special reason to hope that hidden variables ultimately exist. The strict causality that such a theory seeks to buttress may be necessary for the deistic view of God associated with the mechanistic worldview that reigned from Newton to the dawn of the twentieth century, but the God of biblical theism is by no means dependent on a universe in which causal predictability reigns. Physicist Donald MacKay has aptly written that "belief in a sovereign God does not in the least entail a belief that there *must* be 'hidden physical variables' sufficient to determine the behaviour of electrons on the basis of a precedent. For biblical theism all events . . . need

God's say-so in order that they occur at all. The choice of 'God or Chance' is simply not a meaningful alternative. . . . As the book of Proverbs (16:33) has it: 'The lots may be cast into the lap, but the issue depends wholly on the Lord.' "[61]

photon 1	pi-meson	photon 2
p^1	π	p^2
spin ½	spin 0	spin ½
'left'		'right'

In the above diagram the standard EPR experiment is pictured with a pi-meson particle that decays into two photons instead of with protons. Here, a particle with zero spin decays/splits into a photon pair. The combined spins of the two photons must cancel each other out (mathematically) to equal zero because the original particle has 0 spin. Quantum theory maintains that "ghost" particles exist for each particle for either spin and that the actual spin itself remains undetermined until one of the two particles is measured. At this point its corresponding particle must have a counterbalancing reverse spin. It would therefore appear that measuring of the spin of one of the particles instantaneously fixes the direction of spin of the other. In other words, the implication is that when the spin of photon 1 is measured in a direction of our choice, photon 2, from this moment on, spins in the opposite direction. Even if the particles are light-years away from each other, simply choosing to measure one particle seems to instantaneously fix the direction of spin of the other.

The reason that no classical solution exists to the paradox created by this experiment follows from a now-famous theorem given by John Bell in his 1965 paper, "On the Einstein-Podolsky-Rosen Paradox." Bell's theorem, also referred to as Bell's inequality, demonstrates a mathematical inequality that unavoidably arises if the locality of classical physics is applied to quantum theory.[62] As Kevin Sharpe has explained, if this is indeed the case then there would be "a limit to the number of pairs of particles with a certain property. . . . To exceed this limit and thus to break Bell's inequality will mean that quantum theory does not have a simple, classical locality."[63] Henry Pierce Stapp points to the philosophical implications of Bell's theorem when he writes that it "shows that no theory of reality compatible with quantum theory can allow the spatially separated parts of reality to be independent: these parts must be related in some way that goes beyond the familiar idea that causal connections propagate only into the forward light-cone."[64]

Bell himself concluded his landmark paper by observing that "for at least one quantum state . . . the statistical predictions of quantum mechanics are incompatible with separable predetermination. In a theory in which parameters are added to quantum mechanics to determine the results of individual measurements . . . there must be a mechanism whereby the setting of one measuring device can influence the reading of another instrument, however remote."[65]

The EPR experiment and Bell's theorem took on increased significance when it became possible to actually perform the experiment with photons in the laboratory, hence making it no longer a thought experiment. Especially crucial was the remarkable achievement of Alain Aspect of the Institut d'optique théorique et appliquée in Paris. In 1982, Aspect performed a "delayed choice" version of the experiment by switching the orientation of the left detector after the photons had split but before they arrived at their respective detectors. The results of the experiment demonstrated that "the agreement is excellent" with quantum theory. Aspect and his colleagues noted that their "observed violation of Bell's inequalities indicates that the experimental accuracy was good enough for pointing out a hypothetical discrepancy with the predictions of quantum mechanics. No such effect was observed." Even though the researchers admitted that their test was not absolutely conclusive, the results nevertheless argue "against the whole class of supplementary-parameter theories obeying Einstein's causality."[66] Aspect's experiment demonstrated that Bohr and not Einstein was correct about the amount of cooperation/coordination between the two separated particles. In the words of Aspect, the results of his experiment, if correct, "violate Bell's inequalities, which means that we cannot keep a simple picture of the world, retaining Einstein's idea of separability,"[67] that is to say, the idea that the two particles are causally independent of each other and do not constitute a single quantum system.

So what precisely are the implications of the EPR experiment and Bell's theorem for our understanding of reality? Although most physicists have resisted the idea, it seems that some sort of nonlocality exists in which one particle can immediately determine the spin of another at unlimited distances and apart from any apparent local cause. Physicist Nick Herbert has observed that, "what Bell's theorem does . . . for the quantum reality question is to clearly specify one of deep reality's necessary features: whatever reality may be, *it must be non-local*. . . . No local reality can explain the type of world we live in."[68] Similarly, David Bohm has championed the idea that these results point to some sort of underlying "wholeness" within the quantum physical systems of the universe.

Bohm, together with B. J. Hiley and P. Kaloyerou in a 1987 article on the ontological basis for quantum theory, wrote that the quantum behavior of matter "shows a certain kind of wholeness, brought about by the quantum potential. This . . . functions as active information that may reflect distant features of the environment and may give rise to a non-local connection between particles that depends on the 'quantum state' of the whole, in a way that is not expressible in terms of the relationships of the particles alone."[69] And again, with B. J. Hiley, Bohm observed that "physicists have generally had a great deal of difficulty with non-locality and indeed often feel a certain revulsion towards it which is so strong that they would prefer not to consider the ideas even as a possibility. Nevertheless, all the commonly accepted interpretations of the quantum theory that have been proposed thus far imply some kind of non-locality."[70]

In light of Bell's theorem and recent laboratory results of EPR-type experiments, David Bohm has proposed a concept of wholism in which he maintains that the seemingly inexplicable explicate order observed in the nonlocal coordination of particles on the quantum level is due to an underlying implicate order in the universe. Essentially, Bohm's implicate order theory is "a new theory of hidden variables,"[71] the primary hidden variable being that of an underlying implicate order. Bohm, in his 1980 book, *Wholeness and the Implicate Order,* suggests that we have uncovered "the germ of a new notion of order." Bohm contends that "this order is not to be understood solely in terms of a regular arrangement of *objects* or as a regular arrangement of *events*. Rather, a *total order* is contained, in some *implicit* sense, in each region of space and time. Now the word 'implicit' is based on the verb 'to implicate.' This means 'to fold inward.' So we may be led to explore the notion that in some sense each region contains a total structure 'enfolded' within it."[72] Bohm's theory of implicate order points to the dependency of all things based on the connectedness that he believes to permeate quantum theory. Kevin Sharpe has summarized Bohm's idea of implicate order quite simply: "His theory is that everything connects with everything else."[73] In this regard Bohm's implicate order is similar to field theory in its potential as a metaphor for the contingency of the physical cosmos on the continuing sustenance of God.

There are, however, difficulties with Bohm's theory that serve as a caution against making too much of its theological implications. First, as Bohm admits but seems often to forget,[74] the nonlocality indicated by the EPR experiment points to a connectedness that may only apply in certain instances and under certain conditions, for instance, only "over relatively short distances for simple systems." For large-scale systems Bohm recognizes the validity of dividing systems into independent subsystems in a way compatible with classical physics. Therefore, "non-locality will only reveal itself in very subtle ways."[75] Also, most of Bohm's colleagues reject his implicate order and holomovement theories because they feel he has abandoned physics for metaphysics and mysticism. His apparent continuing support of some sort of hidden-variable solution to the EPR paradox has also made his position unattractive for many. John Polkinghorne has rightly noted that quantum theory, while certainly not without significant metaphysical implications, does not justify the sort of comprehensive philosophical system that Bohm wants to create. Polkinghorne contends that quantum theory "is not itself a sufficient basis for a universal metaphysics. . . . Bohm's holomovement and implicate order present grand, even baroque, metaphysical schemes claiming some anchorage in the quantum world. Whatever the merits of these detailed proposals, they rapidly go beyond anything that a sober assessment of contemporary physical theory could be held to sanction."[76]

Bohm's theory, while rich in metaphor, does not reflect the opinion of most physicists, and building too much on Bohm's specific concepts may prove counterproductive to establishing a dialogue with contemporary physics as it manifests itself in more standard and accepted theories. Yet Bohm's ideas underline a growing tendency within physics to recognize the interconnectedness and contingency of matter. At the very least the EPR paradox and Bell's theorem suggest that the metaphysical assumptions associated with classical physics and the classical realism on which it is based need to be reevaluated. Both the nonlocality of Bell's theorem and the various classical and quantum field theories seem to point to an interconnectedness of matter that has significant metaphysical implications.

Neither field theories nor the nonlocality of the EPR experiment can serve as proof that our physical universe depends on a transcendent Creator. Yet such ideas tell us something about the nature of the very physical universe that Christian theology maintains is dependent on the continuing sustenance of God. It is certainly not contrary to the nature of physical reality to be interconnected and dependent. Field theories and the concept of nonlocality may even be useful as metaphors for the sustaining activity of God through which God's immanence is made manifest in every time and every space within the universe that God called into being. Yet as we have seen, we need to exercise caution in this area. Otherwise theology becomes bound to certain scientific theories and our metaphors for the sustaining presence of God become the reality for which "God" (or "Spirit") becomes the metaphor.

MODERN PHYSICS AND THE PROVIDENCE OF GOD

Divine Providence in the Context of Classical Physics
General providence, or *providentia ordinaria*, is the term theology has traditionally employed to designate God's continuing governance of the world. Unlike special providence (*providentia extraordinaria*), which concerns the possibility

of God's direct, even miraculous intervention in the physical universe, general providence has to do with the "ordinary" teleological direction of the process of the universe by its Creator. Karl Barth has defined the two concepts as follows: "By *providentia ordinaria* is meant the divine government as it occurs within the framework of what we can recognise as the laws which underlie the cosmic events of nature and history, and by *providentia extraordinaria* the divine government in so far as it takes the form of miracles."[77] Providence is normally associated with God's direction of the course of human history. Although this is a related question, to be sure, our primary concern is with the question of God's continuing providential governance of the processes of the physical universe as an aspect of continuing creation. To this end we must ask to what extent and in what way the traditional Christian confession of God's providence can be maintained in light of the worldview of classical physics.

The fundamental assumption of classical physics, from Isaac Newton to Albert Einstein, has been that of causal determinism. The Marquis de Laplace took this view to its logical conclusion in his belief that if the exact state of the universe at any given time could be accurately known, then the state of the universe at any past or future time could also be known—thus combining determinism with predictability. Classical physics, in its culmination in the theory of special relativity, has remained essentially Newtonian and Laplacian in this regard. In relativity theory not only is Newtonian determinism retained, but the predictability posited by Laplace is made easier in that it is no longer necessary to know the state of the entire universe to predict its future state at some point in space-time. Because determinism does not depend on predictability, however, the determinism of the Newtonian system remains essentially unchanged in general relativity.

The determinism of classical physics has important implications for the Christian doctrine of divine providence. In a universe that is strictly deterministic one might ask what place is left for the freedom of God in directing its course. Also, what meaning could such a providential direction have if a strict determinism rules the physical universe? Could God be identified in any way with the causal determinism of classical physics?

Already in the last century Albrecht Ritschl rejected such an approach because it makes an identification of God with scientific concepts of causation and does violence to the concept of God. Ritschl contended that the scientific explanation of the physical world would deny the significance of our conception of God "if it equated God, under the idea of 'cause,' with a natural science made comprehensible through observation."[78] Similarly, Karl Barth maintained that "If we had no choice but to think of *causa* or cause as the term is applied in modern science, . . . with all its talk about causality, causal nexus, causal law, causal necessity and the like, then clearly it is a concept which we could not apply either to God or to the creature of God, but could only reject." Barth argues instead that the concept of *causa* can only be retained when it is understood as an analogy, and not as a "master-concept to which both God and the creature are subject."[79]

An identification of God (or divine providence) with the causal determinism of classical physics is not a viable option for theology. Not only is divine providence (and by implication God) reduced to a metaphor in such schemes, but applying such a scientific understanding of causality to divine providence leaves no place for divine freedom or for an intervening or special providence—that is, a *providentia extraordinaria*.

Divine Providence in the Context of Quantum Physics

Unlike classical physics, the fundamental assumption of quantum physics is indeterminism. Since Werner Heisenberg's 1926 formulation of the uncertainty principle, the assumption of a strict determinism as found in classical physics has been irrevocably undermined, though not completely replaced. Ian Stewart expressed well the impact of quantum theory on our worldview when he wrote, "With the advent of quantum mechanics, the clockwork world has become a cosmic lottery."[80] As we have already seen, the strict determinism of classical physics poses certain difficulties for the doctrine of divine providence. The question to be considered here is whether the doctrine of God's providence fares any better within the context of the indeterminism of quantum physics.

Strictly speaking, quantum theory abandons neither causality nor determinism. Foundational for an understanding of the indeterminism of quantum mechanics is the Schrödinger equation. As long as no measurement takes place, quantum theory maintains that Schrödinger's equation remains valid.[81] Schrödinger's equation, however, is linear, which means that several combinations of solutions can exist indefinitely in a complex linear superposition until the actual solution is fixed by measurement/observation. Hence although Schrödinger's equation is a "perfectly well-defined deterministic equation,"[82] its linear nature allows a superposition of multiple possible solutions. It is here that indeterminism enters the picture. Schrödinger's equation demonstrates a causal relationship in which "$H \mid \psi\rangle$ describes how ψ evolves," but because a superposition of possible solutions exists until a measurement is actually taken and all but one possibility is eliminated, an apparent indeterminism prevents accurate prediction and forces the researcher to calculate possible outcomes on the basis of statistical probability.

A similar problem is provided by the decay of radioactive substances. We know such substances decay at approximately a certain rate, but no one can say for certain precisely when a particular atom will decay. The paradox of Schrödinger's cat, which we will look at in the following section, is the classic thought experiment that attempts to relate the uncertainty involved in such processes of radioactive decay to large-scale structures. Entirely satisfactory solutions suggesting how this might be done are still lacking. In essence, we are left with two systems, one predictable, the other unpredictable, one deterministic, the other indeterministic, one describing the large-scale macro-systems of the universe, the other the quantum micro-systems. Both, however, exist within the same interconnected physical universe and, according to the Christian confession, are subject to the same divine providence.

The indeterminism of quantum mechanics seems to allow room for the freedom of God and for a special or intervening providence that classical physics did not allow. Indeed, it could even be possible, as Hawking suggests, to ascribe the randomness of quantum mechanics "to the intervention of God." Yet we would have to agree with Hawking that it would be "a very strange kind of intervention [because] there is no evidence that it is directed toward any purpose. Indeed, if it were, it would by definition not be random."[83] If such fundamental indeterminism is accepted, therefore, one wonders in what sense God can be said to govern the world or to predetermine certain outcomes. Must all the various possible options within God's providential direction of the universe (and of human history) exist in a state of linear superposition until one of them is actually observed and becomes realized as that which exists as a "causal" reality? And in such a case who would the observer be—some human witness or God? Does all this lead to a radical and quasi-scientific form of Berkelian idealism? The answer, it would seem, is no.

First of all, it remains highly debatable how, or even whether, the quantum uncertainty principle is to be applied to the large-scale structures of the universe, that is, to essentially everything that is large enough to see. Even if the most radical advocates of the philosophical implications of quantum theory are correct and "the physical universe . . . dissolves away into a shadowy fantasy"[84] and Christian theology responds by placing God in the role of the Observer whose act of observation determines which of several possibilities is realized, serious problems still exist. That God's knowledge or foreknowledge of an event or outcome could make it a reality is an intriguing possibility. But what do we do with the omniscience and timeless omnipresence of God? In other words, how could we conceive of God not knowing a possible outcome? In such schemes God seems either to become a largely accidental spectator or a strictly deterministic "controller" who has from all eternity known (and consequently determined) the outcome of every event, process, and state. Such problems warn of the danger of binding our concept of God and divine providence too closely to any particular theory, whether it be that of classical or quantum physics. Both theories are a rich source of models, metaphors, and paradigms that theology is free to use in its confession of the providential presence of God in the context of modern, scientific worldviews. Yet any attempt to go beyond this would seem an abuse of both science and theology.

Deterministic Indeterminism and the Providential Freedom of God

The determinism/indeterminism question remains one of the major unresolved philosophical issues separating classical and quantum physics. As physicists search for a Grand Unified Theory that would unify not only our understanding of the four fundamental forces but also of these two streams of physics, speculation has already begun as to the implications of such a theory for the determinism/indeterminism question.[85] Could it be that the unification of physics will bring a unification of the tension between determinism and indeterminism? Or must either determinism or indeterminism ultimately prevail? Roger Penrose, although skeptical that this will prove to be the case, suggests that "it is even possible that we may end up restoring determinism in quantum mechanics."[86] Of course, a number of physicists believe relativity theory may have to be adapted to make room for some degree of indeterminism.[87]

The German physical and theoretical chemist O. E. Rössler has written that "it could turn out . . . that a universe that is chaotic itself ceases to be chaotic as soon as it is observed by an observer who is chaotic himself."[88] Chaos, in other words, may be simply a matter of perspective. A hypothetical chaotic observer would view a chaotic universe as entirely in order—and because the observer views it as such it would indeed become orderly. It is an assertion of the fundamental unpredictability of the quantum and perhaps also the large-scale systems of the universe.

The uncertainty principle of quantum physics has led, in many ways, to a reexamination of the nature of chaos, or what in classical terminology would be called nonlinear systems. Most significant among such reexaminations have been those that propose a sort of compromise between determinism and indeterminism by suggesting that chaos is perhaps not so chaotic as we might imagine. Einstein seems to have suggested something of this nature when, in the course of his resistance to the metaphysical implications of quantum theory, he argued that there are certain unknown causal factors that quantum theory does not take into account, and that these are responsible for the indeterminism indicated by quantum theory.[89]

A great deal of attention has been given recently to the idea of a deterministic indeterminism as a possible harmonization of the implications of classical and quantum physics. Gary Zukav, for instance, in his book *The Dancing Wu Li Masters,* speaks of a "chaos beneath order,"[90] and Ian Stewart, in *Does God Play Dice? The New Mathematics of Chaos,* speaks poetically of the effort to domesticate chaos: "Chaos gives way to order, which in turn gives rise to new forms of chaos. But on this swing of the pendulum, we seek not to destroy chaos but to tame it."[91] On a more rigorously scientific level, Heinz Georg Schuster has attempted, with his 1984 book *Deterministic Chaos,* to analyze mathematically the phenomenon of deterministic chaos within dissipative systems. Schuster defines deterministic chaos, within the context of his study, as "the regular or chaotic motion which is generated by nonlinear systems whose dynamical laws uniquely determine the time evolution of a state of the system from a knowledge of its previous history." Schuster notes that due to new theoretical results and the use of high-speed computers, "it has become clear that this phenomenon is abundant in nature and has far-reaching consequences in many branches of science." Among nonlinear systems that researchers have found, as a function of an external control parameter, to exhibit a transition from order to chaos in a manner that could be characterized as "deterministic chaos" are: the forced pendulum, lasers, nonlinear optic devices, particle accelerators, and certain chemical reactions.[92] That this transition (time evolution) from order to chaos is determined by dynamic laws "from a knowledge of its previous history" is ironically reminiscent of the language of Laplacian determinism.

How do contemporary views of a deterministic indeterminism differ from a Laplacian determinism in which the future state of the universe could potentially be calculated from its present state? Roger Penrose seems to indicate the direction in which such discussions are leading when he writes that he believes that some "new procedure takes over at the quantum-classical borderline which interpolates between" deterministic and probabilistic "quantum jump" parts of quantum mechanics, and that this new procedure "would contain an essentially non-algorithmic element," which would in turn imply "that the future would not be computable from the present, even though it might be determined by it."[93]

In distinguishing between computability and determinism, Penrose represents a break from a strict Laplacian determinism that did not make such a distinction. The concept of a determined but not completely predictable universe also contains possibilities for theological reflection on the providence of God. As a model of God's providential direction of the universe, Penrose's tentative outline of a "correct quantum gravity" (CQG) theory demonstrates how it is possible to conceptualize divine providence and divine freedom as consistent aspects of God's providential sustenance of the physical cosmos. In fact, Penrose suggests that a CQG theory would leave a role for human free will within an essentially deterministic universe.[94]

In a similar vein we might consider the paradox of Schrödinger's cat. Not only was 1935 the year of the proposal of the famous EPR experiment, but it was also the year that saw the proposal of another famous thought experiment of a different nature. Erwin Schrödinger, one of the key figures in the development of quantum mechanics, sought to demonstrate the implications of applying the uncertainty of quantum probability to large-scale structures. Schrödinger proposed a thought experiment in which the fate of a hapless cat becomes contingent on the quantum probability of the decay of a small amount of radioactive substance, which exists within a closed system that also includes the cat. Schrödinger explained the experiment as follows:

> A cat is penned up in a steel chamber, along with the following diabolical device (which must be secured against direct interference by the cat): in a Geiger counter there is a tiny bit of radioactive substance, so small, that perhaps in the course of one hour one of the atoms decays, but also, with equal probability, perhaps none; if it happens, the counter tube discharges and through a relay releases a hammer which shatters a small flask of hydrocyanic acid. If one has left this entire system to itself for an hour, one would say that the cat lives if meanwhile no atom has decayed. The first atomic decay would have poisoned it. The ψ-function of the entire system would express this by having in it the living and the dead cat (pardon the expression) mixed or smeared out in equal parts.[95]

Because of the superposition of various possible states in quantum mechanics, the fate of the cat, if we are to remain consistent with the Schrödinger equation (see previous section), must be calculated by someone outside of the closed box in the same manner as the probability of the decay of the radioactive material. In other words, according to quantum theory, until observed, the cat is "in a complex linear combination of dead and alive. It could be dead plus alive."[96] Of course, this sounds like nonsense. Schrödinger himself believed the cat would be either dead or alive and that at some point between the quantum, micro-level and large-scale reality his equation breaks down and must be adapted to complicated large-scale structures such as cats and the universe.[97] Others, however, have more confidence in Schrödinger's equation than Schrödinger himself had and believe that the cat paradox demonstrates that classical realism does not work. Paul Davies and J. R. Brown, for instance, have written that "the paradox of the cat demolishes any hope we may have had that the ghostliness of the quantum is somehow confined to the shadowy microworld of the atom, and that the paradoxical nature of reality in the atomic realm is irrelevant to daily life and experience. . . . Following the logic of quantum theory to its ultimate conclusion, most of the physical universe seems to dissolve away into a shadowy fantasy."[98]

The prevailing view, however, remains that of Schrödinger himself: that quantum physics must be adapted for large-scale systems.[99] The question we wish to raise, then, is whether the fact of such an adaptation of the indeterminism of quantum physics to the apparent determinism of large-scale structures could serve as a model for a similar adaptation of the providential freedom of God to the apparently deterministic large-scale structure of the universe. Similar to the tension between quantum indeterminism and classical determinism, the doctrine of God's providential direction of the universe (and of human history) has always contained a similar tension between the indeterminism of human free will and the determinism of divine predestination. Even within the divine economy (excluding the problem of human free will), a tension exists between the indeterminism of divine freedom and divine predestination.

Traditionally, theology has described the problem in terms of a primary cause (*causa prima*), or a first cause (*causa princeps*), which is identified with God, and secondary causes (*causa secundae*), or individual causes (*causa particulares*), which are identified with human volition and other causes that belong rightly to "the whole reality of heaven and earth which is distinct from God."[100] Traditional theology proposed a divine concurrence within the "overruling of providence" in which "God co-operates with the operation of *causae secundae*," and "the divine *causare* [causing] takes place in and with their *causare*." The created operations therefore become the divine operations and the secondary causes (*causae secundae*) are essentially reduced to caused causes (*causa causans*), while God remains God's own cause (*causa sui*). Theology, therefore, essentially borrowing Aristotelian categories and terminology, sought to describe providence in terms of a concurrence, that is to say, a cooperation with "the activity of God on the one side and that of the creature on the other." Contemporary theology, however, has not been satisfied with this solution, which Barth says is not a coming together of divine and human/created "causes" but rather a "*concursus* of the Bible and Aristotle."

If God governs the creation in such a way that the universe evolves according to a strict, predetermined order, what place is left for divine freedom? On the other hand, if God is free to intervene in the physical universe, what happens to the traditional doctrine of divine predestination? Theological systems have tended ultimately to opt for one or the other. In a sense, theologians proceed much like physicists in this regard. On the micro-level of miracles, prayer, and human moral decision, we proceed as if God and individual persons were able to alter the course of history or affect in some way the state of the physical cosmos (for example, the human decision to pollute or not to pollute, to engage in nuclear war or not). On the macro-level of the teleological outcome of history or the consummation of creation, the predetermined "plan" of God takes over. Like physicists, theologians would like to know how these two levels fit together. Does one ultimately prevail over the other? While current discussions among physicists cannot provide answers to these theological questions, they may provide useful paradigms for overcoming—or at least learning to live with—the tension between indeterminism and determinism. If physics can learn to live with so-called deterministic chaos, perhaps theology can accept a providential freedom of God that accommodates the determinism of divine predestination and the indeterminism of human and divine freedom without denying the inevitable tension between the two or subsuming one under the other. The mathematician Ian Stewart put the matter well when he suggested, "Perhaps God can play dice, and create a universe of complete law and order, in the same breath."[101]

MODERN PHYSICS AND SPECIAL PROVIDENCE

Special Providence and the Immutable Laws of Physics
Stephen Hawking has written: "Science seems to have uncovered a set of laws that, within the limits set by the uncertainty principle, tell us how the universe will develop with time, if we know its state at any one time. These laws may have originally been decreed by God, but it appears that he has since left the universe to evolve according to them and does not now intervene in it."[102] Hawking is saying that the physical laws reign supreme in the universe and cannot be interrupted or excepted—even by a God who may have originally created them. This assertion comes face to face against the traditional Christian belief in miracles, for a miracle, in the mind of many, is precisely that: an interruption or exception of the physical laws that govern our universe.

The so-called interventionist, special providence of God need not, however, be understood only in terms of the miraculous. It is entirely possible for a "special" act of providence that intervenes in human or natural history to take place without violating any laws of nature. Hence Arthur Peacocke is correct to contend that particular events or clusters of events "can be intentionally and specifically brought about by the interaction of God with the world in a top-down causative way that does not abrogate the scientifically observed relationships operating at the level of events in question."[103] Such a possibility, according to Peacocke, is of value in that it "renders the concept of God's special providential action intelligible and believable within the context of the perspective of the sciences."[104] Miracles, however, by their nature bring into sharp focus the question of God's ability to intervene in the physical universe. Consequently miracles will be the primary focus of our treatment of special providence.

It will be helpful here to clarify what we understand by "miracle." The traditional (Thomistic) doctrine of miracles specified three conditions that an occurrence must meet in order to qualify as a miracle. (1) It must deal with a fact that, in principle, can be verified by the methods of historical investigation (*momentum historicum*). (2) Its occurrence must be inexplicable by natural laws. In other words, it must be not only a highly unlikely or unusual occurrence but also one that is scientifically inexplicable (*momentum scientificum*). (3) Because it is a real event that must have a cause, it can only be seen as having come from God (*momentum theologicum*).[105]

These traditional qualifications of what constitutes a miracle are of continuing value in the dialogue with natural science in general and physics in particular. The last qualification constitutes a theological judgment that does not come directly into play in the discussion with the natural sciences. It would seem, however, that the first two qualifications, the *momentum historicum* and the *momentum scientificum,* could be agreed on by physicists and theologians alike. First, a miracle is in principle a historically verifiable occurrence. Miracles, therefore, are seen as taking place within the realm open to scientific investigation. Second, although there is good theological reason today for broadening the category of "miracle," in the strictest and more traditional sense miracles are occurrences that are not explicable within the context of presently known physical laws. It is precisely here that the issue has usually come to an impasse between theology and natural science. Theology has traditionally maintained that such occurrences not only have taken place in the past, but in principle can happen in the future. Natural science has maintained that the laws of physics that govern the physical processes of our universe are invariable and, therefore, miracles are in principle impossible.

David Hume was perhaps the first, in the context of the emerging, modern scientific worldview, to deny the occurrence of miracles. Hume agreed that "a miracle is a violation of the laws of nature," or more precisely, that a miracle is "a transgression of a law of nature by a particular volition of the Deity, or by the interposition of some invisible agent." On the basis of this definition, Hume sought to disprove the existence of miracles. He argued that there must be "a uniform experience against every miraculous event, otherwise the event would not merit the appellation. And as a uniform experience amounts to a proof, there is here a direct and full *proof,* from the nature of the fact, against the existence of any miracle."[106] For Hume, therefore, a miracle is excluded by definition. Modern science, if not individual scientists, has tended to reject miracles on this same basis.

What is at stake here is not simply a dispute over individual "miraculous" occurrences so much as the question of God's ability to intervene in the created order. God's general providence, as we have seen, takes place apart from any interruption or exception of physical laws. God actively directs and sustains the universe, but within the context of the specific physical laws that God established to govern it. The traditional Christian doctrine of divine providence, however, also includes the possibility of a special providence (*providentia extraordinaria*) that posits the freedom of God to intervene in the normal process or order of the physical universe or human history in a way that presupposes God's ability to interrupt or except the physical laws that govern the universe. The affirmation of this doctrine has been difficult for modern theology but continues to be important. The question is not so much whether the earth actually ceased to rotate in the long day of Joshua as whether the Creator of the universe could, in principle, intervene in such a way. The question of miracles has more to do with the doctrine of God and God's relationship to the physical cosmos than with particular "supernatural" occurrences. Not only is the doctrine of miracles significant for our understanding of God, but the Christian religion is built on two central miracles: the incarnation of God through the virginal conception of Jesus, and the resurrection of Jesus from the dead. Clearly, Christian theology can never reject the possibility of miracles within the context of God's special providence and remain *Christian* theology.[107] But to what extent can such a special providence be maintained in the light of contemporary physics? Any discussion of miracles sooner or later is likely to run up against the "immutable laws of physics" that seem to disallow such occurrences in principle. It is the apparent immutability of such laws that has led Hawking and others to claim that God does not now intervene in the physical world.

The American physicist Richard Feynman has written that "there is . . . a rhythm and a pattern between the phenomena of nature which is not apparent to the eye, but only to the eye of analysis; and it is these rhythms and patterns which we call Physical Laws."[108] It is this rhythm and pattern between the phenomena of nature that science has generally held to be immutable, unvarying in its regularity. But this in no way implies that science has discovered all the laws of nature or that those we currently accept may not at some point need to be adapted to fit new discoveries. In fact, scientists are constantly seeking new laws of nature and revising their understanding of existing laws. Natural science at its best and most realistic operates under the assumption that many of its "laws" may be only provisional approximations. Feynman provides an amusing description of this situation:

We have these approximate symmetries, which work something like this. You have an approximate symmetry, so you calculate a set of consequences supposing it to be perfect. When compared with experiment it does not agree. Of course—the symmetry you are supposed to expect is approximate, so if the agreement is pretty good you say, "Nice!," while if the agreement is very poor you say, "Well, this particular thing must be especially sensitive to the failure of the symmetry." Now you may laugh, but we have to make progress in that way.[109]

Finding "new" laws, then, is a "process of guessing, computing consequences, and comparing with experiment." The bottom line, however, is that whether we know all of the laws of nature or not, such laws do exist and are inviolable.

The inviolable nature of physical law is, as we have seen, presupposed by the traditional doctrine of miracles. Therefore the so-called immutability of the laws of nature constitutes no proof against miracles. From the perspective of theology, one might say that miracles are the exceptions that not only assume but "prove" the rule. Yet the difficulty is not so easily removed. Hume's criticism that miracles by definition cannot happen, remains a problem. Recent changes in the understanding of the nature of physical law, however, especially in quantum theory, may allow possibilities for a theological affirmation of miracles over against scientific understandings of natural law that did not previously exist.

Given the fact that all the laws of nature have not yet been discovered or are not fully understood, a certain difficulty arises in saying what they do and do not permit with reference to the total compass of reality. The laws that describe individual systems may not be satisfactory when seeking to describe the whole. It is similar to the old trick of the mathematics teacher who, using a combination of perfectly valid equations and formulas, is able to demonstrate that $1 + 1 = 1$. All the equations and formulas used are valid within themselves but somehow, taken together, they produce the wrong answer. Ahron Katchelsky, speaking of physical beings and the laws of physical chemistry, points to a similar difficulty: "Our problem is whether the laws governing the behavior of *single* particles suffice for the treatment of organized *assemblies* of particles—even assuming that our knowledge of the laws were complete."[110]

In this light, Hawking's statement that it appears that God, if indeed a Creator God exists, has left the universe to evolve according to the laws of nature "and does not now intervene in it"[111] should be seen as an observation and not made into a rule. But theology should also expect such an observation to hold true generally. After all, what kind of Creator would we confess who found it necessary to continually make adjustments and corrections to a "good" creation? Even if a case of divine intervention (in the sense of a miracle rather than a reparatory tinkering with the universe) were verified, the "laws" of nature could almost certainly be revised to take into account the observation as part of the natural phenomena of the universe.

Perhaps the most radical development in the understanding of the nature of physical law, however, has been that introduced by quantum mechanics, which has replaced the Newtonian understanding of universal law with a quantum-statistical approach. Philosopher Richard Swineburne has noted that natural laws may be either universal in form and state what must happen (classical physics), or statistical in form and state what must probably happen (quantum physics). "From the eighteenth to the beginning of the twentieth century most men believed that all natural laws were universal. Yet since the development of Quantum Theory in this century many scientists have come to hold that the fundamental natural laws are statistical."[112] Erwin Schrödinger, for instance, has written that "physical laws rest on atomic statistics and are therefore only approximate."[113] In light of such a view of natural law, a miracle would seem to be a violation of statistical probability rather than of some absolute set of laws. The precise theological and philosophical implications of such an understanding of miracles, however, remain to be seen.

Quantum Theory, Singularities, and Miracles

If one takes seriously the divine postulate, and additionally contends that the divine Being is Creator of the universe, then the question of miracles (if not their actuality, then at least their potentiality) is unavoidable. The nineteenth-century physicist George G. Stokes was correct when he wrote: "Admit the existence of a God, of a personal God, and the possibility of miracle follows at once."[114] A century after Stokes made this observation, it might reasonably be asked whether aspects of contemporary physics shed a positive light on the theological affirmation of miracles. Such aspects of contemporary physics would prove nothing concerning miracles. They may, however, serve to demonstrate that the theological affirmation of miracles cannot be dismissed out of hand. They may also provide useful models for explaining the Christian doctrine of miracles in a way intelligible to modern persons. Two insights from modern physics are especially relevant here: the uncertainty principle of quantum mechanics and the existence of singularities within classical cosmological models.

Hume's argument against miracles (and successive versions of it) is founded upon a Newtonian understanding of physical law that is today no longer accepted as valid. The Newtonian/Laplacian understanding of physical law was an entirely deterministic one. Today, physical law, within the context of quantum mechanics, is understood statistically. The philosopher of science Mary Hesse writes that "Newtonianism has been replaced in modern physics by . . . quantum theory whose laws are not deterministic but statistical. . . . It is important to notice that according to quantum theory this is not merely a question of *ignorance* of laws which may after all be fundamentally deterministic, but of irreducible indeterminism in the events themselves."[115]

To say, as does Hesse, that the quantum, statistical view has "replaced" the Newtonian view seems a bit premature considering that quantum and classical physics have not yet been unified successfully. Nevertheless, the existence of the quantum-mechanical, statistical view of natural law, even if its precise relationship to the classical view remains uncertain, is of undoubted metaphysical significance. As long as the statistical view of natural law holds true at some level, the "universal" understanding of the classical view loses its character as absolute, deterministic, and universally applicable. But does the appearance of the concept of a statistical understanding of physical law change the standing of the idea of miracle in light of the physical sciences? On the one hand, as Hesse points out, "radical as the transformation from Newtonian to quantum physics is, . . . it does not have any direct effect on the acceptability of the idea of miracle."[116] The fact that laws are viewed as statistical does not mean that they cannot be violated and that such violation would not cause the same logical difficulty as within the strictly classical view. "Statistical laws in science are in fact regarded as violated if events occur which are excessively improbable. . . . There is no question that most events regarded as scientifically 'miraculous' in religious contexts would, if they violate Newtonian laws, also be excessively improbable on well-established quantum laws, and therefore would be regarded as violations of these also." In a sense, however, the "abandonment of the deterministic world-view in physics has made it more difficult to regard the existing state of science as finally legislative of what is and what is not possible in nature."[117]

While it is clear that quantum, statistical laws can also be "violated," what would constitute such a violation cannot be stated with as much precision as in the case of Newtonian laws. Swineburne has written that in the case of quantum, statistical laws, "it is not in all cases so clear what counts as a counter-instance to them."[118] This flexibility within the understanding of physical law has, though not eliminating the difficulty, created a more congenial atmosphere for the concept of miracles. Science, at least to the extent it is influenced by quantum mechanics, is no longer so certain as to what can and cannot happen.[119]

The closest physics comes to providing a working model or metaphor for miracles is in the occurrence of singularities. All Friedmann type universes have at some point in their past history (and, if closed, also in their future) a point (Big Bang or Big Crunch) at which the density and curvature of space-time would have been (or will be) infinite. As Hawking explains: "Because mathematics cannot really handle infinite numbers, this means that the general theory of relativity . . . predicts that there is a point in the universe where the theory itself breaks down. Such a point is an example of what mathematicians call a singularity."[120] At such singularities our ability to make predictions breaks down, providing an example within classical physics not just of insufficient information but of a fundamental unpredictability. Not only are "events" or conditions at singularities not subject to prediction, but singularities themselves, as the name suggests, are unique, nonrepeatable states.

In a sense, then, taken metaphorically, miracles can be compared to singularities. In the case of miracles, as with singularities, we encounter unique, nonrepeatable events at which our ability to make predictions, based on the laws of nature, breaks down. From a theological perspective, one might even say that in miracles we encounter the infinity of the transcendent God, which our human understanding of the physical world is not able to handle. Singularities, of course, are not miracles; and neither are miracles singularities in the sense in which the term is used in physics. The two are not to be literally identified in any way. Yet the idea of a singularity, which we find especially in a Big Bang or Big Crunch, demonstrates that even within the normally deterministic worldview of classical physics there are instances at which predictability and known laws simply break down and science can do nothing other than point to the occurrence and confess its inability to explain or go beyond it. Theology does essentially the same thing in the face of miracles. For this reason, if no other, the concept of singularity has metaphorical value for a theological concept of miracle.

Regarding the question of miracles in the light of modern science and the Christian belief in a transcendent and omnipotent God, we are left with a certain tension and uncertainty that call for restraint in our talk of miracles. We should claim neither too much nor too little concerning the potential of divine, miraculous intervention. Arthur Peacocke has summarized the matter well, writing: "Given that ultimately God is the Creator of the world . . . we cannot rule out the possibility that God might 'intervene,' in the popular sense of that word, to bring about events for which there can never be a naturalistic interpretation. . . . But we have . . . cogent reasons for questioning whether such direct 'intervention' is normally compatible with and coherent with other well-founded affirmations concerning the nature of God and of God's relation to the world."[121]

Divine Intervention as Scientific/Theological Problem

John Polkinghorne, speaking of the conditions of the early universe that allowed the development of human life, mentions the idea of inflated domains in which certain parts of the universe have different properties. According to this view, we live in a domain in which the precise necessary level of expansion is maintained to produce a universe within the "anthropic limits" required for the development of life. Polkinghorne suggests that such an anthropic self-selection of the conditions of our "domain" may have benefits for theism. He explains that "if the idea of inflated domains is the reason why there is a region where the precise balances resulting from that theory's symmetry breaking lie within anthropic limits, then that could be a gain for the theist, who might be loath to invoke direct divine intervention."[122]

But why, we might ask, would theists "be loath to invoke direct divine intervention" in the world? In a sense the invocation of miracles has generally been viewed as a sort of theological "cheating" similar to the invocation of a God-of-the-gaps. When all other explanations fail, we invoke the miraculous intervention of God. Yet as Arthur Peacocke (as previously cited) points out, such intervention is not normally "compatible with and coherent with other well-founded affirmations concerning the nature of God and of God's relation to the world." Contemporary biblical scholars, therefore, often seek every possible way of explaining an apparent miraculous intervention of God recorded in Scripture as taking place within the laws of nature.[123] Whereas past generations of exegetes often did not hesitate to identify an act of intervention as a miracle, contemporary scholars admit the possibility, and then usually only provisionally, when all other explanations fail. Physicist and Anglican priest William Pollard typifies this tendency when he comments that the majority of miracles recorded in Scripture "are the result of an extraordinary and extremely improbable combination of chance and accidents. They do not, on close analysis, involve . . . a violation of the law of nature."[124]

For theology, it is important to distinguish between God's ability to intervene in the affairs of the world through a miraculous interruption of natural law and God's propensity to actually carry out such acts of special providence. From the perspective of the natural sciences it is difficult to engage in dialogue with theology if theology is constantly changing the rules by invoking miraculous intervention. It is like playing tag with someone who retains the right to change the safety zones at his or her convenience. Thus, partly for apologetic reasons, miracles have become something of a theological problem that contemporary theologians are "loath to invoke." There are also theological grounds for this reluctance. As Polkinghorne suggests, a God who is constantly tinkering with creation through special, miraculous intervention begins to look uncomfortably like a God-of-the-gaps.

Yet when all is said and done, the ability of God to intervene in the universe remains a fundamental confession of the Christian doctrine of God. At issue is not so much the immanence of God—that can be maintained apart from the ability to interrupt the laws of nature—but the transcendence of

God. A God who cannot in principle intervene "miraculously" in the universe can hardly be credibly maintained to be its "wholly other" Creator. The transcendence of God, however, is perhaps ultimately more of a stumbling block than the possibility of miracles. A God who transcends the physical universe also transcends the ability of modern science to prove or disprove God's existence. In an age when scientific research stands on the very threshold of understanding the mysteries of the universe, a God who is beyond its grasp remains a hard pill to swallow.

Mary Hesse is correct in her contention that miracles, or divine interventions in general, do not seem to be the main problem, but rather, the doctrine of God's transcendence. She writes: "Difficult to understand from the scientific point of view is theological talk about the special acts of a transcendent God. The offence of particularity is still with us, whether these special acts violate or conform with the laws of nature. The fundamental problem is not about miracle, but about transcendence."[125]

THE PROBLEM OF EVIL

Entropy and Evil

Entropy, which can be defined as the measure or amount of manifest disorder within a system, cannot in itself be said to be negative or evil. Nevertheless, since the discovery of the second law of thermodynamics in the last century, the concept of entropy has played a significant role in the theological discussion of the problem of evil. The principle of entropy, to a greater extent than most discoveries of natural science, has found seemingly unlimited parallels within the various systems contained in every field of study and has spawned both awe and dread in the popular imagination. It should come as no surprise that theology has taken note of similarities between the principle of entropy observed in physical systems and the disorder of human and social systems (sin/moral evil) and the tragedy-producing "disorder" in the physical world (natural evil). Indeed, theologian and physicist Robert John Russell has recently argued that "entropy is a prefiguring of evil on the physical level." In explaining the connection between entropy and evil, Russell writes: "Evil is likened to a disorder, a disfunction in an organism, an obstruction to growth or an imperfection in being. Entropy refers to such disorder, measuring the dissipation of a system, the fracturing of a whole. . . . We need only to think of the pain and cost of natural disasters . . . to recognize the extent of suffering in this world. All these are rooted in the press of entropy, the relentless disintegration of form, environment, organism."[126]

There would certainly seem to be a connection, although not an identification, between entropy and natural evil. The related issue of moral evil that exists within individual humans and social systems also presents interesting parallels. It is natural evil, however, for which we are most likely to find a working metaphor in the phenomenon of entropy. Entropy and evil, as Russell points out, are both "dependent on being, lacking independent existence." Without order, disorder has no meaning or existence. Similarly, without good, evil has no independent existence. As Paul Tillich has written: "Destruction has no independent standing in the whole of reality but . . . is dependent on the structure of that in and upon which it acts destructively. Here, as everywhere in the whole of being, non-being is dependent on being, the negative on the positive, death on life. Therefore, even destruction has structures. It 'aims' at chaos; but, as long as chaos is not attained, destruction must follow the structures of wholeness; and if chaos is attained, both structure and destruction have vanished."[127]

It is interesting here to compare Tillich's idea that "if chaos is attained, both structure and destruction have vanished" with the implications of Ludwig Boltzmann's well-known entropy formula: $S = k \log P$.[128] The formula demonstrates that in isolated systems (like our universe), entropy increases precisely because the probability for disorder increases with the progression of time. Given these circumstances we might conclude that eventually a thermal equilibrium would be reached in which complete disorder and maximum probability are achieved. The equilibrium thus reached denotes such a total state of chaos that no processes continue and there is no more order left for disorder to infect. Within a Tillichian ontology of evil and disorder it would seem that, given such a literal state of thermal equilibrium, we would have to say that the structure of disorder itself ceases to exist inasmuch as it has overcome all order on which it was dependent for existence. Interestingly, physics speaks of the possibility of a thermal equilibrium existing primarily in two contexts within the entire system of the cosmos: in the very beginning and at the very end. Although far from agreement on the matter, some cosmologists posit a chaotic early universe that in its first milliseconds of existence existed in a state approaching thermal equilibrium.[129] Other cosmologists speculate that, on the basis of the second law, our universe must end in a similar state of maximum disorder—perhaps even in a Big Crunch in which conditions would resemble those of the equilibrium believed to have existed at the Big Bang. That both of these states have been associated with so-called states of nothingness or *nihil* presents intriguing possibilities for analogy, if not consonance with the Tillichian ontology of evil.

If, as both Russell and Tillich maintain, entropy and evil are, respectively, dependent on order and good for their existence, could the converse also be true? Are order and good in any way dependent on entropy and evil for either their existence or identity? If we answer the question affirmatively, we find ourselves in the company of a very old theological tradition that dates back at least to Irenaeus and that builds a theodicy on the dependence of good on a certain amount of evil in the world.[130] In this view, "the world exists to be an environment for man's life, and its imperfections are integral to its fitness as a place of soul-making."[131] The idea has found parallels in the thinking of some contemporary physicists and other natural scientists engaged in the study of entropy and system disorder.[132] Philip Hefner gives theological expression to this view when he contends that "chaos provides the possibilities without which there can be no actuality; it is the womb of creativity and actuality. . . . Creation and chaos belong together by nature. Tragedy and the demonic harass the good, because the good contains within itself the seeds of its own destruction, without any external intervention necessary."[133]

Whether one asserts the dependence of entropy/evil on order/good, a converse relationship, or some form of symbiotic interdependence, most contemporary theological and scientific viewpoints assume some sort of linkage between the two. In both theology and the natural sciences, however, the exact nature of this relationship is disputed. It is possible, therefore, for theology to find corresponding models in the natural sciences for a number of divergent perspectives in regard to the question of the relationship between good and evil. Given such a context, prudence would seem to call for restraint on the part of theology in not making too much of any particular scientific model. The main issue, however, remains the relationship between entropy and evil in general, for which there seems to be much more justification for drawing analogies.

One cannot equate evil with entropy, yet both concepts provide insights and metaphors useful in the explanation of the other. Both theology and physics seek to explain the nature of and reason for the existence of disorder within otherwise orderly systems. Russell summarizes the matter well: "Although the characteristics of entropy and evil do not give direct support to one another, if evil is real in nature, entropy is what one would expect to find at the level of physical processes. Conversely, if a real arrow of time is coupled to entropy in physical processes, one would expect to find dissipative, disruptive, yet subtly catalytic processes in history and religious experience."[134]

Rampant Evil and Dysteleological Cosmological Models

We have seen that at least on the level of analogy and metaphor a certain connection exists between entropy and evil. Although views of entropy and evil within both physics and theology are diverse, they seem to fall into two general categories: (1) entropy/evil is genuine, uncontrolled disorder and leads to no end other than further disorder; and (2) entropy/evil is confined within certain established limits and/or is part of some larger teleological movement toward an ordered or planned end. In the Christian theodicy tradition this division is roughly paralleled by the Augustinian and Irenean types of theodicy.[135] We will look first at the dysteleological models and their theological counterparts.

In regard to God's present activity in relation to evil (natural and moral), four views have been held.[136] Each view makes two assumptions: that God is good and that genuine evil and disorder exist. All four views attempt to explain the relationship between these two premises. Two of these views exist within the general framework of a disorder run rampant. First is the view that God, for reasons unknown, governs the world in such a way that evil is simply permitted to have free rein (*gubernatio permissa*). The second view is that God governs the world so as to impede evil (*gubernatio impedita*), apparently to the best of God's ability, but that evil is too all-encompassing and God is at best only able to restrain it somewhat. In both cases evil exercises more or less a free rein and leads to no particular ordered end. Ironically, there is a parallel here with what John Hick has identified as the Augustinian stream in Christian theodicy. While the theology of Augustine is normally associated with a sovereign, omnipotent God, his view of evil as primarily human-connected and disjunct from God has tended to give evil, in so-called Augustinian theodicies, an independent existence.[137]

The parallel to these views is found within physics in the various dysteleological models in which an ever-increasing entropy is not part of some greater teleological direction, but leads rather to nothing other than even greater levels of disorder. The "heat death" of the universe, first predicted in 1854 by the German physicist Hermann von Helmholtz based on his study of the implications of the second law,[138] is the earliest and perhaps classic example of a dysteleological cosmological model. As John Barrow and Frank Tipler explain, the heat death of the universe "denies the Universe is progressing toward some goal; but rather is using up the store of available energy which existed in the beginning. The Universe, in other words, is not teleological, but *dysteleological!*"[139]

The idea of the heat death of the universe—that is, the notion that the universe will eventually wear down and come to an end—was popularized by the British astrophysicists James Jeans and Arthur Eddington in the 1920s.[140] Eddington compared the running down of the universe with the shuffling of a deck of cards in which "the order will never come back however long you shuffle." This situation stems from the second law, which establishes an irreversible arrow of time, because the "progress of time introduces more and more of the random element into the constitution of the world."[141]

Eddington noted that we can do nothing to prevent "the inexorable running-down of the world by loss of organization and increase of the random element. Whoever wishes for a universe that can continue indefinitely in activity must lead a crusade against the second law of thermodynamics. . . . At present we can see no way in which an attack on the second law of thermodynamics could possibly succeed, and I confess that personally I have no great desire that it should succeed in averting the final running down of the universe."[142] Analogically, we find here a parallel with the view that for some reason God allows evil to run its spiraling course of destruction. Evil exists by God's permission, and we can do nothing to stop it. Evil becomes merely an unpleasant fact we must learn to accept, just as, according to Eddington, we learn to accept the fact that the universe seems to be programmed to wear out.

"Domesticated" Evil and Teleological Cosmological Models

There are two remaining options for reconciling the existence of a loving and good God with the existence of evil, both of which are related analogically to teleological cosmologies. Both theological models for comprehending evil contend that God exercises control (and thereby responsibility) over evil, thus denying evil a separate existence and giving it a place in the overall teleological direction of the universe. The first view is that God directs the evil in the world toward some greater or final purpose or goal (*gubernatio directa*). Evil, in this Irenean model, is employed by God to bring about the good. The second view holds that the extent of evil or disorder is limited by God and cannot exceed a certain determined limit (*gubernatio determinata*).

The teleological models of entropy find their theological counterpart in the Irenean school of thought inasmuch as evil, in this perspective, has no independent existence but is subject to (and even a part of) God's overall plan.[143] This tradition finds full expression in the thought of Friedrich Schleiermacher, who developed even more clearly than Irenaeus an instrumental view of sin and evil. Schleiermacher contended that "sin has been ordained by God . . . in relation to redemption; for otherwise redemption itself could not have been ordained."[144] Hence God directs sin and evil to fulfill the greater purpose of redemption.

Corresponding, at least analogically, to the idea that God restricts evil, is the view of some scientists that entropy has a maximum limit set on it. One possible model of such a maximum-limit entropy is found in the Poincaré recurrence theorem, which attempts to demonstrate that "almost any mechanical system with finite potential energy, finite kinetic energy, and bounded in space must necessarily return to any previous initial state. Thus, whatever the state of the Universe now, the entropy as defined by Boltzmann would almost certainly have to decrease in the future back to its present value."[145] The Poincaré recurrence suggests, therefore, a model in which entropy at some point reaches a maximal limit and decreases to a previous value.

Similar to the Poincaré recurrence is the possibility that the second law breaks down or reverses itself in models of a contracting universe. In such models "entropy would rise to a maximum at the point of maximum expansion of a closed universe and thereafter begin to decrease, with a return at the final singularity to the conditions which prevailed at the initial singularity." Barrow and Tipler further observe that "in order for such a return to occur, the disintegration of radioactive materials [as one example] must be counterbalanced by a spontaneous regeneration even today, and this could be searched for."[146] The possibility of verification for such a model, in fact, has been examined independently by W. J. Cocke and John Wheeler.[147]

Also worthy of note in this regard is the limitation on entropy/chaos that Gary Zukav has seen within the randomness of quantum systems. He writes: "The world view of particle physics is a picture of *chaos beneath order.* At the fundamental level is a confusion of continual creation, annihilation and transformation. Above this confusion, limiting the forms that it can take, are a set of conservation laws. They do not specify what must happen, . . . they specify what can*not* happen. They are permissive laws."[148]

An example of a view of entropy that is analogous to the view that God directs evil (*gubernatio directa*) can be found in the physical chemist Ilya Prigogine. Working from the perspective of thermodynamics, Prigogine seeks to demonstrate that the irreversibility of time must not be seen as a purely negative progression of isolated systems of states from greater to lesser order. Especially in relation to human existence, Prigogine believes that it is false to view the irreversible arrow of time and its accompanying increase in entropy as essentially threatening to human existence. Rather, the "arrow of time does not oppose man against nature. Far from that, it stresses the embedding of mankind in the evolutionary universe which we discover at all levels of description." Crucial for Prigogine is his use of thermodynamics, in which irreversibility exists, rather than dynamics, in which reversibility is the common assumption. It is only with irreversibility that, according to Prigogine, an evolutionary, teleological paradigm works. Prigogine and Isabelle Stengers have therefore written that "it is . . . of great importance that an evolutionary paradigm can now be established in physics. . . . The immense importance of irreversible processes shows that this requirement is satisfied for most systems of interest. Remarkably, the perception of oriented time increases as the level of biological organization increases and probably reaches its culminating point in human consciousness."[149]

Also relevant in Prigogine's view is the idea that identical systems will end in different states. It is here that the truly revolutionary nature of his research into thermodynamics can be seen. Prigogine, in his 1980 book *From Being to Becoming,* suggested that irreversibility means that dissipative systems, surprisingly, evolve from states of lesser to greater order.[150] According to Russell, Prigogine's research "suggests that, as one drives a system far from thermodynamic equilibrium, new forms of extraordinary order appear," and also that "temporal irreversibility is fundamental in nature, and that entropy plays a catalytic role during processes of unusual complexification."[151]

Entropy has also been defined by some as "the increase of possibilities of transformation or organization, or the increase in the number of 'accessible states.'"[152] Such views have been presented by Kenneth Denbigh and Ahron Katchelsky. Katchelsky suggests that in "flow" systems things do not always move in the direction of thermodynamic equilibrium. Speaking of the circulation of heat flow, Katchelsky writes, "The flow pattern is a compromise between stabilizing and transforming factors which maintain a balanced existence within a narrow temperature range."[153] Speaking of this flow pattern as applied to biological systems, Katchelsky speculates that a "jump from a lower to a higher level of organization across a range of instability" may be "basic to biological evolution" in which "micromutations would act as a destabilizing factor which disturbs the fine balance of the flow process . . . leading to a finite jump to new organizational setups."[154] Therefore, from this example from biology, which Katchelsky believes is also relevant for physics, we see that "disorder" (in this case micromutations) can actually lead to increased possibilities for transformation and organization that may lead the system to a more ordered state.

The correspondence between theological models of evil and scientific models of entropy is both striking and significant. This correspondence would seem to be more than coincidence, but rather an indication of a certain amount of common ground between theology and physical science in the entropy/evil question. Although the nature of the disorder and the systems described by theology and physical science is clearly distinct, there is a sense in which science and theology address the same questions: namely, what is the ultimate nature, purpose, and extent of the disorder (entropy/evil) within otherwise ordered/good systems? In addressing these questions in its consideration of the problem of natural evil, theology is certainly concerned with the nature of the physical universe and entropy within physical systems. Similarly, physics and the other natural sciences are not unconcerned with metaphysical/philosophical questions in their search for answers to the questions posed by entropy. There is, therefore, an overlapping of interests between theology and natural science which, at least in part, may explain some of the similarities in the respective models of entropy and evil. The existence of such common ground opens the way not only for the possibility of fruitful dialogue but also for a cooperation between theology and science in the sharing of ideas and models.

Theodicy and Modern Physics

With all the rich parallels between entropy and evil, one might naturally inquire whether the research results of modern physics relevant to entropy and disorder suggest any new possibilities for theodicy. I believe that in essence they do not. They do, however, seem to have given new life to a whole class of long-derided[155] Leibnizian theodicies that suggest that we live in the best of all possible worlds. The German physicist Carl Friedrich von Weizsäcker has made an interesting suggestion in this regard. Von Weizsäcker, beginning with Leibniz's contention that we live in "the best of all possible worlds," takes up the question anew in the light of modern physics. He writes: "As God created the world all possible worlds stood before his eyes; he chose one of them, the best, and gave it existence. Thus our world became real, it became 'the world.' Yet every possible world could have potentially been 'the world'; only they were denied the predicate of existence."[156]

Only with the advent of modern physics have we been in a position to address the basic assumption of Leibniz's theodicy from the perspective of physical science. Do we really live in the best of all possible worlds? Are there really other possible worlds? Von Weizsäcker writes:

> Curiously, the uniqueness of the world becomes a philosophical topic through Leibniz's thought in this regard. The idea of "possibility" that enables us to think about things separate from the predicate of existence allows us to set up the fiction of other, thought-up worlds alongside of the one world that we all know. This fiction only serves, however, to distinguish the "real" world from among all possible worlds through specific characteristics, thereby reemphasizing its contingency. Its characteristics are the conditions of its existence. It is real because it is how it is; and it is unique, because its characteristics are unique, that is to say, optimal. . . . Therefore the idea of possibility cannot encompass the concept of the world. There are possibilities in the world, but not possible worlds.[157]

Although von Weizsäcker, unfortunately, does not flesh out many of the details of his proposed theodicy, he seems to suggest a revival of sorts of the theodicy of Leibniz. He contends that Leibniz's basic philosophical train of thought in this area is built on considerations that are at home in the world of physics, where they are without question legitimate.[158] Leibniz's famous claim that we live in the best of all possible worlds, [159] despite the criticisms directed against it, may be legitimated from the perspective of modern physics, which suggests that we not only live in the best of all possible worlds, but perhaps even the only possible "real" world. For von Weizsäcker, it would seem, our world (entropy and all) becomes the only possible world because it is the only "real" world.

Since von Weizsäcker penned his arguments, the many-worlds interpretation of quantum mechanics, if indeed it is someday accepted over the Copenhagen interpretation, at least seriously weakens any support physics might lend to a Leibniz-style theodicy. If Barrow and Tipler and other proponents of the many-worlds theory are right, it may be that all possible worlds, even an infinite number of worlds, do exist or have existed. Barrow and Tipler's own version of the many-worlds interpretation of quantum mechanics is that there is "only one Universe, but small parts of it . . . split into several pieces."[160] While the focus on only one universe may save the Leibnizian theodicy within modern physics, it remains uncertain what effect the possibility even of a single universe that splits and realizes many or even all possibilities would have on the idea that only one universe (or a very limited number of universes) is possible. Part of the difficulty rests with the tentative and speculative nature of the many-worlds interpretation itself in its numerous versions. Nevertheless, the very possibility of a many-worlds interpretation would seem to place a question mark over von Weizsäcker's suggested revival of a Leibnizian theodicy based on modern physics.

A variation, however, might be possible in some of the strong anthropic principle (SAP) models of the many-worlds interpretation in which our world is seen as being the only one in which the evolution of information-processing life is possible. Although admitting that Leibniz did not believe the world to have been created for humanity, Barrow and Tipler find support in Leibniz's "best of many possible worlds" argument for their own version of the many-worlds interpretation as a component of the strong anthropic principle.[161] Renewed support for a traditional, *theo*-centric theodicy, therefore, may be an ironic offshoot of anthropic principle arguments for our world being the most hospitable of many possible (or real) worlds for human existence.

Apart from the many-worlds question, other aspects of contemporary physics and cosmology are bound to have an impact on the formulation of any modern theodicy. Perhaps chief among these are the various versions of the anthropic principle. Apart from anthropic versions of the many-worlds interpretation, the SAP itself presents some interesting possibilities. Similar to the best of all possible worlds argument, the SAP, with or without many-worlds, seems to suggest that the world must be as it is for theologians to exist who can talk about theodicy. Evil, then, becomes a necessary component of the kind of world required for the nurture of sentient, moral beings.

Perhaps even more intriguing is the possibility suggested by the so-called final anthropic principle (FAP), especially John Wheeler's concept of a "participatory universe."[162] In such models humanity, by its very act of participation in the universe and in its collective final observership, is made the explanatory principle of the origin and development of the universe. In other words, we are responsible for the universe being here and for its being the way it is. In such a model humanity, and not God, becomes responsible for the evil/entropy within the world because we apparently require it in some way. While such a view would appear to free God from responsibility for evil, it would also seem to virtually eliminate God from the picture by making God redundant.

A related theodicy that suggests that "evil" may be necessary in our universe has been detected in what Willem Drees considers to be Freeman Dyson's theodicy of diversity. Drees writes: "Dyson suggests a theodicy based on a principle of diversity. If maximum diversity is the perfection, perfection is only possible if all tensions which can be co-present are present." Thus, "the possibility of failure is a risk that is necessary in a non-deterministic process moving towards maximum diversity."[163]

We close our considerations of theodicy by returning to the view that there may have been only one set (or at best a very few possible sets) of laws of physics for a Creator to choose that could govern the development of the universe. Both Einstein and Hawking have suggested that there may be only one possible world from the perspective of theoretical physics. Einstein, for instance, once asked "whether God could have made the world in a different way; that is, whether the necessity of logical simplicity leaves any freedom at all."[164] Similarly, Hawking suggests that if his no-boundary proposal is correct, then God would have had "no freedom at all to choose the initial conditions" of the universe and very little if any choice in choosing the laws that the universe obeys in light of the fact that "there may well be only one, or a small number, of complete unified theories" sufficient to allow a universe in which human beings could exist.[165] A theodicy based on such a perspective would seem to explain evil as a necessary part of the best (or only) world that God could have created. In other words, if God could not have created a better world, or perhaps even any other world, then God had no choice about the "evil" in the world and cannot be held accountable for it. Once again, however, the appeal of such an option is severely limited in that it seems necessary to "tie God's hands" in order to make the argument work.

The fact that most perspectives on theodicy arising out of physics lead in this direction points to an inherent weakness of natural theology to rise above the level of mere causal argumentation. Either God had the ability to make the world other than it is or God did not. Only if God is made to appear to have had no other choice can God's "causing" of our world be seen as noncapricious from the perspective of natural theology alone. Theodicies, therefore, arising out of a natural theology based on data taken from physics seem inevitably to weaken God over against the physical universe.

SUMMARY: GOD'S CONTINUING ACTIVITY IN THE UNIVERSE IN LIGHT OF CONTEMPORARY PHYSICS

Speaking about God in the context of continuing creation presents special difficulties. In many ways it is easier to speak of what God may have done in the past (original creation and creation out of nothing), or about what God may do in the future (consummation of creation), than what God is doing in the present. Similarly, it is often easier to speak of transcendence than of immanence. The activity of an immanent God in our present era is much more open to verification (and falsification) than the activity of a primarily transcendent God who acts on the universe in the primordial past or in the distant future. This is not to say that transcendence and immanence are not compatible, for a balanced doctrine of God must take both into account. Yet the present activity of a God who is also immanent in the physical universe presents certain unique challenges for theology. We have spoken repeatedly in this chapter—indeed almost exclusively—of analogies and models for understanding the activity of God in terms of a continuing creation as opposed to the more concrete treatment, for example, of *ex nihilo* models of cosmogony found in the preceding chapter. In the case of a *creatio originans* and a *creatio ex nihilo*, we saw physics borrowing terminology and models from theology to elucidate concepts difficult to explain within the normal scope of physics. In the case of *creatio continua* the borrowing of metaphors and models seems primarily to be taking place in the other direction.

Contemporary physics, through its classical and quantum field theories and the nonlocality suggested by the EPR experiment, points to the interconnectedness and dependence of physical reality. The physical sciences cannot address directly the fact that physical reality may depend on the continuing sustenance of a transcendent God. The bare fact of interconnectedness alone, however, reveals the contingent nature of the physical universe and provides a foundation on which theology can build a confession of the continuing sustenance of God in a way that is intelligible to the modern mind. In doing this, theology is free to make use metaphorically of such concepts as field theory and nonlocality. But theology must also be careful that neither God nor God's activity is literally identified with any specific theory or concept of physical science. To do so would seem to lead inevitably to a situation in which "God" becomes the metaphor for the physical theory, rather than vice versa.

In regard to God's continuing work of providence, we have also seen that God is not to be identified with the processes of the physical world, although God's presence is certainly to be seen *in* them. God is not identical with the physical processes of the world but neither is God some yet-to-be-discovered additional factor that we must take into our calculations. God providentially directs the processes of the universe, but does so within and through the laws that God created and established for this purpose. Arthur Peacocke expresses this idea well when he writes, "the processes revealed by the sciences are in themselves God acting as Creator and God is not to be found as some kind of *additional* factor added on to the processes of the world. God, to use the language usually applied to sacramental theology, is 'in, with and under' all-that-is and all-that-goes-on."[166] This is, of course, not an identification of God with physical processes. It is, rather, a recognition that God works through them and is to be seen in them. There remains a fundamental distinction between saying that God is "in, with and under" all-that-is, and saying that God *is* all-that-is and all-that-goes-on.

In traditional Christian theology not only is the identification of God with the physical world rejected, but also all views that emphasize the immanence of God to the exclusion of God's transcendence. A God who is not transcendent is not capable, even in principle, of miraculous intervention because such a God would be necessarily subject to and limited by the laws of nature. Miracles remain a difficult point in the dialogue between science and theology. Yet their theological importance must be affirmed—and along with it the importance of confessing a God who transcends the realm of the physical universe and the laws that govern it while at the same time remaining free to intervene in it. It is important, however, that such intervention normally takes place within the laws that God has established to govern the universe through what theology calls "general providence." Even from the perspective of theology, miracles remain the exceptions that serve to reinforce the rule. God is no cosmic tinkerer, and God's creation is not in need of periodic adjustment. Nevertheless, as transcendent Creator, God remains in principle free to intervene—even miraculously—within the universe.

In regard to God's continuing work of creation and the problem of entropy, the biblical picture of a world in which order and good ultimately triumph over entropy and evil seems to go against many of the results of research into the second law of thermodynamics.[167] As Robert John Russell has put the question: "Are we somehow to be freed from the tyranny of entropy, and is the universe to shine forever as the resplendent creature of

God—a *new* heaven and earth?"[168] From the perspective of Christian theology the answer would seem to be that this is exactly what will take place. A God who is both transcendent and immanent can, in providential governance of the universe, break the dissipative spiral of entropy and evil.

In the final analysis, it would seem that modern physics has not made the confession of God's work of continuing creation any more difficult than it was previously. In fact, the advances of modern physics have proven a rich source of models and metaphors that theology is free to use in confessing God's ongoing immanence through the continuing work of creation. In some ways contemporary physics, by undermining Newtonian determinism and raising significant questions about the nature and character of physical law, has produced an emerging worldview more hospitable to the confession of a Creator who is immanent in the work of continuing creation than that based on the physics and other natural sciences of the last century.

The dialogue with physics, even in the fields most closely concerned with questions of God's immanence, seems once again to point to the importance of confessing God's transcendence. If God were only immanent, not only would God be confined by physical law, but advances in physics would seem on the verge of making God homeless. If God is not transcendent and is not to be equated with the universe itself, then God's dwelling place would seem to be restricted to the ever-shrinking gaps in our knowledge of the physical universe. Of such a nontranscendent deity it can rightly and without regret be said that Newton put him out of work and modern physics has left him little living space. The nontranscending God-of-the-gaps, therefore, in the light of modern physics, is not only unemployed but is fast becoming homeless. The transcendent God of Christian theism, however, is neither out of work nor out on the streets. God is to be seen and experienced in all the intricate workings of our physical universe. Our conclusion, therefore, is that E. O. Wilson is wrong in his assessment that, because of modern physics, "God's immanence has been pushed to somewhere below the subatomic particles or beyond the farthest visible galaxy."[169] The ever-tinkering God-of-the-gaps has rightly suffered this fate in the face of the advances of modern physics. The immanence of the transcendent God of Christian theism, however, becomes only clearer and more awe-inspiring as the ongoing processes of creation are more fully understood. To paraphrase the psalmist: Even the subatomic particles and the farthest galaxies display the glory and the immanence of God.

Chapter Five

Can God Survive the Consummation of the Universe?

All the stars of the heavens will be dissolved and the sky rolled up like a scroll; all the starry host will fall like withered leaves from the vine, like shriveled figs from the fig tree.

—Isaiah 34:4 (NIV)

Then I saw a new heaven and a new earth; for the first heaven and the first earth had passed away, . . . And I saw the holy city, the new Jerusalem, coming down out of heaven from God. . . . And the city has no need of sun or moon to shine on it, for the glory of God is its light.

—Apocalypse of John 21:1, 2, 23.

The Natural God ends in heat death or in universal collapse. The Natural God either fades in force forever, or else shrinks to a point perhaps forever—two kinds of natural death.

—Joel Friedman

I hope . . . to hasten the arrival of the day when eschatology, the study of the end of the universe, will be a respectable scientific discipline and not merely a branch of theology.

—Freeman Dyson

If life evolves in all of the many universes in a quantum cosmology, and if life continues to exist in all of these universes, then all of these universes, which include all possible histories among them, will approach the Omega Point. At the instant the Omega Point is reached, life will have gained control of all matter and forces not only in a single universe, but in all universes whose existence is logically possible . . . and will have stored . . . all bits of knowledge which it is logically possible to know. And this is the end.

—John Barrow and Frank Tipler

ESCHATOLOGY AS EMERGING SCIENTIFIC DISCIPLINE

In the history of philosophical and theological thought a strong connection has always existed between creation and eschatology inasmuch as a beginning normally implies an end. With the tremendous focus on questions of origin in connection with the Big Bang theory, the appearance of eschatology as a serious topic of discussion among physicists is not surprising. Eschatology's coming into its own as a concern of physics, however, predates the Big Bang theory by nearly a century. Modern physicists were first led to speculate about the end of the universe as a result of the implication of the second law of thermodynamics that our universe is running down. The so-called heat death of the universe, first predicted in 1854 by the German physicist Hermann von Helmholtz[1] and popularized in the 1920s by the British astrophysicists James Jeans and Arthur Eddington,[2] qualifies as the first modern "scientific eschatology."[3]

Yet only in more recent times has eschatology truly become a field of study within physics and cosmology. This most recent development in scientific eschatology (also referred to as "physical eschatology") can be attributed to the American physicist Freeman J. Dyson, through whom "the study of the survival and the behavior of life in the far future became a branch of physics"[4] as the result of his 1979 paper, "Time without End: Physics and Biology in an Open Universe." In this seminal paper Dyson expressed the hope that his work would "hasten the arrival of the day when eschatology, the study of the end of the universe, will be a respectable scientific discipline and not merely a branch of theology."[5] Indeed, as John Barrow and Frank Tipler note, "although the papers on life in the far future are not numerous, they have shown the progression required of physical science. . . . The discussion is now based entirely on the laws of physics and computer theory. This is in sharp contrast to the vague speculations which were typical of eschatological discussions prior to Dyson."[6]

One reason for the resurgence of interest in eschatology as a field of physics with the appearance of Dyson's article is the optimistic emphasis he placed on the future of intelligent, information-processing life. The old heat death theories painted such a bleak picture of the destiny of the universe and its life forms that few were inspired to investigate the distant future. Dyson demonstrated, however, that the possibility exists for the indefinite continuation of intelligent life in our universe. This, in turn, has encouraged the study of the conditions of our physical universe in the distant future in order to determine whether and to what extent they may be compatible with the continuation of intelligent life. Before Dyson's article (and to some extent this is still true) physicists paid little attention to questions that could truly be called eschatological. Steven Weinberg's well-known book, *The First Three Minutes,* is perhaps typical of the interest of most physicists in eschatology. As Dyson lamented: "He takes 150 pages to describe the first three minutes, and then dismisses the whole of the future in five pages."[7] Even then the prospect seems dim. Weinberg concludes, "The more the universe seems comprehensible, the more it also seems pointless."[8] Little wonder that it was more appealing for physicists and cosmologists to look at the origin of the universe than at its end. Even after the appearance of Dyson's article and others of a similar nature, eschatology continues to receive only passing mention at the conclusion of many books on cosmology. The situation, however, appears to be changing. This new willingness of physicists to tackle eschatological questions opens new possibilities for dialogue with theologians, who often have approached the subject with no less reluctance and apprehension.

Not only has the work of Dyson and others on the fate of life in the remote future kindled interest in scientific eschatology among physicists, but also recent advances in physics itself have made possible the examination of the structure of the universe in the far future much more feasible. As philosopher of science Milton Munitz explains:

> In recent decades, discussions of the future of the universe have been widened and deepened by taking into account the concepts and laws of elementary-particle physics. . . . Recent theories of microphysicists have made possible the description and explanation of physical processes under conditions of extremely high and extremely low temperatures and densities. . . . Thus, while investigations by physicists and cosmologists of the end of the universe still lag in number and refinement of detail compared to investigations of the origin of the universe, there has been a recent increase of attention to this topic to redress the balance somewhat.[9]

Scientific eschatology, especially that branch concerned with the possibility of life in the remote future, has rightly claimed its place as a scientific discipline alongside of questions of the origin of the universe and the origin of life. It remains to be seen, however, what impact this will have on Christian eschatology. Scientific cosmogonies and theories of the origin of life have played substantial roles in contemporary theological formulations of the doctrine of creation. With few exceptions, however, theologians have taken little note of recent developments in scientific eschatology.[10] As scientists make more progress in their examination of the fate of the universe and the life forms within it, however, and these findings begin to be incorporated into a general scientific picture of our universe, future theological eschatologies will have to take into account the various scientific eschatologies. As Karl Heim wrote in 1952: "Every light which at least in some degree illuminates the darkness of the future is valuable for us. Therefore the question which we put to natural science is this. Does it provide us with any certainty about the future and end of the world?"[11] One can only hope that the dialogue between theology and science in the field of eschatology will begin with more mutual understanding and less suspicion than that which characterized much of the early dialogue over creation.

OPEN OR CLOSED UNIVERSE?

Dark Matter and Friedmann Universes
Since the discovery that we live in an expanding universe, the most significant question for scientific eschatology has been whether our universe is open or closed. Is there enough matter in the universe to halt its expansion and eventually bring everything back together in a so-called Big Crunch? If less than the critical mass exists, will the universe continue expanding forever? The entire issue rests with the amount of matter in the universe. Calculating the approximate mass of the universe, however, has proven to be no easy task. From what is visible to observation it would appear that there is far too little matter to bring the universe's expansion to a halt. Yet if that were all the matter that existed, the universe would be expanding much more rapidly than it is. Physicists, therefore, have speculated that an unseen "material" called dark matter exists within the so-called empty spaces of the universe. The question is how much dark matter there may be.

Recent findings from the Hubble space telescope, using its powerful lens to detect gravitational distortions that are telltale signs of the presence of significant amounts of dark matter, have suggested that there is insufficient matter in the universe to bring its expansion to a halt.[12] Another recent space venture, however, has turned up evidence suggesting the contrary. NASA's Cobe space probe created a scientific sensation recently when an announcement was made at a meeting of the American Physical Society (the same group at which cold fusion was announced to similar fanfare three years earlier, for those who keep track of such fiascoes) that it had detected fluctuations in the background radiation of the early universe that confirm the predictions of Big Bang theorists as to why the universe is now so "lumpy."[13] Besides being an incredible confirmatory boost to the Big Bang theory, the Cobe discovery also suggests that the universe may be closed. The data produced by Cobe, if correct, indicate that the fluctuations in the evenness of the universe began to form about 300,000 years after the Big Bang. In order for such fluctuations to have developed so quickly as a result of gravitational attraction, however, the universe must have significantly more mass in it than physicists had previously suspected—probably enough to cause its eventual collapse.[14] Essentially, the clues from the latest available information seem to have shifted from favoring an open to a closed universe between the Hubble announcement in February 1992 and the Cobe announcement in April 1992. It will be some time before additional observations are able to supplement or confirm the Hubble and the Cobe findings—let alone explain the seemingly contradictory evidence as to the total mass of the universe. We will have to wait for some additional time after that until the top physicists and cosmologists can begin reaching some consensus as to what precisely all this means and incorporate these data into their cosmological models. In the meantime, as prudence would seem to require, we will discuss the eschatological implications of models of both open and closed universes.

Basing his calculations on Einstein's theory of relativity, the Russian physicist and mathematician Alexander Friedmann in 1922 developed a model of a closed universe that predicted not only its expansion but its eventual recollapse. Friedmann made two fundamental assumptions about the universe in his calculations: that the universe looks the same in whatever direction we look (with all galaxies moving away from us), and that this would be true from any other point in the universe as well. Since Friedmann's original calculations, two other models of an expanding universe have been developed that correspond to his assumptions, the open and the flat cosmological models.[15] In an open universe of the Friedmann type the universe continues expanding indefinitely with an ever-decreasing restraint of gravitational attraction. In the flat model the universe also continues expanding but at just the critical speed needed to prevent its recollapse. For practical purposes, however, the flat universe is also an open universe in that it undergoes unending expansion and also seems to meet its end in a gradual running out of energy that physicists refer to as heat death. The three possible Friedmann type universes are illustrated by the following diagram.

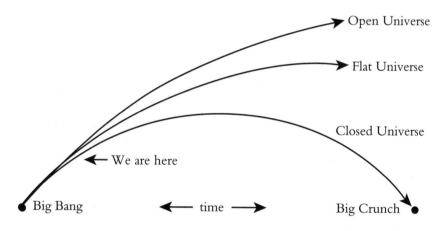

The above diagram is certainly an oversimplification, but is useful in illustrating the distinction between the three major Friedmann type models of the universe. Just as each model charts its distinct course, so each has its separate eschatological implications, with those of the open and flat models being sufficiently similar that we shall treat them together under the category of the open model universe. We will look first at the scientific eschatologies associated with open and closed universes, and then deal with the specific theological questions and problems that each model presents.

The Future of Life in an Open Universe (Dyson)

Since the time of Helmholtz the possibility of the heat death of the universe has loomed over scientific eschatology like an unscalable wall of pessimism. Even in the early days of the second law when classical physics assumed an eternal universe, the idea that the universe would eventually run out of energy and become a dark, heatless, uninhabitable scattering of dead matter was received with little enthusiasm by a scientific community enthralled by Darwinian optimism. While the concept of a static, eternal universe long since has been abandoned, the open universe model has inherited the melancholy weight of the heat death. In the few works on the remote future of our universe and life within it written before Dyson, this mood seemed unbroken. P. C. W. Davies's 1973 paper, "The Thermal Future of the Universe," is typical of such efforts. Davies, who argued that an open universe would end in complete opaqueness, concluded his paper with a good news/bad news scenario. "A sufficiently resourceful intelligence could maintain life indefinitely (though with increasing difficulty) in permanent thermodynamic disequilibrium, by using the radiation field as an energy source." In opaque models of the universe, however, which Davies believes more accurately represent our universe, "the photons would eventually disappear, the whole Universe reaching a uniform temperature (true heat death), and life would become impossible."[16]

Freeman Dyson has sought to change this pessimistic outlook. He addresses the question that naturally comes to human beings when we consider the distant future of the universe: What happens to life—specifically human life—in the universe's distant future? To this question Dyson applies a sort of Darwinism to the open model of the universe, which he believes gives an "enormously greater scope for the activities of life and intelligence" than a closed universe.[17] He asks whether it is conceivable, given the past adaptation of life to its changing environment, that intelligent life might evolve from present-day humans into some form capable of survival in the distant future of an open universe.

A critical assumption made by Dyson is that "it is impossible to calculate in detail the long-range future of the universe without including the effects of life and intelligence." If a purely natural selection could produce intelligent life, Dyson wonders whether it might also be possible for such intelligent life "to guide the physical development of the universe for its own purposes."[18] After making this seminal assumption Dyson, making no apologies "for mixing philosophical speculations with mathematical equations," states his aim of establishing "numerical bounds within which the destiny of the universe must lie."[19]

A secondary assumption made by Dyson concerns what he considers the "most serious uncertainty affecting the ultimate fate of the universe," the question "whether the proton is absolutely stable against decay into lighter particles." When it is not, then all matter is ultimately transitory and must eventually dissolve into radiation. The unending existence of matter being seen as prerequisite for the indefinite continuation of life, Dyson assumes the proton to be absolutely stable, despite the theoretical work of Yakov Zeldovich, Barrow and Tipler, G. Feinberg, and others that suggests the contrary.[20] More recently, however, Dyson, unable to ignore any longer the mounting evidence that matter may be ultimately unstable, has taken this new "challenge" to life into account. He writes:

> My theoretical physicist colleagues have recently found serious reasons to believe that all matter may be unstable. According to their latest theoretical models . . . the nuclei of all atoms will disappear into positrons and photons and neutrinos with a lifetime of the order of 10^{33} years. . . .
>
> This will be the supreme test of life's adaptability. I do not know whether we can survive without protons. But I do not see any reason even then to declare the situation hopeless. If the assumptions of abstraction and adaptability are correct, the patterns of life and consciousness should be transferable without loss from one medium to another. After the protons are gone, we shall still have the electrons and positrons and photons, and immaterial plasma may do as well as flesh and blood as a vehicle for the patterns of our thought. Perhaps the best possible universe is a universe of constant challenges, a universe in which survival is possible but not too easy.[21]

Dyson assumes two basic possible models for the universe, the closed and the open. He considers the open universe to provide the best chances for the indefinite continuation of life. And if the universe turns out to be closed, according to Dyson, "we shall still have about 10^{10} years to explore the possibility of a technological fix that would burst it open."[22] Dyson poses three questions that must be answered if we are to determine whether life in the distant future in an open universe will be possible: (1) Does the universe freeze into a state of permanent physical quiescence as it expands and cools? (2) Is it possible for life and intelligence to survive indefinitely? (3) Is it possible to maintain communication and transmit information across the constantly expanding distances between galaxies?[23] For intelligent life to exist indefinitely, these crucial questions must be answered no, yes, and yes, respectively. While Dyson is optimistic about the answers to the first two questions, the last one, dealing with communication, poses some uncertainty.

In regard to the first question, Dyson believes the traditional heat death picture, in which all processes and movement come to an end, is incorrect. He writes: "So far as we can imagine into the future, things continue to happen. In the open cosmology, history has no end."[24] This conclusion would seem to be supported by the theoretical work of Barrow and Tipler, published about six months before the appearance of Dyson's article. In their joint work, "Eternity Is Unstable," they develop a "novel picture of the universal heat death" in which an open universe becomes increasingly irregular—and even unstable—in the far future. They conclude that "the future state of non-flat, ever-expanding universes is characterized by a cumulative shear distortion in the expansion flow. That of the ever-expanding flat models is analogous to a relativistic vortex, for the dominant instability is due to the vorticity of the matter flow lines. In both cases the final state is characterized by increasing irregularity."[25] Similarly, Steven Frautschi has written, "Modern cosmology does not terminate in the classical heat death of the 19th century. The classical heat death was characterized by statistical equilibrium of matter at constant temperature and entropy. An expanding universe never achieves equilibrium and never reaches a constant temperature."[26]

The second critical question that Dyson takes up is whether it is possible for life and intelligence to survive indefinitely. In regard to life as we know it—for example, human life—the answer seems to be no. The conditions in the far future in an open universe will be incompatible with human life forms. For this reason Dyson puts his hope in the ability of life, especially intelligent life, to evolve in a direction that will allow it to survive in the distant future. If we assume that life is based on structure rather than conscious matter, "then it is possible to talk about life and intelligence in abstract terms, independent of the details of organic chemistry and the physiological properties of flesh and blood."[27] Dyson explains, "It is conceivable that in another 10^{10} years life could evolve away from flesh and blood and become embodied in an interstellar black cloud (Hoyle, 1957) or in a sentient computer (Capek, 1923)." Dyson further speculates that if it should turn out that matter can only avoid ultimate collapse into black holes if it is subdivided into minuscule dust grains, "then the preferred embodiment for life in the remote future must be something like Hoyle's black cloud, a large assemblage of dust grains carrying positive and negative charges, organizing itself and communicating with itself by means of electromagnetic forces."[28]

For those keen to draw parallels between modern scientific theories and biblical images, Dyson's proposal would certainly add an interesting twist to the phrase, "You are dust, and to dust you shall return" (Gen. 3:19). Dyson's suggestion raises serious questions about the nature of life and its ultimate value. In his model intelligent life can, in theory, continue forever, given the right conditions within an open universe. But we must ask what kind of life this is. Is it life with passion, emotions, existential decisions, and other attributes that are for us key components of intelligent life? Or is life simply reduced to the ability to compute and, if Dyson is correct about his third point, perhaps also to communicate with other such forms? We already begin to see a sort of reductionism in Dyson that we will observe in successive scientific eschatologies. What seems to be lacking from the picture is any kind of eschatological future for the individual. Is it really comforting to the individual person alive today to know that "information processing" carried on by cosmic dust clouds may be able to exist in the remote future?

As for more traditional, biological life forms, Dyson reaches "the sad conclusion" that the slowing down of metabolism described by his biological scaling hypothesis "is insufficient to allow a society to survive indefinitely" because life forms would not be able to radiate excess waste in the form of heat with sufficient rapidity.[29] Thus the ironic problem for life in the distant future of an open universe is "not how to keep warm, but how to keep cool!"[30] To escape this impasse Dyson sees only one strategy for biological life: hibernation. "Life may metabolize intermittently, but may continue to radiate waste heat into space during its periods of hibernation. When life is in its active phase, it will be in thermal contact with its radiator." This strategy of hibernation would, according to Dyson, allow life to achieve at one time its two main objectives. First, in such a scenario, "subjective time is infinite; although the biological clocks are slowing down and running intermittently as the universe expands, subjective time goes on forever. Second, . . . the total energy required for indefinite survival is finite." In fact, Dyson calculates that the indefinite survival of a society with the complexity of the present human species would require "about as much energy as the sun radiates in eight hours." And the energy contained in an entire galaxy "would be sufficient to support indefinitely a society with a complexity about 10^{24} times greater than our own."[31]

Where this supply of finite energy might come from is a matter of some difficulty. Frautschi suggests either positronium formation or black holes as energy sources, with black holes holding the most promise.[32] In order to utilize the energy radiated from black holes, however, they must be towed together so that they amalgamate.[33] Precisely how this would be done is left up to the anticipated highly intelligent life forms of the far future. "A sufficiently resourceful intelligence inhabiting a critical universe learns how to move black holes, bringing them together from increasingly widely separated locations and merging them to increase the entropy."[34]

An apparent problem with the use of black holes as an indefinite energy source is that, according to Stephen Hawking's demonstration that black holes radiate energy, they will not last forever.[35] As Jamal Islam explains: "Hawking has shown that when . . . quantum phenomena are taken into account black holes are not really black, but give off radiation such as electromagnetic waves or neutrinos. In this manner a black hole can lose mass, become smaller, and eventually disappear!"[36] But fortunately, for those placing their hopes on some sort of utilization of black holes as an energy source in the remote future, Hawking has recently reversed his earlier opinion on the apparent radiation of energy from black holes. Hawking, and most other physicists as well, now agree that, on the basis of quantum theory, "the particles do not come from within the black hole, but from the 'empty' space just outside the black hole's event horizon."[37]

Assuming for the sake of argument that there will be sufficient energy for societies to be able to survive indefinitely in an expanding universe, Dyson addresses the question of whether two such societies would be able to communicate with each other—communication being for Dyson an essential function of intelligent life. The problem here is not only that of finite energy but also the great distances that would exist between the two societies and the rapid speed at which they would be moving away from each other. Dyson concludes, assuming that such communication would be via electromagnetic signals, that "it is in principle possible to communicate forever with a remote society in an expanding universe, using a finite expenditure of energy." In summary, Dyson expresses his scientific optimism for the remote future of life in our universe: "I have found a universe growing without limit in richness and complexity, a universe of life surviving forever and making itself known to its neighbors across unimaginable gulfs of space and time."[38]

Dyson contends that these conclusions seem possible only within an open universe. In a closed universe "the biological clocks can never speed up fast enough to squeeze an infinite subjective time into a finite universe."[39] Frank Tipler, however, has recently suggested that the opposite may be true: that an infinite subjective time for life forms in the distant future would be possible only in a closed universe.

The Future of Life in a Closed Universe (Tipler)
Frank Tipler has expressed his eschatological vision most clearly in his 1988 article, "The Omega Point Theory: A Model of an Evolving God"; his 1989 article, "The Omega Point as *Eschaton*: Answers to Pannenberg's Questions for Scientists"; and in his recent best-selling book, *The Physics of Immortality*.[40] Tipler maintains, despite all its metaphysical and even theological overtones, that his "Omega Point theory, including the resurrection theory, is pure physics."[41] To further make the point that he has no predisposition to undergird

any theistic or Christian viewpoint, he notes that he considers himself an atheist; he writes, "I certainly do not believe in the God of the traditional Christian metaphysics."[42] Tipler hopes, therefore, that his Omega Point theory will be taken seriously by scientists as a theory of physics and not a personal attempt to make an apology for theism.

In his 1989 article Tipler responds to a question Wolfhart Pannenberg put to scientists. Pannenberg inquired: "Is the Christian affirmation of an imminent end of this world that in some way invades the present even now, reconcilable with scientific extrapolations of the continuing existence of the universe for billions of years ahead? . . . Scientific predictions that in some comfortably distant future the conditions for life will no longer continue on our planet, are hardly comparable to Biblical eschatology."[43] Tipler responds, "it is definitely true that the universe will exist for billions of years in the future." He then proposes to provide "a physical foundation for Pannenberg's interpretation of eschatology" by showing that "the future makes an imprint on the present" inasmuch as "the physics required to sustain life in the far future must be in place now, since the most fundamental laws of physics do not change with time."[44] Yet Tipler would seem to intensify the problem indicated by Pannenberg between scientific and biblical eschatology. Indeed, he proposes an indefinite continuation of life into the future that bears perhaps even less resemblance to the apocalyptic biblical imagery than the scientific predictions of an end to life in the universe at some "comfortably distant future."

In contrast to Dyson, who found that an open cosmology presented the only possibility for the indefinite continuation of life, Tipler attempts to demonstrate the possibility of an indefinite continuation of life in a closed universe.[45] But what, for Tipler, constitutes life? Barrow and Tipler believe that three conditions must be met in the far future in order to say that life continues to exist. "(1) Information processing—the running of programs—continues along at least some future-endless timelike curve γ all the way to the future c-boundary of the Universe; (2) the amount of information processed . . . between now and the c-boundary is infinite; and (3) the amount of information stored . . . diverges as the leaves of the [curvature] foliation approach the future c-boundary."[46]

Similar to Dyson's definition, we see in this definition a reduction of life to information processing that poses serious problems from the perspective of theological anthropology. John Polkinghorne notes with concern this definition of life "as a computer-like capacity for information-processing and storage," but believes that it is possible to make use of Barrow and Tipler's arguments "without subscribing to so reductionist a point of view, since a capacity is surely a necessary condition for life, even if one may doubt its sufficiency."[47] Setting aside for the moment the question whether information processing and storage can be equated with intelligent life, we turn to Tipler's specific model explaining how such information processing could continue indefinitely in a closed universe.

As with Dyson and the indefinite continuation of life in an open universe, the question of whether sufficient energy will be available for an infinite amount of information processing to take place between now and the "Final State" also presents a problem for Tipler's model of life in the remote future in a closed universe. Tipler believes that "the laws of thermodynamics will permit an infinite amount of information processing in the future, provided there is sufficient available energy at all future times."[48]

Energy is a problem in closed as well as in open cosmologies because the energy required for information processing and storage is inversely proportional to the temperature. Therefore, while the problem in an open universe is to find and utilize efficiently small amounts of energy, the problem in the final stages of a closed universe is that very large amounts of energy will be required as the temperature approaches infinity near the final singularity. Thus, whereas "in the flat universe only a *finite* total amount of energy suffices to process an infinite number of bits," in a closed universe "an ever-increasing amount of energy is required per bit near the final singularity." Tipler suggests that this energy will come from a shear effect produced by an unevenly collapsing universe. He explains that most closed universes are expected to undergo a shear effect when they collapse; that is, they will actually *expand* in one direction while at the same time collapsing in the others. According to Tipler, "this shearing gives rise to a radiation temperature difference in different directions, and this temperature difference can be shown to provide sufficient free energy for an infinite amount of information processing between now and the final singularity."

Assuming that the shear effect theory holds up, the next (and biggest) hurdle to overcome is that of the final singularity itself that awaits the end of a closed universe. How is it possible to speak of the indefinite continuation of life in a universe that will eventually come to an abrupt end? For Tipler the solution of the energy problem also provides the solution to this problem. Tipler believes sufficient energy exists for an infinite amount of information processing between now and the final singularity, "even though there is only a *finite* amount of proper time between now and the end of time in a closed universe. Thus although a closed universe exists for only a finite proper time it nevertheless could exist for an infinite subjective time, which is the measure of time that is significant for living beings."

It is in this "infinite subjective time" that, according to Tipler, life will completely engulf the universe and will "incorporate more and more material into itself, and the distinction between living and non-living matter will lose its meaning." As Barrow and Tipler explained in their 1986 book, *The Anthropic Cosmological Principle:*

> . . . if life evolves in all of the many universes in a quantum cosmology, and if life continues to exist in all of these universes, then *all* of these universes, which include *all* possible histories among them, will approach the Omega Point. At the instant the Omega Point is reached, life will have gained control of *all* matter and forces not only in a single universe, but in all universes whose existence is logically possible; life will have spread into *all* spatial regions in all universes which could logically exist, and will have stored an infinite amount of information, including *all* bits of knowledge which it is logically possible to know. And this is the end.[49]

Concerning the nature of life at the Omega Point, Barrow and Tipler add in a footnote: "A modern day theologian might wish to say that the totality of life at the Omega Point is omnipotent, omnipresent, and omniscient!"[50]

Tipler seeks, therefore, to demonstrate a formal equivalence between the totality of space-time and the Omega Point. In the development of his Omega Point theory Tipler is indebted not only to Pierre Teilhard de Chardin, but also to John Wheeler's participatory anthropic principle, which is built on the logic of the Copenhagen interpretation of quantum mechanics, which holds that the properties of particles at the quantum level are determined by the observer's choice of what to measure. Wheeler takes this logic a step further and applies it to the entire universe. As Tipler explains: "Wheeler conjectures that *all* the properties of *all* the particles in the universe are determined by the collection of all the acts of observer-participancy in the past, present, and future. In particular, these acts collectively bring into existence all the observers themselves. Thus . . . the creatures collectively are responsible for creating the entire universe and themselves."[51]

John Wheeler, in his 1979 article "Beyond the Black Hole," described the participatory universe as a "self-excited circuit" that, based on "billions upon billions of acts of observer-participancy," literally becomes the explanation of its own creation.[52] Wheeler illustrates his participatory universe as if it were a large letter U (for universe) that, "starting small [picture a thin U beginning at upper right], . . . grows [thickening underside of U] and in time gives rise [Wheeler draws an eye onto the fat upper left extension of the U that looks back at its thin beginning] to observer-participancy—which in turn imparts 'tangible reality' to even the earliest days of the universe."[53] As Wheeler states in a paper he wrote with C. M. Patton: The "'participator' replaces the 'observer' of classical physics." Therefore, "it is impossible in principle to separate what happens to any system, even the universe, from what this participator does."[54] Tipler takes Wheeler's concept of all time and all space converging at some teleological point a step further and endows this point of convergence (the Omega Point) with theological significance.[55] For Tipler, the Omega Point is not only the culminating fulfillment of an in-process deity who exists necessarily, but it also implies a resurrection in its intersection and union with all points of space-time. Concerning the theological implications of the Omega Point theory, Tipler could already write in his 1989 article:

> We can say, quite obviously, that life near the Omega Point is omnipresent. As the Omega Point is approached, survival dictates that life collectively gain control of all matter and energy sources available near the Final State, with this control becoming total at the Omega Point. We can say that life becomes omnipotent at the instant the Omega Point is reached. Since by hypothesis the information stored becomes infinite at the Omega Point, it is reasonable to say that the Omega Point is omniscient; it knows whatever it is possible to know about the physical universe (and hence about itself).
>
> . . . all the different instants of universal history are collapsed into the Omega Point; "duration" for the Omega Point can be regarded as equivalent to the collection of all experiences of all life that did, does, and will exist in the whole of universal history. . . . The Omega Point in its immanence counts as a Person because at any time in our future the collective information processing system will have, or will be able to generate, subprograms which will be able to pass the Turing test. High intelligence will be required at least collectively in order to survive in the increasingly complex environment near the Final State.[56]

We see here a transition in language as Tipler clearly moves from speaking of all persons to the *Person* who is the Omega Point. As Tipler summarizes his view, "the indefinitely continued existence of life is not only physically possible; it also leads naturally to a model of a God who is evolving in His/Her immanent aspect (the events in spacetime) and yet is eternally complete in His/Her transcendent aspect." Put quite simply, despite his effort to maintain God's completeness in transcendence, Tipler seems to present an eschatological pantheism in which the universe (along with all that is, was, and will be in it) becomes God. And, if we remember that Tipler is seeking to provide a physical basis for Pannenberg's concept of the future impacting the present inasmuch as the physical laws that lead inevitably to the Omega Point must already be in place, then in Tipler's model it would seem that the world is also in some sense now a part of the Divine.

For Tipler, it is precisely in this coming together of all persons who have ever lived in the Omega Point resolution of the history of the universe that his concept of resurrection is to be found:

All timelike and lightlike curves converge upon the Omega Point. In particular, all the light rays from all the people who died a thousand years ago, from all the people now living, and from all the people who will be living a thousand years from now, will intersect here. The light rays from those people who died a thousand years ago are not lost forever; rather, these rays will be intercepted by the Omega Point. . . . All the information which can be extracted from these rays will be extracted at the instant of the Omega Point, who will therefore experience the whole of time simultaneously just as we experience simultaneously the Andromeda Galaxy and a person in the room with us.[57]

Here again, in Tipler's portrayal of resurrection, we encounter an anthropological reductionism in which the eternal existence of our light waves and their eventual reading or processing at the Omega Point constitute resurrection/eternal life. This is seen even more clearly in his book *The Physics of Immortality,* in which an entire chapter is devoted to the physics of resurrection from the dead. Here he contends, for instance, that the physical mechanism of the resurrection of the individual consists of the individual's being "emulated in the computers of the far future."[58] For Tipler, all that is essential to the human person is of such a nature that it will be capable of being saved on a supercomputer of the future. The reduction of the individual, however, to the information that can be gathered from the light waves that he or she left behind would seem to be in conflict with traditional Christian anthropology in which the individual is viewed as more than a collection of data.

Pannenberg, in his evaluation of Tipler's model, is generally positive, noting that "in the general thrust of Tipler's project there is a remarkable convergence with Christian theology."[59] As for problems with Tipler's model, Pannenberg is primarily concerned with where Christology would fit into such a model. He proposes some possible ways in which Christ, especially in his incarnation and resurrection, might already encounter (converge with) humanity as the Omega Point.[60] As to possible problems of reductionism in Tipler's view of intelligent life, Pannenberg mentions only that "Tipler's consideration of resurrection by simulation disposes of some of the resources that allowed classical eschatology to answer the problem" of the evil of death that was seen as being overcome in a resurrection of the individual, and not in a merely simulated resurrection through processing of all the data obtainable from light waves from the individual's lifetime. Otherwise, Pannenberg's evaluation of Tipler's concept of resurrection is positive, commenting that "such a 'simulation' seems sufficient to secure identity with the former person."

John Polkinghorne is much more critical on this point than Pannenberg. Insightfully evaluating the overall eschatology presented by Tipler and Barrow in various joint and individual writings, Polkinghorne identifies some crucial problems with this model, especially in its anthropological reductionism. His critique is also largely valid for Dyson's open cosmological model, which, as we have already noted, contains a similar reductionism. Polkinghorne writes that the "physical eschatology" of Barrow and Tipler, found in their vision of a final anthropic principle:

> offers at best the prospect of endlessly accumulating information. It is a hope bleaker even than those centered on the future of the Race or the Party. Christianity offers the hope of a destiny beyond death for the *individual*. I do not think that either an infinitely accelerating sequence of information-processing events in a collapsing universe, or a never exhausted sequence of such events in a decaying universe, represents sufficient fulfillment of cosmic process to deny the charge that the physical universe as we know it is ultimately condemned to futility. To think otherwise would indeed be "to sacrifice the individual on the altar of a cosmic plan."[61]

Ian Barbour levels similar criticisms against the eschatological formulations of Dyson and Tipler. Barbour is especially concerned that for Dyson and Tipler eschatological salvation rests not with God but with human-type intelligence and technology. The projections of both Dyson and Tipler, he points out, are "highly speculative and rest on many unverified assumptions. They seem to me inconsistent with the biblical message, not because they disagree with some of the imaginative future scenarios in the Bible, but because they reflect views of humanity, God, and the future that are at odds with basic biblical convictions." Barbour further explains that in Scripture the person is viewed as a whole composed of body, spirit, and mind and not simply as an intellect capable of information processing. Barbour also notes that "Dyson and Tipler propose a technologically based salvation that seeks control of the cosmos, whereas the Bible speaks of the need for personal transformation and social reconstruction in response to God. Though biblical eschatology takes many forms, all agree that future fulfillment will be the work of a personal God as well as humanity, not the work of humanity apart from God."[62]

Despite these criticisms, however, we can agree with Pannenberg that a "remarkable convergence with Christian theology" can be seen in Tipler's Omega Point theory. Aside from the apparent support for the existence of a Supreme Being and an eschatological resurrection, which Pannenberg commends, Tipler's theory also presents possibilities for comparison with the biblical/theological concept that God will become "all in all" (1 Cor. 15:28), as well as the biblical/theological view that the destiny of human beings cannot be separated from that of the rest of the physical universe (Rom. 8:18-22). Nevertheless, Tipler's theory, like Dyson's and Wheeler's, remains a highly speculative model that, if it is taken up at all by the scientific community, is likely to undergo substantial change. Precisely what significance it may have for Christian theology, therefore, is uncertain. Clearly, Christian theology cannot bind itself to any such theory. Tipler's Omega Point theory may, however, if accepted as "pure physics" by the scientific community, serve to establish some common ground of dialogical interest between Christian and scientific eschatology and may even help to make such concepts as God and resurrection intelligible within the context of modern scientific thought. In doing so, however, theology must be careful in its enthusiasm for newfound dialogue not to buy into the reductionism that seems to be inherent in such models.

Theology should not expect too much from natural science. Given that a "natural" theology built on a "natural" revelation has some validity, Tipler's claim to have reached his conceptions of God and resurrection on the basis of natural science alone cannot be dismissed out of hand. Yet such theories cannot be expected to go beyond general ideas of God and perhaps also some sort of afterlife. We should not be surprised, therefore, that "a place for Christology is missing in Tipler's concept of the universe."[63] Neither should we expect that an easy identification can be made between the Omega Point, for example, and the God of Christian theism.

THE CHALLENGE OF CHRISTIAN ESCHATOLOGY IN LIGHT OF MODERN COSMOLOGY

We have surveyed some recent scientific eschatologies that address the question of life in the distant future. Now we turn our attention to Christian eschatology in light of the possible eschatological destinies of the universe emerging out of modern physics and cosmology. Pannenberg's question to scientists deserves attention from theologians as well: "Is the Christian affirmation of an imminent end of this world . . . reconcilable with scientific extrapolations of the continuing existence of the universe for billions of years ahead?"[64] Another question with which theology must deal that is perhaps even more troubling has to do with the nature of the eschatological end of the world. The biblical vision, however apocalyptic, leaves room for a new heaven and earth and a bodily resurrection from the dead. Ultimately, it is more of a transition to a new era ushered in by God than a literal end. By contrast, the fate of the universe in either an open or closed cosmological model would seem to include an end much more absolute in character than that of biblical eschatology.

The problem for theology is how such things as resurrected bodies, new heaven and new earth, and heavenly Jerusalem, all of which have a certain physical quality, could be conceived of as existing eternally, without end in regard to age and the extension of space and time. As Ian Barbour asks: "Dyson and Tipler think that a future *heat death* or *freezing death* can be avoided. But if they cannot be avoided, would that contradict biblical assumptions? Would such a future imply that the universe is meaningless. . . ?"[65] Whatever cosmological model we consider, however, certain aspects of the present structure of our cosmos appear to impede the realization of the biblical eschatological vision.

Theologian Karl Peters, in fact, has suggested that the eschatological vision of the Bible, which is embedded in the cosmology of its time, cannot be made intelligible in the context of modern cosmology. He writes: "It is . . . difficult to speak of the culmination of the universe in a manner consistent with both science and the Christian vision of a new heaven and a new earth. The primary reason is that the cosmology in which the original Christian universal, future eschatology was embedded has been superseded by the cosmology of twentieth-century science."[66] Peters further contends that:

> a universe in which the overcoming of evil by good, in which justice is finally served, is vastly different from the current scientific picture of an expanding universe with billions of galaxies each with billions of stars. It is so different that it is difficult to see how the details of biblical eschatology can be translated into the current scientific world view as a future, universal eschatology. This applies . . . even to the notion of the creation of a new heaven and a new earth. If the expanding universe is indeed open, expanding forever, then how can one speak of God recreating the universe? If the universe is closed, then it is likely to end in a "big crunch" of mammoth black-hole proportion. Again, it is difficult to see how a new creation can take place.[67]

As a solution to this dilemma Peters suggests two possible options. "Two types of eschatology consistent with the scientific picture of creation are . . . 'realized interpersonal eschatology,' and 'local, future societal or planetary eschatologies.'" Concerning the possibility of a local eschatology within a universe headed, as a whole, toward thermal equilibrium, Peters writes: "The potential energy of the universe is sufficient . . . , when coupled with fundamental laws and forces of nature, to create a series of increasingly complex structures in some local regions of the universe." By "realized interpersonal eschatology" Peters is speaking of small communities that realize the overcoming of evil within themselves and serve as "the catalyst towards future, societal and planetary eschatological communities . . . in which . . . the gradual emergence of a Teilhardian *omega point* is realized: the reduction of evil to a minimum, the gradual conquering by science of disease and hunger, the eclipsing of hatred and war."

The difficulty with Peters's proposal is that it leaves little room for traditional Christian eschatology. As Peters admits, even localized eschatologies cannot hold out indefinitely against the march of entropy and are only temporary "islands of matter, life, and intelligence." And Peters's realized eschatology, which sounds like a human-initiated postmillennialism that takes place quite apart from the eschatological activity of God (science and "humans taking responsibility" usher in the omega point), is a subjective experience of the overcoming of evil in small communities that bears little resemblance to the universal and future-oriented eschatological vision of the Bible. Essentially, Peters seems to allow science to write the eschatological script and then attempts to redefine the term *eschatology* in a way that would not bring it into conflict with modern cosmology. This attempt to "rescue" theological eschatology, however, seems to be a capitulation to the natural sciences.

Returning to Pannenberg's question, we would suggest several possible approaches to the problem that he raises apart from redefining the traditional understanding of biblical eschatology. One might point out, for example, that the imminent end of the world is more an expectation than an affirmation of theology. From the perspective of biblical theology it would seem that it is important that Christians always await the imminent "end of the world" without any actual timetable being set. Of course, when physicists predict an apocalyptic "Big Crunch" or a heat death of the universe long after human life would have become extinct, it would certainly seem problematic to reconcile this with the apocalyptic vision of the Bible. A more fruitful response to this dilemma, I would suggest, calls for a distinction between the theological and scientific apocalyptic visions. Pannenberg seems to point to such a solution in volume three of his *Systematic Theology* when he writes that "biblical eschatology, which portrays an imminent end of the world—even if no specific timetable is set (Mk 13:22)—is not congruent with scientific extrapolations which point toward the remote future in regard to a possible end of the world. It cannot, therefore, be easily contended that both have to do with the same event."[68]

Biblical eschatology is concerned primarily with this planet and its human inhabitants. Mention of the stars and "the heavens" in biblical apocalyptic literature (e.g., Isa. 65:17; Matt. 24:29; 2 Peter 3:10; Rev. 21:1) would appear primarily significant insofar as they are seen as part of the earth's environment. The earth itself and its inhabitants remain the primary focus of the apocalyptic events described.[69] The end that it speaks of is not an absolute end inasmuch as it allows for a bodily resurrection and creation of a new heaven and new earth. The oft-made assumption that the apocalyptic *parousia* of Christ and consummation of creation is to be equated with a much more radical end of the entire universe in the remote future as predicted by physicists would seem unwarranted. It is entirely possible to understand biblical apocalyptic literature as speaking of a renewal or transformation of the world rather than its absolute destruction and subsequent re-creation.[70] If such identification between the *parousia* and the end of the universe is avoided, then the focus of the difficulty shifts from the biblical expectation of the imminent end of the world to the problem of the biblical concept of eternity. It is the problem of eternity, therefore, that emerges as an underlying concern in the reconciliation of biblical and scientific eschatologies.

As Emil Brunner has pointed out, the biblical and Christian concept of eternity is not identical with those of classical philosophy or the natural sciences, both of which have tended to limit the idea of eternity to an unending extension of space-time processes. According to Brunner, however, "this is not the Christian concept of eternity. The Bible does not speak of an eternity which man essentially possesses in himself and which he can recognize as his own true being. It speaks rather of the eternity that comes to man, which lays hold of him, which is bestowed upon him." Brunner explains that the Christian conception of eternity differs from that of philosophy and the natural sciences inasmuch as the Christian concept does not have "a formal, empty and purely negative character as negation of time. It is full of positive content. Eternity as we apprehend it in faith is the presence of the self-communicating love of God. . . . Neither the negation of time, nor infinite duration as such, are the factors which determine this understanding, but only the Spirit of God who is present and effectual in faith."[71]

We encounter here essentially three basic concepts of eternity: (1) The philosophical/scientific concept that might generally be defined as the unlimited or unending extension of space-time structures and processes. (2) The concept of eternity as applied to God. God, as the "Lord of time" (Brunner), is eternal because God has created time. As such, God is not dependent on space-time structures and processes for God's own eternity because God is "prior" to these realities. God is eternal in that God's being is unbounded, not just in the sense that God has no space-time beginning or end but also in that God is not subject to the concepts of space and time. (3) Because God has chosen to create space-time and be revealed to human beings within the context of our space and time, the intersection of the physical, created reality with the eternal God produces what Brunner has rightly distinguished as a "Christian concept of eternity."

In this study, because we are examining eschatological visions that are specifically scientific, we will be using the term normally in the first sense inasmuch as this is the only eternity that natural science can speak of in relation to the physical universe. The problem remains, however, precisely how the concepts of an eternally existing universe (in the sense of unending duration of space-time processes) is to be understood over against God's eternity as well as the Christian concept of an eternity with this God.

CHRISTIAN ESCHATOLOGY AND OPEN COSMOLOGICAL MODELS

The Second Law and the Heat Death of the Universe

If the first law of thermodynamics and its principle of the conservation of energy were the sole basis of the scientific predictions for the future of our universe, the future of our cosmos would indeed seem optimistic. As theologian Karl Heim wrote: "A closed system is a system into which no energy is introduced from outside, and from which no energy can be lost. If we start from the exact formulation of the law of energy, there would seem to follow from it quite a simple consequence for the question of the future of the world: the universe cannot perish; for is it not a closed system?"[72] Heim was well aware, however, that the second law made such optimism difficult if not impossible. He wrote that since the discovery of the second law, "there has lowered over mankind, like a dark thundercloud which will one day shed its load, the picture of the heat death of the universe . . . in which the whole sum of energy in the universe will have dissolved into masses with equal temperatures and equal radiation." Therefore "'scientific eschatology' consists in the expectation of the point of time, to which the world relentlessly draws near, in which all life of the mind and with it all knowledge will be annihilated, along with all works of art and cultural achievements. . . . It is altogether improbable that the cosmos will escape this fate."[73]

Indeed, despite the implications of the second law, Dyson and others have argued that an open universe presents chances for the continuation of life indefinitely. Little reason for optimism remains, however. Models such as Dyson's are highly speculative and require a tremendous amount of luck (for example, the universe must be open, the proton must be absolutely stable against decay, life must be based on structure) and no small amount of manipulation (for example, intelligent life must direct its own evolution toward non–flesh-and-blood forms that hibernate, black holes must be towed, and so on) in order to have any chance of being theoretically viable. And even if the reductionist views of information-processing cosmic dust clouds that pass for "life" in the remote future are theoretically feasible, there are doubts as to whether this would make the universe any less futile than if it actually ended in an absolute heat death. In this section we shall examine the ramifications of the more standard (and more pessimistic) model in which the open universe ends in something very much like the heat death first predicted in the last century in light of the second law of thermodynamics.

As theologian Ted Peters has written: "The application of the second law of thermodynamics measured in terms of entropy to the macrocosmos leads to the notion of temporal finitude. If the universe in its entirety is moving irreversibly from order to disorder, from hot to cold, from high energy to dissipative equilibrium, then . . . the universe will eventually die. Even though in far-from-equilibrium sectors or microcosms within the larger whole we will find creative activity and the emergence of new structures, the overall advance of the cosmos is in the direction of eventual dissipation and heat death."[74] Important here is that the second law points to the temporal finitude even of an ever-expanding open universe. Steven Weinberg describes in brief the fate of an open universe in the remote future as follows: "Our descendants, if we have any then, will see thermonuclear reactions slowly come to an end in all the stars, leaving behind various sorts of cinder: black dwarf stars, neutron stars, perhaps black holes. Planets may continue in orbit, slowing down a little as they radiate gravitational waves but never coming to rest in any finite time."[75] The irony of such an ever-expanding universe is that its apparent infinity seems to be confronted with the problem of finiteness at every turn. Arthur Eddington expressed this dilemma very well when he contended that when the universe falls prey to the final heat death, "time will *extend* on and on, presumably to infinity, but there will be no definite sense in which it can be said to *go on*."[76]

Of interest at this point is the position taken by the British mathematical physicist E. A. Milne. Questioning the standard interpretation of the second law, Milne argued that the universe would not end in heat death. Milne, in his 1950 Cadbury lectures on "Modern Cosmology and the Christian Idea of God," wrote: "It has often been claimed that the second law of thermodynamics implies that the universe is doomed to what is called a 'heat-death' . . . I believe this conclusion to be mistaken; it is not an inevitable consequence of the second law of thermodynamics as applied to the universe as a whole, and I do not believe it to be true of the universe as it is."[77]

Milne's critique is essentially based on the way in which a universal heat death is deduced from the available data. The second law, according to Milne, cannot be proved to be irreversible as it applies to the entire universe.[78] A heat death of the universe cannot, therefore, be legitimately deduced. As an alternative to the heat death model, Milne suggested a cosmological model in which the increase of entropy is a local phenomenon and the universe has no end. He wrote:

If we cannot infer a "heat-death" for the whole universe, what *can* we infer about the final state of the whole universe? The answer is that it *has no final state.* . . . For, always, to a given observer there will be systems near the spatial confines of the universe that appear to have *just been* created, systems that are arbitrarily young. As his telescope ranges to fainter and ever fainter systems or galaxies, he will count more and more of them, and, on the *t*-scale, assign to them distances converging on the distance *ct,* where *t* is the present age, to him, of the universe. . . . Between himself and this distance he will be able to observe an unending set of local situations in which the local entropy is increasing, but the more distant ones will possess an entropy which has barely increased since creation. . . . There is no need of any appeal to any principle of rejuvenescence. For the universe as a whole has no age and no size, only an age and a size when a particular observer is singled out, at a particular stage of his experience.[79]

In Milne's model the universe is a place of "infinite variety." This means, as Milne suggests, that several planets may well exist in the universe in which biological evolution has produced intelligent life. What would such a variety of life-containing planets mean for our view of God? Milne asks: "Is it irreverent to suggest that an infinite God could scarcely find the opportunities to enjoy Himself, to exercise His godhead, if a single planet were the sole seat of His activities?" It is indeed an interesting concept that an infinite God would most naturally create an infinite universe with an infinite number and variety of life forms.[80] From the perspective of theology, however, one would have to say that an infinite God is certainly capable of finding an infinite number of "opportunities to enjoy Himself" within the context of a single, finite planet. Milne, in fact, suggested essentially the same idea in regard to God's activity in connection with the evolutionary process. He wrote: "It is . . . consonant with our idea of an infinite transcendental God, who has created the universe as a transcendental point-singularity, to regard Him as fully employed in the subsequent history of this universe, in causing an infinite number of occasions for the exercise of the occurrence of mutations." For Milne this means that God did not simply wind up the universe and leave it alone, but that God "created the universe, and therewith also endowed it with the only law of inorganic nature consistent with its content, . . . and then He tended his creation in guiding its subsequent organic evolution on an infinite number of occasions in an infinite number of spatial regions. That is of the essence of Christianity, that God actually intervenes in History."[81]

In this way Milne seeks to correlate the traditional Christian idea of God's intervention in history with the natural process of biological evolution. Within Milne's model, however, a distinctive point for eschatology is that

God's involvement with the infinitely complex evolutionary process is also infinite in time; that is, it and the universe never come to a final end. Because most physicists, however, remain convinced that some form of heat death will be the likely end of an open universe, this possibility must be addressed seriously by theology.

What Does God Do When the Lights Go Out?
As astrophysicists have known for some time, the hydrogen that fuels the nuclear reactions that light the stars will at some point in the remote future run out. Physicist Jamal Islam describes the scenario as follows: "All of the stars in a galaxy like our own will reach their final states in about 100 billion years. The galaxy then will be a system of black holes, neutron stars, white dwarfs, and other small cold bodies like planets, asteroids, and dust. . . . From this time onwards the sky will be pitch black."[82]

Given such a fate for the universe, the problem for Christian eschatology might be put bluntly as: "What does God do when the lights go out?" The biblical answer to such a question would seem to be found in Revelation 21:23: "The [heavenly] city has no need of sun or moon to shine on it, for the glory of God is its light. . . ."[83] Precisely how this passage is to be understood, however, has not been settled by the commentators. Many, such as Wilhelm Bousset, believe that God and the Lamb simply replace the sun and the moon, which cease to exist.[84] R. H. Charles, however, suggests that, "as in Isaiah the sun and the moon do not cease to exist: their splendour is simply put to shame by the glory of God Himself." Hence "the glory of God lights the heavenly city," but the sun and moon "still give light to the world outside the city."[85] Such an interpretation would seem to fit well with our earlier suggestion that the biblical, apocalyptic end of the world is not to be identified literally with the end of the physical universe predicted by modern physics. In Charles's interpretation the so-called extinguishing of the sun and moon has to do with the heavenly city and those who dwell within it. In the rest of the cosmos outside the city, things apparently continue much as before. Therefore it is not so much that the sun and moon must necessarily be seen as being extinguished in the biblical, apocalyptic vision, but that for the inhabitants of the heavenly city they are simply made redundant in the presence of the illuminating glory of God.

Of course, no credible exegesis would claim that this verse was intended to address the dilemma posed by an open universe. As George E. Ladd comments: "It is doubtful that John intended to give astronomical information about the new world; his purpose is to affirm the unsurpassed splendour which radiates from the presence of God."[86] Nevertheless, the passage provides insight into the nature of the divine that is relevant to the question at hand. Whether God will provide (or radiate) literal light is not the point here, but rather, that God is and will be *sufficient* for the needs of God's people—and indeed of God's entire creation.

What do we mean here by sufficient? Put one way, we might say that according to the biblical view God, as sustainer of the universe, is the ultimate energy source. Precisely how this functions is beyond speculation from the standpoint of theology. Based on the Christian understanding of continuing creation, however, it would seem an entirely valid deduction that if the universe is at present absolutely contingent and dependent on God in the divine all-sufficiency, then God will continue to be sufficient for the sustenance of the universe even when, in the remote future, its purely physical energy sources would seem to be unable to continue to provide the energy needed to sustain the basic functions necessary to support life.

A concept of eternity, understood within the context of God's own eternity, need not, therefore, be a stumbling block for Christian faith. The remote future of an open universe poses no insurmountable problem for Christian faith, which places its hope in the sustaining activity of a transcendent Creator. Because the eternity of the transcendent God is neither defined nor limited by our conceptions of the universe's eternality (or lack thereof), God's continuing sustenance of that which is created and taken up within God's eternal love is not threatened by any scientific vision of the remote future of the universe. This sustaining activity can perhaps also be understood in "noninterventionist" terms—at least insofar as God's present sustenance is generally understood in a noninterventionist way. God does not need to wind up the universe again or give it an injection of hydrogen. God alone is sufficient. From the perspective of Christian theology, we are able to confess that God created the universe out of nothing and will sustain God's people and creation (in some form) through all eternity out of no other source than the fullness of God's own being.

The Possibility of a "Flat" Universe

The so-called third solution that corresponds to Friedmann's assumptions is what is commonly known as a "flat" model in which the universe is expanding at precisely the rate necessary to avoid eventual collapse. Although essentially an open model inasmuch as it does not recollapse, the flat model is different enough from standard open models to merit attention in its own right in regard to the problems and possibilities it poses for Christian eschatology. In a standard open universe the rate of expansion itself continues to decrease less and less until a relatively stable rate is achieved as the galaxies become less and less restrained by their mutual gravitational attraction. In a flat universe, however, the galaxies continue moving away from each other but only at precisely the rate of expansion necessary to prevent an eventual recollapse. In other words, the standard open cosmologies have a hyperbolic geometry, while a flat cosmology has a so-called Euclidean (or flat) geometry—hence its name. In this model, at some point in the remote future the galaxies would appear, from the perspective of humanlike observation on our planet, to come to a relative standstill. Of course the pinpoint precision that would be necessary to obtain such an exact critical rate of expansion, especially in the early universe, is phenomenal. Even today, some 10 to 15 billion years after the presumed initial singularity, if the rate of expansion is slightly more or less than the critical rate, then the universe will either eventually "break loose" in a never-ending expansion of the standard open model or recollapse as in a closed model.

If our universe were purely the result of chance, one would have to say that the flat model would merit little attention inasmuch as the odds are stacked phenomenally against it. Given the fact, however, that our universe today is still close enough to the critical rate of expansion that we are not yet able to say whether it is open or closed, many physicists are intrigued by the possibility that the universe might be so "designed" that it maintains eternally a critical rate of expansion. Also, from the perspective of those who believe that the appearance of design in the universe is no accident, such as theists and proponents of the strong anthropic principle, there is a certain attraction in a cosmological model that requires such phenomenal precision.

In a flat universe the problem of communication over incredibly long distances would seem to be partly overcome inasmuch as the distances and speed of separation between the various parts of the universe in the remote future would be significantly less than that of a standard open universe. From the perspective of Dyson, therefore, it would seem that at least one of the problems confronting information-processing life, namely communication between societies, would become significantly less problematic.

Also, the situation regarding energy in the remote future is somewhat different in a flat universe. Although the "running down" implied by the second law toward something similar to a heat death remains unavoidable, a flat universe presents new possibilities for energy. Barrow and Tipler explain that in a flat universe "the rate of expansion . . . will be sufficiently slow so that almost all of the electrons and positrons in the plasma will recombine. The particles will recombine into positronium when the total energy of an electron-positron system becomes negative. The only energies the particles will have in a flat universe is the Coulomb energy of attraction and the random thermal energy of motion."[87] Because of the instability of a flat Friedmann model universe, which does not "isotropise at large times," there would seem to exist perpetually the Coulomb energy of attraction and the thermal energy of motion, which would seem to be sufficient to forestall the prediction that the universe will suffer heat death at some point of absolute thermal equilibrium in the remote future. This also means, however, that a flat universe would be filled with high levels of radiation, which presents its own problems for the long-term survival of carbon-based life forms.[88]

Also intriguing in the flat universe model is the possibility of an eternal unpredictability. At no point in the remote future could we be certain whether the rate of expansion was precisely the critical rate or whether a very slight variation from the critical rate existed that would make a decisive difference in the even more remote future. From the perspective of theology there is a certain amount of attraction to the idea that our universe may be designed to be so perfectly balanced between an open and a closed cosmology that human intelligence is left forever guessing.

Although a flat universe presents a scenario with some intriguing differences from that of an open universe, Christian theology seems in the end to be faced with precisely the same problems: namely, an eternally expanding universe in which conditions become increasingly inhospitable for carbon-based life forms. To what extent, then, can God's people be said to exist in resurrected bodies in a new heaven and new earth within a universe in which nothing similar to physical life or our present world system will be able to exist? Must God take God's people into another dimension or intervene in clockmaker fashion to rewind the universe? While such possibilities cannot be ruled out, their postulation does little to counter the impression that modern cosmological models present serious difficulties for Christian eschatology.

CHRISTIAN ESCHATOLOGY AND CLOSED COSMOLOGICAL MODELS

Black Holes as Foretaste of Universal Annihilation

> All the stars of the heavens will be dissolved and the sky rolled up like scroll; all the starry host will fall like withered leaves from the vine, like shriveled figs from the fig tree.
>
> —Isaiah 34:4 (NIV)

The Russian physicist I. L. Rozental describes what the future of a closed universe will look like as follows:

> The age of the closed Metagalaxy [universe], short compared with the times characteristic of the extinction of many cosmic objects (dwarfs and neutron stars), will not allow such objects to simply "die peacefully." Turbulent processes accompanying the swift contraction of the Metagalaxy in its final stages will raze them to the ground. . . . At $t_1 = 10^6$ years, the

remaining stars of the main sequence will start decaying. At $t_1 = 100$s, the white dwarfs and at $t_1 = 10^{-4}$s, the neutron stars will be destroyed, respectively. At that time, the Metagalaxy will consist of loose protons, neutrons, electrons, photons, neutrinos, and black holes. . . . This entire conglomeration will fuse to form something like a huge black hole. Traditional cosmology further envisions a subsequent collapse leading to a singular state.[89]

Confronted with the probability that our universe, if closed, will end in "something like a huge black hole," it is helpful to know something of the nature of black holes. The term *black hole,* coined in 1969 by John Wheeler, denotes a region of space-time that has collapsed on itself and from which nothing, not even light, can escape because the gravity is too strong. Stephen Hawking, who led the way in research into black holes in the 1960s and 1970s, writes: ". . . according to general relativity, there must be a singularity of infinite density and space-time curvature within a black hole . . . [that] would be an end of time for the collapsing body. . . . At this singularity the laws of science and our ability to predict the future would break down."[90] The border of a black hole is what physicists call an event horizon. Hawking, in rather pessimistic terms, writes:

> The event horizon, the boundary of the region of space-time from which it is not possible to escape, acts rather like a one-way membrane around the black hole: objects, such as unwary astronauts, can fall through the event horizon into the black hole, but nothing can ever get out of the black hole through the event horizon. . . . One could well say of the event horizon what the poet Dante said of the entrance of Hell: "All hope abandon, ye who enter here." Anything or anyone who falls through the event horizon will soon reach the region of infinite density and the end of time.[91]

Indeed, a black hole sounds more like the bottomless pit or abyss (Rev. 20:3) of biblical apocalyptic into which Satan is cast than the new heaven and new earth in which God's people are supposed to spend eternity. If this is indeed the fate of our universe—to collapse into a huge black hole—one can immediately see the difficulties presented to Christian eschatology. The new Jerusalem, millions of resurrected bodies, and the new heaven and new earth (to mention a few of those parts of the biblical eschatological expectation that would seem to have a decisively physical aspect) must all exist after some point in time in the remote future within a few cubic centimeters of infinitely dense space in which time and space, for all practical purposes, have come to an end and from which nothing can escape. In the face of such a destiny, Tipler's "infinite subjective time," or a "fifth dimension," would seem, however inadequate, to be the only known options for preserving a concept of eternity that bears any relationship to some sort of space-time structure. But even with such solutions we are either confronted with a "real" time that continues ticking down to the final collapse or, in the case of a fifth spiritual dimension, the sense that God is forced to abandon a project that has gone bad. In either case the Christian concept of eternity finds its future overshadowed by the prospect of an all-engulfing black hole that can only be circumvented with a bit of theological sleight of hand.

If our universe is closed, however, its final destiny must not necessarily be the dark abyss of a black hole. The possibility exists that a closed universe that ends in a remarkably similar state to that from which it presumably sprang will once again explode into a state of expansion, creating a new space-time.

Possibility of an Oscillating Universe

Within a closed universe model an irreversible Big Crunch is not the only possibility. We are referring to what has been variously known as an eternal return, or a cyclic, oscillating, pulsating, or reprocessing universe. John Wheeler is one among several physicists who has been reviving this ancient concept, which goes back at least to the cosmologies of the ancient Greeks,[92] and applying it to closed universe models. Wheeler and Patton compare the universe with an electron and ask:

> Why not take a model universe . . . and let the quantum dynamics of this system systematically crank ahead through the phase of collapse to whatever happens afterwards? The electron travelling towards a point centre of positive charge arrives in a finite time at a condition of infinite kinetic energy, according to classical theory, just as the universe arrives in a finite proper time at a condition of infinite compaction. But, for the electron, quantum theory replaces deterministic catastrophe by probabilistic scattering in (x,y,z)-space. Why then for the universe should not quantum theory replace deterministic catastrophe by probabilistic scattering in superspace? . . . In brief, this picture considers the laws of physics to be valid far beyond the scale of time of a single cycle of the universe, and envisages the universe to be "reprocessed" each time it passes from one cycle to the next.[93]

Or, as Wheeler has elsewhere written, "Little as one knows the internal machinery of the black box [the phase of final collapse in which the physics are unknown], one sees no escape from this picture of what goes on: the universe transforms, or transmutes, or transits, or is *reprocessed* probabilistically from one cycle of history to another in the era of collapse."[94] George Gamow put the concept of an oscillating universe perhaps more simply when he wrote: "We conclude that our universe has existed for an eternity of time, that until about five billion years ago it was collapsing uniformly from a state of infinite rarefaction . . . and that the universe is now on the rebound."[95]

Somewhat surprisingly, there has been considerable negative reaction to the possibility of such a cyclical universe on the part of both physicists and theologians. Much, though certainly not all, of the scientific opposition to the idea of an oscillating universe stems from the fact that what has happened or will happen in any other cycle apart from our own (if there are other cycles) is pure speculation and in principle beyond the reach of modern science. Theologians' hostility to the idea of an oscillating universe has much more to do with the theology of creation than with eschatology because, if true, an eternally cyclic universe would undermine the idea that the universe had an absolute beginning—an idea made scientifically kosher by the Big Bang theory and one that continues to generate enthusiasm among many theologians.

If our universe is indeed closed, many physicists would prefer to view it as simply having an end. Sir Arthur Eddington, writing in 1935 shortly after the discovery of an expanding universe had brought the question of an eternal cycle of expansion and collapse into vogue, said:

> From a moral standpoint the conception of a cyclic universe, continually running down and continually rejuvenating itself, seems to me wholly retrograde. Must Sisyphus for ever roll his stone up the hill only for it to roll down again every time it approaches the top? That was a description of Hell. If we have any conception of progress as a whole reaching deeper than the physical symbols of the external world, the way must, it would seem, lie in escape from the Wheel of things. It is curious that the doctrine of the running-down of the physical universe is so often looked upon as pessimistic and contrary to the aspirations of religion. Since when has the teaching that "heaven and earth shall pass away" become ecclesiastically unorthodox?[96]

Eddington expressed a similar opinion, also in 1935, in his book *The Nature of the Physical World*. He wrote: "I am no Phoenix worshipper. . . . I would feel more content that the universe should accomplish some great scheme of evolution and, having achieved whatever may be achieved, lapse back into chaotic changelessness, than that its purpose should be banalized by continual repetition. I am an Evolutionist, not a Multiplicationist. It seems rather stupid to keep doing the same thing over and over again."[97]

Eddington has admitted that his dislike of an oscillating universe is based largely on personal philosophical and religious grounds, not on specific scientific problems with the theory itself. We will therefore comment briefly on the theological aspects of his judgment. First, it must be pointed out that Eddington's use of the biblical reference to heaven and earth passing away is problematic. The concept of heaven and earth passing away occurs in biblical apocalyptic almost always in connection with the creation of a new heaven and a new earth. An absolute end of everything—that is, an end that can in no way simply be considered a transformation—is foreign to the thought of the Bible.[98] This is why many ecclesiastics have found the predicted end of the universe problematic, not because they have never heard the verse "heaven and earth will pass away." Hence we must reject Eddington's implication that the hope that the universe will in some way and in some form prove to be eternal is antibiblical.

Another interesting point to note in Eddington's comment is the view that the physical world must "escape from the Wheel of things." Here one detects a hint of Buddhistic logic—that the world is somehow only struggle and that the ultimate answer to the pain and suffering involved in this struggle is to escape from the cycle of existence. It is indeed an interesting concept to apply the idea of escape not only to the individual but to the entire universe. Eddington's comments along these lines—for instance, that a cyclic universe would be nothing but futile repetition—would seem to imply that the ultimate end of the universe is not only a goal of its evolutionary existence but also an ultimate answer to the problem of suffering. While the suggestion that the universe needs to escape from its existence may fit well with certain forms of Buddhist thought, it finds little correspondence with Christian theology. Such a view implies that something is fundamentally wrong with God's good creation, something that cannot be resolved or redeemed. This in turn has implications for our view of a God who would create a universe whose best of all possible destinies is to complete whatever "evolutionary achievement" it is capable of and then to "escape the Wheel of things." Certainly Christian theology recognizes the sufferings and groanings of creation (Rom. 8:20-22). But Christian theology also confesses that the "frustration" to which the creation was subjected due to human sin finds its resolution in God's redemption, not in escape from the cycle of existence.

The reception of oscillating universe theories in more recent times has not been much better than that given by Eddington. John Wheeler has attempted to find a home for an oscillating universe within the anthropic principle. As Barrow and Tipler write: "Wheeler has speculated that the Universe may have a cyclic character, oscillating *ad infinitum* through a sequence of expanding and contracting phases. At each 'bounce' where contraction is exchanged for expansion, the singularity may introduce a permutation in the values of the physical 'constants' of Nature and of the form of the expansion dynamics. Only in those cycles in which the 'deal' is right will observers evolve." Barrow and Tipler, however, criticize the suggestion as being untestable and too speculative and do not explore its possibilities within the context of the anthropic principle.[99]

Steven Weinberg criticizes the oscillating universe model on the grounds that it does not provide the hoped-for eternity that it seems to promise. If the second law holds true through the final contraction and "bounce" of an oscillating universe, such a series of oscillations would eventually run down. This would also imply that there must have been a beginning to the series, which means that the oscillating universe does not provide the hoped-for avoidance of the "problem of Genesis." Weinberg explains:

> Some cosmologists are philosophically attracted to the oscillating model, especially because, like the steady-state model, it nicely avoids the problem of Genesis. It does, however, face one severe theoretical difficulty. In each cycle the . . . entropy per nuclear particle is slightly increased by a kind of friction as the universe expands and contracts. As far as we know, the universe would then start each new cycle with a new, slightly larger ratio of photons to nuclear particles. Right now this ratio is large but not infinite, so it is hard to see how the universe could have previously experienced an infinite number of cycles.[100]

Although the oscillating universe model does not have a great deal of support among physicists, it tenaciously remains an intriguing theory with some vocal advocates.[101] If the recent NASA-Cobe discovery suggesting that the formation of unevenness in the microwave background radiation of the universe occurred early proves correct, indicating that the universe may be closed, then one would expect a resurgence of interest in models of an oscillating universe. In such an event theology would have to take seriously the implications of an oscillating universe.

Although cosmological models of an oscillating universe that follow a so-called Big Bang–Big Crunch pattern are recent, the idea of a cyclic universe itself is very old, going back at least to the ancient Greeks in the West and, even earlier, to China and India in the East and Egypt and Babylon in the Middle East.[102] It is therefore not surprising that we find the first (and until now almost the only) serious attempt to integrate a cyclic universe cosmology with Christian theology already in the thought of the third-century theologian Origen. Origen wrote:

> Not for the first time did God begin to work when He made this visible world; but as, after its destruction, there will be another world, so also we believe that others existed before the present came into being. And both of these positions will be confirmed by the authority of holy Scripture. For that there will be another world after this, is taught by Isaiah, who says, "There will be new heavens and a new earth, which I shall make to abide in my sight, saith the Lord;" and that before this world others also existed is shown by Ecclesiastes, in the words: "What is that which hath been?

Even that which shall be. And what has been created? Even this which is to be created: and there is nothing altogether new under the sun. Who shall speak and declare, Lo, this is new? It has already been in the ages which have been before us." By these testimonies it is established both that there were ages before our own, and that there will be others after it. It is not, however, to be supposed that several worlds existed at once, but that, after the end of this present world, others will take their beginning.[103]

Such a cyclic universe raises several theological problems. If everything repeats itself, does this include human actions? If so, what of human free will? Are these cycles unending? If they are, in what sense can we speak of God as Creator? And, perhaps most significantly, has Jesus died on the cross in each cycle, making his death nonunique and trivial? In an extended passage in his *De Principiis* Origen addresses several of these crucial theological problems. In answer to those who, in Origen's day, suggested that each cycle is an exact repetition of the one before it, he wrote:

> I do not understand by what proofs they can maintain their position . . . For if there is said to be a world similar in all respects (to the present), then it will come to pass that Adam and Eve will do the same things which they did before . . . and everything which has been done in this life will be said to be repeated—a state of things which I think cannot be established by any reasoning, if souls are actuated by freedom of the will, and maintain either their advance or retrogression according to the power of their will. For souls are not driven on in a cycle which returns after many ages to the same round, so as either to do or desire this or that; but at whatever point the freedom of their own will aims, thither to direct the course of their actions. . . . So therefore it seems to me impossible for a world to be restored for the second time, with the same order and with the same amount of births, and deaths, and actions.
>
> But this world, which is itself called an age, is said to be the conclusion of many ages. Now the holy apostle teaches that in that age which preceded this, Christ did not suffer, nor even in the age which preceded that again; and I know not that I am able to enumerate the number of anterior ages in which he did not suffer.[104]

For Origen, therefore, it is clear that a cyclic universe neither destroys free will nor makes the death of Christ a repeatable (or repeating) event. Regarding the role of God as Creator, Origen is not so clear. We know from other parts of his writing that he maintained an original creation out of nothing.[105] Whether this applies to the creation of the first cycle[106] or to our current universe is not certain. If the latter, it would not be entirely clear what he understood by an "out of nothing" creation, unless each world is created new by God out of nothing—a view that does seem to be hinted at in Origen's thought.[107]

Interestingly, recent contributions of quantum theory to the oscillating universe model have supported Origen's view that the cycles of the universe would not simply be "doing the same thing over and over again" as Eddington seems to have held. In fact, not every cycle may be suitable for life—a possibility that may even allow us to consider our present cycle unique in this regard. This would certainly be no more anthropocentric than the common theological (and in some circles scientific) belief that our planet is the only one capable of sustaining intelligent life.[108] In regard to the diversity of cycles suggested by the application of quantum theory to the oscillating universe model, Patton and Wheeler write: "Even without the actual quantum geometrodynamic calculation, . . . can one conclude that any given cycle of expansion and contraction is followed, not by a unique new cycle, but a probability distribution of cycles? According to this expectation, in one such cycle the universe attains one maximum volume and lives for one length of time; in another cycle, another volume and another time; and so on. In a few such cycles life and consciousness are possible; in most others, not."[109]

Wheeler, in a manner similar to his participatory universe theory, applies findings from the microscopic world of quantum physics to the macroscopic realm of the entire universe. In this case, Wheeler adopts the picture of the course charted by probabalistic quantum mechanics for the shattered electron to the universe as a whole as it enters and emerges reprocessed from the Big Crunch phase. Thus a unique feature of Wheeler's oscillating universe is that it has a probabalistic variety of new cycles, apparently awaiting the "final observation" of the participatory observer to become "real." Wheeler's model describes "the beginnings of alternative new histories for the universe itself after collapse and 'reprocessing' end the present cycle." Needless to say, Wheeler's model is speculative even by the standards of traditional oscillating universe models. Nevertheless, it serves to demonstrate that the models of an oscillating universe that are currently being proposed and discussed, especially those that take into account quantum theory, represent something far removed from the mere doing of the same thing over and over again of which Eddington complained. In this context Origen's advocacy of the necessary uniqueness of cycles, which he based on theological grounds, would seem to receive support from recent developments in the scientific discussion of an oscillating universe.

Origen's cosmology, while no less speculative than the theory of the oscillating universe, is not without theological value. Just as Origen wrote his theology in the context of a worldview in which a cyclic universe was the dominant cosmology, so also must we write our theology within the context of the cosmological models that dominate our modern worldview. In the event that an oscillating model of the universe again becomes dominant, and to the extent that it is already accepted as a credible cosmology, modern theologians would be wise to review carefully the work of Origen, who, writing more than sixteen hundred years ago, demonstrated that Christian theology and a cyclic universe must not be seen as incompatible. Origen's view, for instance, that free will prevents the cycles from ever being exact repetitions would seem to counter Eddington's argument that a universe in which everything repeated itself would be senseless. Origen also demonstrated that the uniqueness of the Christ event cannot be sacrificed in order to suit the needs of a cyclic cosmology. While modern theologians may be uncomfortable with how Origen does this, making our own age a unique culmination of ages because of the Christ event, he has shown at least one possible solution to the problem. If the need arose, modern theology could certainly rise to the challenge and present other possibilities.

None of this is to suggest, however, that a theology should be built on a specific scientific theory (although it would certainly not be the first such case). Theology, however, has the responsibility to demonstrate to what extent and in what ways Christian faith is compatible with cosmologies that may in fact prove to be an accurate description of our universe. If this is not done, we cannot claim to have avoided building a theology on a specific cosmology. Rather, when we ignore a particular cosmological model for the simple reason that it seems incompatible with Christian faith, or that more "compatible" models are on the market, then we are in fact building our theology on the hope that a particular model will be rejected by the scientific community. Sometimes it is necessary for theology to ask the speculative "what if" questions, if only to show that possible responses do exist. Theology, of course, cannot be expected to take account of every cosmological theory that comes through the pipeline. The persistent cyclic or oscillating universe models, however, would seem to be potentially too significant to ignore.

Is a Noninterventionist Model Possible?

Perhaps the most difficult problem posed by a closed cosmological model is that of divine intervention. If we proceed on the assumption that the universe must continue indefinitely in some form in order for Christian expectations of an eternal existence in resurrected bodies in a new heaven and a new earth to be fulfilled, then the prospect of a final Big Crunch poses serious difficulties. Of course, the assumption that the physical universe must in some form continue to exist may itself be false. A purely spiritual existence (which is merely spoken of symbolically in physical terms in Scripture) or an eternity with God in another dimension are conceivable possibilities. Considering the fact, however, that biblical prophecies and promises seem to be bound specifically to this present universe, the adoption of these options would present additional problems.

If we look to some version of Tipler's infinite subjective time as a way out of this dilemma that would allow us to work with a noninterventionist model, we would be confronted with the problem of the traditional understanding of eternity. The question then would be whether the subjectification of eternity necessarily involved in such a model would be acceptable to Christian theology. Regardless of the subjective experience of infinity that is made possible by an infinite amount of information processing, the hard fact remains that real time continues to tick down to the Big Crunch. What meaning, then, does a subjective infinity have in the face of an unavoidably objective, finite space-time?

But why should nonintervention be the preferred theological response to this dilemma? Intervention, that is to say the alteration of the fate of the universe by the Divine Will by means of an interruption or alteration of the existing laws of Nature, not only goes against the pattern of God's previous relationship with the world but seems to imply a deistic type God who needs to intervene in the universe in a nontrivial way from time to time to "wind it up" with a shot of extra energy to prevent its collapse. For this reason theologians have been reluctant in the face of predictions of a heat death or Big Crunch simply to suggest that God intervenes dramatically to put the universe back on course.

Although the Christian God is a God who intervenes in history, there is good reason for the reluctance to posit God's intervention as a "fix" to every problem confronting theology. Christian theology recognizes that God is by nature free to intervene in any way and at any time within creation. What God may actually do in the future of our universe is certainly beyond speculation and, in any case, will probably prove more remarkable, both in its simplicity and effect, than anything that human speculation could anticipate. If God's activity, however, is restrained by anything, it is God's own nature. Given the fact that God's past "intervention" has generally taken place in correspondence with the natural processes that Christians believe God set in motion, God's radical alteration of the course of the entire natural universe would seem, if we can use the phrase, out of character for God. If such large-scale intervention is posited as a way around problems posed by scientific eschatology, additional difficulties are created for theology. On the theological level we would have to ask what such a necessary intervention in the cosmic process says about God's good creation (Gen. 1:31). If God intends an alternate future for the universe other than that for which it is now "programmed," why did God simply not design it differently from the beginning?

On a purely practical level the proposal of an intervening rescue of the physical universe would impede dialogue between theology and the natural sciences in the field of eschatology. What, after all, would be left open to discussion? Would this mean that whatever futures scientific cosmological models may predict would be largely irrelevant for theology? If they do not fit our pattern, would we simply posit a divine act of cosmic intervention to bring them into line? Such an approach would belittle the value of natural science just as much as when some creation scientists suggest that God created the world approximately ten thousand years ago with the mere appearance of great age and evolutionary process.[110]

On the other hand, theology must remain independent from science and not limit itself to the possibilities and framework provided by a knowledge of the natural world alone. Physics talks about eschatological possibilities from within the structure of our universe while theology, whose true object is the transcendent God, speaks about possibilities from without. Physicists can only discuss those possibilities physically present in the universe. Theologians, on the other hand, when they properly understand their task, must speak of the possibilities provided by the love of a transcendent God. Theology, therefore, cannot ignore physics and the various possible futures that it predicts for our universe and for intelligent life. But neither can theology surrender its task to speak about eschatology, or to speak eschatologically, by limiting itself to the possibilities pointed to by the results of physics.

Hence we are left with the paradoxical problem of contemplating how a God who intervenes in human history (incarnation) has promised to intervene once again on a comprehensive scale (*parousia*) will provide a future for God's people without redesigning the foundation stones on which the universe is built. With closed universe models the idea of an oscillating universe provides possibilities, as does Tipler's concept of an infinite subjective time. Neither alternative, however, is free of its own theological and scientific problems. In the end, theology, in dialogue with natural science, must do better than simply to hope that a seemingly theology-friendly cosmology will win the day.

Could God Survive the Consummation of the Universe?
A final question that must be raised in the context of our discussion of the implications of scientific eschatology for the doctrine of God is whether, given that one of the worst-case scenarios for the remote future of the universe turns out to be correct, a divine being could survive either the heat death of an open universe or the Big Crunch of a closed universe. Crucial here is the doctrine of God's transcendence. If God were entirely immanent, then the consummation of the universe—especially in a closed cosmological

model—would seem to pose a threat to the being of God. If God does not transcend the physical universe, how can God be said to transcend its consummation in either a heat death or Big Crunch? If God is not wholly other, then it would seem that God could not, in principle, survive the consummation of the universe. In a recent attempt at formulating a pantheistic "Natural God" who is equated with the evolving, unifying "Force of Nature," Joel Friedman discusses the prospects that such a God faces at the end of the universe. He writes: "The Natural God ends in heat death or in universal collapse. The Natural God either fades in force forever, or else shrinks to a point perhaps forever—two kinds of natural death." Hence Friedman's Natural God dies an unavoidably natural death. The only hope such a God has of surviving indefinitely is to be found in the possibility of an oscillating universe. As Friedman writes: "The Natural God may well be the Natural Phoenix, rising from the 'ashes' of universal collapse, and so on. The Natural God may thus be an Eternal Cycle of Force. This however is a matter of speculation. No good scientific evidence now exists for an eternal pulsating universe."[111]

Process theology would also seem to be confronted with this problem. The process philosopher and theologian Charles Hartshorne has argued that the thought of process theology is pan*en*theistic rather than pantheistic. Nevertheless, God includes the world within God's being. The physical world, therefore, in Hartshorne's thought, becomes literally a part of God and is in this sense identified "concentrically" with God.[112] The question then is how this universe could come to an end without an integral part of God also coming to an end according to the thought of process theism. While the image of the nontranscendent God-in-process-with-the-universe "going down with the ship" might have a certain appeal for theodicy or for an eschatological "God is dead" perspective, such a God falls short of being the Creator God of Christian faith. Given these problems, we would therefore suggest that once again the insights of modern physics into the nature of the universe indirectly reinforce the significance of the doctrine of God's transcendence. A nontranscendent God, in the face of any final end of the universe, would seem either a hapless spectator or the perpetrator of some sort of cosmic suicide. God, however, is maintained by Christian theology to be the conductor of the final act (if indeed our universe has a final act), not just a spectator with better than average chances of finding a way to survive the consummation of the universe. In the Christian view God is the one who is doing the consummating. The summary of the matter for Christian theology, to adapt a phrase from Aquinas, is that God is the unconsummated consummator of the universe.

SUMMARY: GOD AS ESCHATOLOGICAL CONSUMMATOR IN LIGHT OF CONTEMPORARY PHYSICS

What we have described as scientific eschatology remains clearly a young and highly speculative discipline.[113] Nevertheless, Christian theology cannot afford to ignore what light modern science is able to shed on the future of the universe that God created, any more than it can ignore what modern science has to say about the origin of the universe. An important emphasis of modern scientific eschatology has been the fate of life in the remote future of the universe. Freeman Dyson and Frank Tipler have demonstrated, respectively, that an indefinite continuation of "life" in either an open or closed universe is theoretically possible. Some serious questions remain, however, concerning the tendencies in both the Dyson and Tipler models to reduce life to information processing and storage and to deemphasize the eschatological future of the individual. Ultimate hope for the individual, as Polkinghorne asserts, "can be grounded in God alone. Only he is the one in whom 'what is mortal is swallowed up in life' and through whom 'the creation itself will be set free from its bondage to decay and obtain the glorious liberty of the children of God.' "[114]

With the work of Dyson and Tipler, along with others who have focused on the possibility of an indefinite continuation of life, physics has moved decisively away from the pessimism expressed as late as 1977 by Steven Weinberg, who concluded his reflections on the remote future with the observation that "this present universe has evolved from an unspeakably unfamiliar early condition, and faces a future extinction of endless cold or intolerable heat."[115] The appearance of a certain form of scientific hope opens new possibilities for dialogue with theology and the distinctive forms of hope expressed in the Christian faith. We must agree with Polkinghorne, however, that a tremendous gulf remains between the hope of an infinite continuation of information processing and storage offered by the models of Dyson and Tipler, and the hope of personal resurrection and eternal life with God expressed in Christian faith.

While Pannenberg is certainly correct that the field of scientific eschatology poses some of the most difficult questions to Christian theology, we would suggest a shifting of the emphasis that he proposes. In light of the tendency to identify scientific predictions of the end of the universe with the apocalyptic vision of the Bible, the fact that the biblical vision speaks of an imminent occurrence over against the scientific prediction of an end that is still billions of years in the future is certainly problematic. If, however, the inappropriateness of identifying the events of scientific and biblical apocalyptic is recognized and the biblical "end" of the world is viewed as a transformation to a new heaven and earth and not an absolute end, then the focus of the problem shifts decisively to that of the question of eternity. Specifically, Christian theology is faced with the task of explaining, within the context of modern cosmologies, in what way it understands the concept of eternity within a universe that in all probability will encounter either thermal equilibrium or a Big Crunch at some point in the remote future. That is to say, how can the future of a universe apparently noneternal by its own criteria (as well as finite humanity) be taken up into the eternality of the Creator—an eternality of a decisively different order from that which the physical universe could potentially possess—which is precisely what Christian faith expects to happen.

The field of eschatology, however, presents problems not only for theology but also for natural science. The ultimate view of the fate of our universe in the light of scientific inquiry alone, despite the efforts of Dyson and Tipler, remains bleak. Only the active presence of the transcendent God of Christian faith redeems the future of the physical universe. Attempts to posit an eternal universe without taking into account the almighty Creator have not been successful. As Karl Heim pointed out: "We cannot assume an infinite source of power unless we reckon with the Almighty God. And we may not have recourse to do this so long as we are thinking in a purely scientific way. All possible ways have already been tried, in order to imagine a world without a God, which maintains itself in motion."[116]

Concerning God as active consummator and redeemer of the cosmos, we have seen once again, as was the case in preceding chapters, the importance of maintaining God's transcendence. Only in this way can Christian theology speak credibly of a God who is the unconsummated Consummator of creation. And only in this way can the "wholly other" quality of God's eternity be preserved not only *from*, but essentially *for*, a finite universe and its mortal inhabitants.

Chapter Six

Summary and Conclusions

The boundaries between physics and metaphysics have become blurred. Questions that would have been considered metaphysical in another age enter into discussions of the origin of the universe, and physicists speak of anthropic principles, which sometimes seem to be more philosophical than scientific.
—Richard Morris

In too many cases popular cosmological works depict God in out-dated concepts that theology itself has long since left behind. . . . [But] it is no more appropriate for cosmologists to operate with medieval notions of God . . . than it is for theologians to operate with medieval scientific concepts . . .
—Russell Kleckly

THE IMPACT OF MODERN PHYSICS AND COSMOLOGY ON THE THEOLOGICAL DISCUSSION OF GOD

At the end of our study the question that must be asked in all earnestness on the part of theology is: What does contemporary physics actually contribute to the theological discussion of God? The question is by no means an easy one. Testimony to this fact is the wide diversity of opinion that continues to exist among theologians as to the relationship between theology and natural science in general.[1] Regardless of which of a variety of models for relating science and theology one chooses, the main question from the perspective of theology remains whether and to what extent natural science is relevant for theology. And by "relevant" we mean in a sense that goes beyond simply providing the background or worldview against which theology speaks of God.

With this question we encounter the issue of so-called natural theology. In the introduction to this study the recognition of the validity of natural theology (or at the very least a natural knowledge of God) was presupposed. At the conclusion of our examinations I would suggest that not only can the study of the creation reveal something about our Creator, but scientists—including physicists and cosmologists—are to some extent themselves natural theologians. Whether they are aware of it or not, modern physicists and cosmologists have been engaging in natural theology to the extent that they seek to go beyond the mere data of the universe and address the fundamental metaphysical questions of its origin, purpose, and ultimate destiny.[2] Hence the "theology" coming out of modern physics is not only directly relevant for a theology based primarily on special revelation, it is also subject to its critique. More and more it is the case that the writings of modern physicists and cosmologists must be critiqued not only as natural science but as natural theology as well.

The fact that modern physics has entered the arena of metaphysical and theological discussion can only be regarded as something positive for theology. Whether the metaphysical speculations of contemporary physicists are weighed on the whole to be supportive of or contrary to long-held theological beliefs, the most important contribution of modern physics to theology is dialogue. Theology in the modern world runs the risk of becoming disengaged and isolated from the special sciences. Inasmuch as this actually occurs, theology also becomes irrelevant for large segments of modern society. For this reason the recent move toward metaphysics by physicists and cosmologists is generally greeted with enthusiasm by theologians. The bottom line for theology is: even if we do not agree with what physicists are saying about the existence and nature of God, creation *ex nihilo,* continuing creation, or the eschatological future of intelligent life; at least we would seem to have some common ground of interest on which to build a dialogue.

Yet however beneficial dialogue for its own sake is, it is never a substitute for content. That theologians and physicists are beginning to talk is good. That they are addressing seriously questions regarding the existence of God, the origin and purpose of the universe, the nature of mind, and the future of life can only be welcomed. But what impact is this dialogue having on theology? At least five areas are to be noted.

First, the dialogue with physics reminds theologians that God as Creator has something to do with the physical world. Knowledge of the physical world is, therefore, relevant as prolegomena to the knowledge of God. This relationship between Creator and creation is important for both physicists and theologians. As Wolfhart Pannenberg has maintained, "If the God of the Bible is creator of the universe, then it is not possible to understand fully or even appropriately the processes of nature without any reference to that God."[3] This does not mean that God should somehow become a hypothesis of physics. Past attempts in this direction have led to an ever-shrinking God-of-the-gaps. Rather, the recognition of the connection between Creator and creation means for the physicist (and for natural scientists in general) that unless one is able to prove conclusively that there is no Creator, one cannot proclaim with absolute confidence that the beginning, end, or purpose of the universe has been fully understood on the basis of empirical research alone. If the universe is, as Christian faith maintains, a product of the creative activity of a transcendent God who is involved in history, then no comprehensive statement about the origin or destiny of our universe is complete without reference to this God. Because God remains transcendent as well as imma-nent, however, natural science can do nothing other than proceed with its investigations as if there were no transcendent Creator. The very possibility of God's existence, however, serves as a continual reminder that there may literally be far more to our universe than what can ever meet the human eye.

For theology the intricate connection between Creator and creation has even more profound implications. Thomas F. Torrance expresses this well when he states: "Any attempt to explicate knowledge of God outside of or apart from those structures of space and time [that God created] is inevitably and essentially irrational. We cannot know God apart from the way in which he interacts with the world he has made or apart from the way in which we are constituted his creatures within that world. . . . It is only from within the . . . universe and through the medium of its contingent realities that we may articulate the knowledge God gives us of himself, even though he infinitely transcends the universe."[4]

Theology, unlike natural science, begins with the fundamental presupposi-tion of God's existence based on God's self-revelation to humanity within history. The inherent circularity in this presupposition is unavoidable. Theol-ogy not only accepts this basic tautology, but builds the entire theological structure of the Christian faith on it. As a closed system Christian faith is an epistemological fortress of certitude. Yet theology, however much it may en-joy the comfort of such a fortress, is forced out of the structures of this system by the very nature of the self-revelatory God it confesses. If God created the physical universe, then the knowledge gained from the investigation of this universe cannot be seen as being unconnected to its Creator.

Physicists like Stephen Hawking, Frank Tipler, Paul Davies, Charles Misner, and others are addressing more and more the question of the exis-tence and nature of God precisely because they recognize that an integral connection must exist between the knowledge of the universe and the knowledge of any God who may have created it. This does not mean, how-ever, that physics is about to replace theology, as some have predicted, or that theology must take its cues from the natural sciences. In this regard physics is subject to the same limitations as natural theology inasmuch as both take the observable, physical world as the starting point and basis of their epistemological systems. Concerning natural theology John Polkinghorne has observed: "However valuable natural theology may be in pointing to the divine and affording insight into his creation, it will only at best be able by itself to bring us to the Cosmic Architect or Great Mathematician. The God and Father of our Lord Jesus Christ is to be sought by other means."[5] Therefore from the standpoint of Christian theology, special revelation, as found in the biblical records of the Old and New Testaments, remains (and must necessarily remain) the foundation of the Christian epistemological system. What the current dialogue with physics demonstrates, however, is that if theology is to take seriously its contention that God is the Creator of the physical universe, then we can no longer (if this were ever indeed possible) speak about God apart from the context of the knowledge of the physical universe gained through empirical investigation. Therefore, even though theology and the natural sciences have fundamentally distinct methods and epistemological systems, we cannot proceed as if the two realms have nothing to do with each other.

Second, contemporary physics is forcing theology more and more either the emphasize the transcendence of God with renewed vigor and clarity or to abandon the doctrine altogether. The very idea of a transcendent being beyond the grasp of empirical investigation is fundamentally at odds with the basic working assumptions of natural science. As many have pointed out, the universe is, by definition, all that exists. Hence if there is a God, this God must exist within the very universe that is in principle open in every regard to scientific investigation. John Barrow and Frank Tipler express this view succinctly when they write: "If the Universe is by definition the totality of everything that exists, it is a logical impossibility for the entity 'God,' whatever He is, to be outside the Universe if in fact He exists. By definition, nothing which exists can be outside the Universe."[6]

If the immanence of God in the universe is emphasized to the exclusion of God's transcendence, there are serious repercussions for other aspects of the traditional doctrine of God as well. Such a God could, in principle, be shown not to exist. The doctrine of a creation out of nothing would become untenable. Theology would be forced to accept some sort of dualism between the divine being and some eternally coexisting raw material or, at the very least, fundamental physical laws. Or, if an ontological pantheism is adopted, then we would have to say that God created the universe out of God's own substance. Another possibility is that found in the models of Frank Tipler and John Wheeler in which, as we have seen, the universe evolves into "God." Either way, there is no room for the wholly otherness of God. The universe is either created out of God's own substance or the universe creates God out of its substance.

Additionally, the Christian understanding of miracles (including the incarnation and resurrection) would have to be radically reinterpreted if God is not transcendent as well as immanent. Such events would be seen, then, not as the intervention of a God who is wholly other than the laws of nature, but simply as affirmations of the Christian community, which attaches special significance to certain events that seem to it otherwise inexplicable. The emphasis, then, is shifted from God to humanity (specifically the believing community) as the foundation for a doctrine of miracles. Similarly, the apocalyptic intervention of God in the future, as portrayed in the Bible, would become untenable. In fact, without a doctrine of divine transcendence one could justly ask in light of the scientific eschatology coming out of contemporary physics and cosmology whether God could survive the consummation of the universe. If God is indeed entirely immanent within the universe, the answer would seem to be an unavoidable no. Joel Friedman'a pantheistic Natural God who either ends in heat death or universal collapse would seem to be the God of the future, given the assumption of nontranscendence.[7] In such a model, God is no longer the eschatological consummator but the one consummated.

The results of modern physics, therefore, if not also its underlying assumptions, are forcing theologians to reconsider the issue of God's transcendence.[8] Many aspects of modern physics have also demonstrated the potential implications for theology if the wholly otherness of God is not maintained. Indeed, much more is at stake than the so-called choice between immanence and transcendence, for the doctrine of God's transcendence stands at the very heart of Christian theism. Its rejection, as Barrow and Tipler have observed, serves inevitably to remove the barrier between God and world, between Creator and creation, leaving some form of pantheism in the place of theism. Ironically, it is the knowledge of the physical universe gained through modern physics that illustrates clearly the fate of a God who ceases to be confessed as transcendent. Christian theology, therefore, confesses a God who "is both present in every point and time of our world and yet remains the one who made the world out of nothing and whose existence is underived."[9]

Third, the traditional arguments for the existence of God (namely, the ontological, cosmological, and teleological) are, for better or worse, being resurrected from the dustbins of theological life through the dialogue with modern physics. In the twentieth century one is pressed to find a single theologian of note (philosophers, who have experienced a recent resurgence of interest in the subject, are excluded) who has employed any of the three traditional arguments for the existence of God. Ironically, one need not look so hard among twentieth-century physicists. Edmund Whittaker, Siegfried Müller-Markus, Freeman Dyson, Charles Misner, and Frank Tipler have all openly employed at least one of the traditional "proofs" in order to argue for the existence of a Supreme Being. Although in the instances of at least Tipler and Dyson it is questionable how much resemblance the God for whom they argue bears to the God of traditional theism, the fact remains that teleological, cosmological, and even ontological arguments for the existence of a Supreme Being are being revived among modern physicists. As to why this is so, one can only speculate that the answer has something to do with the fact that, given the ever-increasing scope of theoretical physics, God is seen more and more as a hypothesis which, being not unrelated to the physical universe and its laws, is in principle subject to either verification or falsification.

The opportunities presented to theology by this rather unusual turn of events are tantalizing. The possibility of entering into direct dialogue with physicists over the logical coherence and scientific viability of the God postulate is almost too enticing to pass up. There are, however, certain inherent dangers in this development for theology. First, although many of those currently employing traditional-style proofs are arguing for the existence of God, the logic of these same arguments can just as easily be employed in an effort to disprove the existence of God. If theology suddenly reverses itself on the consensus, held unofficially since Kant, that the existence of God cannot be proven, in order to accommodate these "new" arguments, it could not easily deny the validity of the same logic if suddenly the tide turns and leading physicists begin employing the same type of arguments to disprove the existence of God.

A second danger has to do with the kind of God who might be argued for (or against) by modern physicists. It is difficult to join fully such discussions without tacitly accepting the conceptions of God assumed by them. In all too many cases the God in question is designed to fit the argument rather than vice versa. This is especially to be seen in Frank Tipler's Omega Point God and in Freeman Dyson's Universal Mind God. In the more traditional conceptions of God, as for example in the case of Whittaker and Müller-Markus, the danger is a revival not just of Thomistic arguments for the existence of God, but also of Thomistic conceptions of God as well. While it is granted that a neo-Thomism may not displease everyone, twentieth-century theology has generally distanced itself from the images of God that Thomism contained and gave rise to, such as the concepts of God as First Cause, Unmoved Mover, or Cosmic Architect.

Fourth, the theological discussion of creation and eschaton, beginning and end, can no longer take place in isolation from our knowledge of the physical world—if, indeed, this were ever truly possible. Since modern physics began early in this century to move away from the concept of a static, eternal universe and to speak of the universe as having in all likelihood a beginning and end, theological treatments of creation and eschatology have been forced increasingly to take the cosmogonies and eschatologies of physicists into account. The picture of the physical universe painted by modern physics will, in its essential form, more and more constitute the intellectual background against which Christianity proclaims its faith in a Creator and Consummator God.

As most parish clergy have discovered, for example, it is difficult to instruct a confirmation class concerning the Christian doctrine of creation without the question being raised: "But what has this got to do with the Big Bang?" At this point, one is faced with essentially three options: (1) Dismiss the Big Bang theory as being contrary to our particular interpretation of biblical teaching and therefore necessarily false (conflict theory); (2) explain that science and religion are addressing entirely different questions and therefore the Big Bang theory, correct or not, is essentially irrelevant for theology (compartment theory); or (3) seek to correlate in some way the scientific theory and Christian belief without equating them or binding them too tightly to one another (complementarity theory). What one cannot do is ignore the question. Especially in regard to creation and eschaton, the worldview of contemporary physics will, in all likelihood, determine more and more the way in which the average person thinks about the beginning and end (or perhaps the lack thereof) of our universe.

Fifth, a rebirth of a new physico-theology appears to be taking place. Although the physico-theology of the seventeenth and eighteenth centuries is generally perceived as having collapsed in the latter part of the nineteenth century in the face of the critique of Kant and the undermining of the adaptation argument by Charles Darwin,[10] a resurgence of aspects of a physico-theology today among both theologians and physicists is unmistakable. The use of the traditional arguments from many physicists is one indication of the revival of the thought that evidences of the existence and nature of God can be gathered from the investigation of the physical world. Even more pointed, however, is the *mixture* (to be distinguished from *dialogue*) of theology and science that seems to be taking place on the part of some theologians as well as a few physicists.

The seventeenth and eighteenth centuries saw the rise of a natural theology that failed to recognize properly its own limitations and boundaries. It was assumed that the existence of God, as well as God's chief attributes, could be demonstrated from the physical world. The mixing of theology and natural science produced a physico-theology that has been derided by scientists and theologians alike. To the extent that the proper boundaries and limitations of both natural science and theology are not observed today, it can be said that we have witnessed in recent years the rebirth of a new physico-theology. One needs only to consider the Omega Point theory of Frank Tipler to see a classic example of physico-theology, complete with an argument for the existence of God, a description of God's nature, and a theory of the resurrection based on "pure physics." Indeed, the table of contents of Tipler's recent book *The Physics of Immortality,* with chapters on free will, resurrection, heaven and hell, and the ontological argument for the existence of God, reads more like a dogmatics text than a treatise on cosmology. And all this, according to Tipler, is based purely on the implications of modern physics and cosmology with no reference to a special revelation.

In the introduction to this study we stated that the metaphysical and theological implications of contemporary physics should be considered as prolegomena to the doctrine of God. The question that must now be asked (and this has already been addressed in the preceding chapters) is: What picture of God is emerging from this "pre-word" from physics. In short, the God emerging from the metaphysical speculations of modern physicists can generally be said to be exclusively immanent, deistic (in the sense of being nonintervening) and, perhaps most surprisingly, fathomable. It is no accident that Stephen Hawking has made the bold claim that a Grand Unified Theory would allow us to know the mind of God.[11] The most frustrating thing for a natural scientist is that anything could, in principle, be beyond the reach of empirical research. By making God, if there is indeed a God, entirely immanent in the physical world, God too becomes in principle a legitimate object of empirical investigation—even if that investigation is directed toward demonstrating God's absence rather than presence.

THE CONTINUING DIALOGUE BETWEEN PHYSICS AND THEOLOGY: GUIDELINES AND SUGGESTIONS

If physics and theology are to achieve a meaningful dialogue, that dialogue must be mutual. Neither can dominate the other, claiming sole right to set the agenda or have the final word. In the Middle Ages theology did both. In the twentieth century, physics, as the unofficial new queen of the sciences, is in danger of taking over this role. If it is to bear fruit, the dialogue must also develop in such a way that it is a dialogue between *disciplines.* At least from the side of theology there is a danger that, because of the amount of specialized knowledge involved, the dialogue may be left to those few who are trained in both physics and theology.

When one surveys the theological literature dealing with the impact of modern physics, one cannot help but notice that most of the active dialogue partners are physicists who have also (usually later) been trained as theologians. We might mention, for instance, Robert John Russell, John Polkinghorne, Willem Drees, Ian Barbour, William Pollard, and Stanely Jaki in this group. Others, like Arthur Peacocke, are scientists trained in a related field. The names of those who are not trained physicists or scientists who have ventured into the dialogue to any significant degree are few. Among twentieth-century theologians of note we might mention here Karl Heim, Wolfhart Pannenberg, Ted Peters, Philip Hefner, and Thomas F. Torrance. The danger is that the physics-theology dialogue become a dialogue *within individuals* and not *between disciplines,* with those who do not feel adequately trained in the other discipline remaining spectators.

If theologians need to enter the fray more boldly, physicists often seem to suffer the opposite problem. Indeed, among the physicists writing about theological and metaphysical issues it is difficult to name those who appear significantly conversant with theological and philosophical methodologies and positions. Two notable exceptions to this pattern, whatever one may think of the anthropic principle, are John Barrow and Frank Tipler. Politeness suggests, however, that we forego naming examples of those who seem to enjoy addressing theological and philosophical questions but who have not found the time to become conversant with the most basic aspects of these disciplines. This situation is also detrimental to dialogue; it smacks of arrogance to pass judgment on a wide array of philosophical and theological questions on the assumption that qualifications as a physicist alone give one license to address meaningfully interdisciplinary issues apart from any other special competence.

It would seem helpful, therefore, if physicists—especially those who feel compelled to explain the relevance of their research for philosophy and theology—would familiarize themselves with basic concepts and streams of thought in contemporary philosophy and theology.[12] When this is not done one runs the risk, at best, of reinventing the wheel. At worst, one is continually interacting with "straw men" positions that are no longer held by contemporary theologians. Most frequent, perhaps, is the tendency of physicists to treat centuries-old conceptions of God as if still current. For many physicists, for instance, it seems that a refutation of Aquinas's cosmological argumentation or William Paley's teleological argumentation is sufficient ground to reject the rationality of belief in the existence of a Supreme Being. That few reputable theologians since the time of Immanuel Kant have made use of such arguments seems to have gone largely unnoticed. Stephen Hawking, who has been accused of both deism and neo-Thomism in regard to his understanding of God, is a case in point. As Russell Kleckley has observed,

"Hawking clearly assumes a concept of God consistent with the God of deism and the metaphorical watchmaker God of William Paley. While [some cosmologists] . . . react . . . against the anthropomorphic God of extreme theism, Hawking goes to the other extreme by depicting God in deistic terms before questioning the validity of the God-concept altogether."[13] Ted Peters has similarly pointed out that "the God who is being rejected by Hawking is the God of deism." This outmoded conception of God, in turn, is an obstacle to fruitful dialogue with contemporary theology. As Peters explains regarding Hawking's question, "What place, then, for a creator?" "His question is oblique in that it does not open the gate to more fruitful discussion. It presupposes deism, so it fails to open up the discussion of theism."[14]

Imagine the complaints if theologians were to point out the misconceptions, logical fallacies, and incongruities of twelfth-century science, dismissing thereby the relevance and value of twentieth-century science. What Russell Kleckley has written about popular cosmologists (many of whom are trained physicists) could just as easily be said of physicists in general who have ventured to address the question of God: "The notion of God as First Cause, either as the originator of something like the Big Bang or as the teleological Grand Designer, may still be firmly implanted in the popular mind, but theology has long since moved beyond the classical versions of those views. . . . It is no more appropriate for cosmologists to operate with medieval notions of God in order to advance their own prejudices than it is for theologians to operate with medieval scientific concepts for the same purpose."[15]

A related concern is the problem of language. One finds, for instance, in the *creatio ex nihilo* question a situation in which physicists seem eager to claim the philosophical advantages of an *ex nihilo* origin of the universe—no unexplained beginning, no in principle epistemologically unknowable "point beyond," and no need of a Creator. Unfortunately, as was seen in chapter 3 of this study, these same physicists exhibit marked deficiencies in their understanding of what precisely is meant, theologically and philosophically, by *creatio ex nihilo*. When one borrows terminology from another discipline, especially when one intends to take over the implications that go along with the terminology, one must make the effort to learn precisely what it means in the context of the discipline from which it comes.

These warnings concerning adequate familiarity with the dialogue partner's field and the use of terminology apply equally to theologians. Contemporary theologians have had a tendency not only to misunderstand specific scientific theories but, even more detrimental to healthy dialogue, have often been guilty of a selective reading of scientific material—essentially raiding the storehouses of science to find whatever seemed at the moment usable in support of a specific theological opinion and leaving all else untouched. What physicist has not come to dread the misuse by theologians of such concepts as entropy, Big Bang, field theory, the second law of thermodynamics, and the uncertainty principle, to name just a few theological favorites? Jeffrey Wicken expressed this problem clearly in his criticism of no less a theologian than Wolfhart Pannenberg in his use of the concept of field theory. As noted in chapter 4, Wicken contends: "If we want to use the word *energy* or *field* in science-theology discourse, let us do so in some way commensurate with their understandings in physics. Talking about 'spirit' as 'energy' and granting it by implication the status of physical law runs dangerously close to usurping the hard-won denotative language of science for physicalizing theology. This serves neither enterprise." [16]

Theologians and physicists, if they are to engage one another profitably in dialogue, must understand the role(s) of their own discipline in relation to that of the other. As many are coming to realize, the long-enforced separation between physics and metaphysics is neither correct nor practicable. Not only do metaphysical assumptions often influence physical theories (versions of the strong anthropic principle and oscillating universe models are cases in point), but the theories and models of physics necessarily impact metaphysical views of reality. This later instance can be seen, for example, in the case of the two great revolutionary advances in physics in our century: relativity theory and quantum mechanics, both of which have altered irreversibly the philosophical discussions of the nature of time, space, causality, and other fundamental metaphysical questions. While philosophical questions are, especially for modern physicists, unavoidable, the physicist as physicist has no special competence to address metaphysical or theological questions. The nature and implications of the physicist's research, however, suggest a natural interest in such questions and provide a legitimate entry into the metaphysical arena. Physicists, therefore, cannot be expected to remain silent about the metaphysical implications of their research. For their part, theologians and philosophers, long accustomed to having free rein in the field of metaphysics, must accept that physicists and cosmologists (and others are likely to follow) have joined the discussion.

Theology, of course, has in principle no special competence to pass judgment on specific theories arising from the natural sciences. Its tendency to do precisely this in the past, as in the case of the Copernican theory and the theory of evolution, have led only to conflict and embarrassment for theology. What, then, is the role of theology vis-à-vis physics? In relation to physics itself, theology's role would seem to be to make physicists mindful of indications of the interconnectedness of all things, the remarkable order and fine-tuning of the universe, the apparent indications of teleological direction, and other pointers toward a reality that transcends the mere physical structures of our universe. In short, a primary task of theology in regard to physics itself is to warn against reducing the totality of reality to what can be seen, measured, explained within the context of specific theories, or otherwise accounted for on the basis of empirical inquiry alone.

Within the Christian community the task of theology, in the light of modern physics, is to make sense of the Christian affirmations concerning creation and consummation. While theology may find some theories seemingly more compatible with Christian doctrine than others, it has no special competence to pass judgment on any specific scientific theory or model. While recognizing that scientific theories are constantly being adapted and even replaced, theology is responsible to find models that show how Christian affirmations about Creator and creation can be understood in light of currently viable scientific theories—these being the only theories relevant to the task of theology at the moment. If theology chooses to sit out a round of scientific development and await the appearance of more "favorable" theories, it sacrifices its credibility and the effectiveness of its apologetic function with regard to contemporary science in the modern world.

Notes

INTRODUCTION

1. John Updike, *Roger's Version* (New York: Alfred Knopf, 1986), 10f.

2. Robert Jastrow, *God and the Astronomers* (New York: W. W. Norton, 1978), 116.

3. So Carl Sagan in his introduction to Stephen W. Hawking, *A Brief History of Time: From the Big Bang to Black Holes* (New York: Bantam Books, 1988), x.

4. Hawking, *A Brief History of Time,* 173f.

5. Cf. Frank Tipler, *The Physics of Immortality* (New York: Doubleday, 1994), chap. 13.

6. Hawking, *A Brief History of Time,* 175.

7. John Houghton, *Does God Play Dice?* (London: Inter-Varsity Press, 1988).

8. Hermann Bondi, "Religion Is a Good Thing," in *Lying Truths,* ed. R. Duncan and M. Weston Smith (Oxford: Pergamon, 1979).

9. Cited in *Has Science Discovered God?* ed. Edward H. Cotton (Freeport, N.Y.: n.p., 1931), vi.

10. Siegfried Müller-Markus, "Science and Faith," in *Integrative Principles of Modern Thought,* ed. Henry Margenau (New York: Gordon & Breach, 1972), 492.

11. Emil Brunner, *The Christian Doctrine of Creation and Redemption,* trans. Olive Wyon (Philadelphia: Westminster, 1952), 5.

12. Thomas F. Torrance, *Reality and Scientific Theology* (Edinburgh: Scottish Academic Press, 1985), 33ff.

13. Richard Schlegel, "The Return of Man in Quantum Physics," in *The Sciences and Theology in the Twentieth Century,* ed. A. R. Peacocke (Notre Dame, Ind.: University of Notre Dame Press, 1981), 159.

CHAPTER 1

1. S. M. Markus (Siegfried Müller-Markus), *Der Gott der Physiker* (Basel: Birkhäuser, 1986), 13f.

2. Harold P. Nebelsick, *Circles of God: Theology and Science from the Greeks to Copernicus* (Edinburgh: Scottish Academic Press, 1985), xiii.

3. Cf. for example Stephen Hawking, *A Brief History of Time: From the Big Bang to Black Holes* (New York: Bantam Books, 1988), 3.

4. For this and the following biographical information, see Robert S. Westman, "The Copernicans and the Churches," in *God and Nature: Historical Essays on the Encounter between Christianity and Science,* ed. David Lindberg and Ronald Numbers (Berkeley: University of California Press, 1986); Fred Hoyle, *Nicolaus*

Copernicus: An Essay on His Life and Work [1883–84] (London: Heinemann, 1973), 16ff.; and Leopold Prowe, *Nicolaus Coppernicus,* 2 vols. (Osnabrück: Otto Zeller, 1967).

5. Cf. Edward Rosen, *Three Copernican Treatises* (New York: Octagon, 1971), 406f., for a convincing counterpoint to the view that the relative absence of conflict was due to the simple fact that no one read the book.

6. Hoyle, *Nicolaus Copernicus,* 32f.

7. For this and the following biographical information, see Stillman Drake, "A Biographical Sketch," in *Galileo: Man of Science,* ed. Ernan McMullin (Princeton, N.J.: Scholar's Bookshelf, 1967); Raymond Seeger, *Galileo Galilei: His Life and His Works* (Oxford: Pergamon Press, 1966); and William R. Shea, "Galileo and the Church," in *God and Nature.*

8. It should be noted that Galileo, the first modern astronomer, was not completely free from the folly of astrology. On 16 January 1609, just months before undertaking his revolutionary astronomical studies, he was persuaded by the dowager Grand Duchess Christina to provide a horoscope for Ferdinand I. Galileo predicted a long and active life on the basis of the stars. Ferdinand died twenty-two days later. Cf. Seeger, *Galileo Galilei,* 13.

9. Ibid., 12.

10. Ludovico Geymonat, *Galileo Galilei: A Biography and Inquiry into His Philosophy of Science,* trans. Stillman Drake (New York: McGraw-Hill, 1965), 43f.

11. Jerome J. Langford, *Galileo, Science and the Church,* rev. ed (Ann Arbor: University of Michigan Press, 1966), 52.

12. Cf. ibid., 78.

13. For this and the following see ibid., 97ff.

14. Drake, "A Biographical Sketch," 62.

15. Alfred North Whitehead, "The First Physical Synthesis," in his *The Interpretation of Science,* ed. A. H. Johnson (New York: Bobbs-Merrill, 1961), 5.

16. Geymonat, *Galileo Galilei,* 137.

17. Ibid., 139.

18. Drake, "A Biographical Sketch," 63f.

19. Cf. "Galilei: Mißverständnis ausgeräumt" and "Schmerzliches Mißverständnis im 'Fall Galilei' überwunden," in *L'Osservatore Romano* 22, nos. 45 and 46 (6 November and 13 November 1992).

20. Kepler, while living in Linz, Austria, was denied permission to take communion by the local pastor, Daniel Hitzler, because of crypto-Calvinistic views of the Lord's Supper. This "excommunication" did not carry the same significance as that within contemporary Catholicism. Kepler continued to worship with the other Lutherans in Linz, and when he desired communion, he simply went to a nearby parish outside of town where the pastor did not feel compelled to enforce Hitzler's "excommunication." For an account of the incident, see Arthur Koestler, *The Watershed: A Biography of Johannes Kepler* (London: Heinemann, 1961), 205ff.

21. Ibid., 116f.

22. Cited in Richard S. Westfall, "The Rise of Science and the Decline of Orthodox Christianity: A Study in Kepler, Descartes, and Newton," in *God and Nature,* 222.

23. Cf. Willy Hartner, "Galileo's Contribution to Astronomy," in: *Galileo: Man of Science,* 181f.

24. Koestler, *The Watershed,* 123.

25. So Harold Nebelsick, *Renaissance and Reformation and the Rise of Science* (Edinburgh: T. & T. Clark, 1992), 196, 203.

26. Francis Bacon, *The Advancement of Learning* [1605] (London: Dent, 1965), 8 (1.1.3).

27. James R. Moore, "Geologists and Interpreters of Genesis in the Nineteenth Century," in *God and Nature,* 323.

28. Bacon, *Advancement of Learning,* 209f. (2.25.3).

29. Moore, "Geologists and Interpreters," 323.

30. Westfall, "The Rise of Science and the Decline of Orthodox Christianity," 225.

31. Ibid., 226.

32. René Descartes, cited by Norman Kemp Smith, *New Studies in the Philosophy of Descartes* (London: Lowe & Brydone, 1966), 81.

33. Isaac Newton, "Four Letters to Dr. Bentley Containing Some Arguments in Proof of a Deity," in *Isaac Newton's Papers and Letters on Natural Philosophy,* ed. Bernard Cohen (Cambridge, Mass.: Harvard University Press, 1978), 280.

34. Richard H. Popkin, "Newton's Biblical Theology and His Theological Physics," in *Newton's Scientific and Philosophical Legacy,* ed. P. B. Scheurer and G. Debrock (Dordrecht: Kluwer, 1988), 81.

35. Cf. ibid. for a concise and convincing account of Newton's religious convictions. Also, Frank Manuel, *The Religion of Isaac Newton* (Oxford: Clarendon Press, 1974), 57–63.

36. Isaac Newton, *The Mathematical Principles of Natural Philosophy,* trans. Benjamin Motte, vol. 2 (London, 1729), 389–92.

37. David N. Livingstone, *Darwin's Forgotten Defenders: The Encounter between Evangelical Theology and Evolutionary Thought* (Grand Rapids: Eerdmans, 1987), 112ff., 116f., 125ff., 128ff., 140ff.

38. George Frederick Wright, "The Passing of Evolution," in *The Fundamentals,* vol. 7 (Chicago: Testimony Publishing Co., 1910–1915), 10.

39. James Orr, "Science and the Christian Faith," in *The Fundamentals,* vol. 4, 102.

40. Ibid., 103f.

41. William Paley, *Natural Theology: Evidences of the Existence and Attributes of the Deity, Collected from the Appearances of Nature* (London: Faulder, 1802).

42. Charles Hodge, *What Is Darwinism?* (New York: Scribner, 1874), 173. The suggestion that the theory of evolution might actually "strengthen rather

than weaken the standard argument from design" (Wright) had not yet been put forward at the time Hodge wrote.

43. For this and the preceding, cf. H. Hunter Dupree, "Christianity and the Scientific Community in the Age of Darwin," in *God and Nature*, 362, 365.

44. John William Draper, *History of the Conflict between Religion and Science* (London: Henry S. King, 1875), 367.

45. Cf. Andrew Dickson White, *A History of the Warfare of Science with Theology in Christendom*, 2 vols. (New York: D. Appleton and Company, 1896).

46. Albert Einstein, "Zur Elektrodynamik bewegter Körper," in *Annalen der Physik* 17:10 (September 1905): 891–921.

47. Albert Einstein, *Sitzungsberichte, Preussische Akademie der Wissenschaft* (25 November 1915): 844ff. Cf. also "Die Grundlage der allgemeinen Relativitäts-theorie," in *Annalen der Physik* 49 (1916): 769–822.

48. George Bernard Shaw, "Too True to Be Good: A Political Extravaganza," in *Too True to Be Good, Village Wooing and On the Rocks* (London: Constable, 1934), 84f.

49. Hans Reichenbach, "The Philosophical Significance of the Theory of Relativity," in *Albert Einstein: Philosopher-Scientist*, ed. Arthur Schlipp (London: Cambridge University Press, 1970), 289.

50. Cited by Erwin Hiebert, "Modern Physics and Christian Faith," in *God and Nature*, 431.

51. Cf. Reichenbach, "The Philosophical Significance of the Theory of Relativity," 293–96.

52. Ibid., 290.

53. Paul Davies, *God and the New Physics* (New York: Simon and Schuster, 1983), 100f.

54. Cited in Roger Hahn, "Laplace and the Mechanistic Universe," in *God and Nature*, 256.

55. For this and the following see Hawking, *A Brief History of Time*, 53ff.

56. Ibid., 55.

57. See Albert Einstein, "Reply to Criticisms," in *Albert Einstein: Philosopher-Scientist*, 666ff., for a 1949 summary of his reasons for opposing this aspect of quantum physics.

58. Banesh Hoffman, *Albert Einstein: Creator and Rebel* (London: Hart-Davis, MacGibbon, 1973), 193f.

59. Hawking reminds us that "even Einstein, when he formulated the general theory of relativity in 1915, was so sure that the universe had to be static that he modified his theory to make this possible, introducing a so-called cosmological constant into his equations" (*A Brief History of Time*, 40).

60. It should be noted that the Russian physicist Alexander Friedmann (1888–1925), who apparently took Einstein's theory more seriously that Einstein himself at this point, was able to predict in 1922 (seven years before Hubble's results were

published) an expanding, nonstatic universe (see Markus, *Der Gott der Physiker,* 214).

61. The concept of the finiteness of the universe has recently been challenged, however, by Stephen Hawking's theory of a "no boundary condition universe," that is, a universe with no space or time beginning or end. Cf. Hawking, *A Brief History of Time,* 135ff.

62. Cf. Wolfhart Pannenberg, *Theology and the Philosophy of Science,* trans. Francis McDonagh (Philadelphia: Westminster Press, 1976).

63. Davies, *God and the New Physics,* 2.

64. E. O. Wilson, *On Human Nature* (Cambridge, Mass.: Harvard University Press, 1978), 192.

65. Karl Barth, *Church Dogmatics* III, 2 ed. G. Bromiley and T.F. Torrance (Edinburgh: T. & T. Clark, 1960), 13.

66. Karl Barth, *Dogmatics in Outline* (New York: Harper & Row, 1959), 59.

67. Cf. Barth, *Church Dogmatics* III, 2, 437–640.

68. John Honner, "Not Meddling with Divinity: Theological Worldviews and Contemporary Physics," *Pacifica* 1 (1988): 256.

69. Langdon Gilkey, *Religion and the Scientific Future* (London: SCM Press, 1970), 18ff.

70. Werner Heisenberg, *Physics and Beyond* (New York: Harper & Row, 1971), 82f.

71. Wolfhart Pannenberg, "Theological Questions to Scientists," in *The Sciences and Theology in the Twentieth Century,* ed. A. R. Peacocke (Notre Dame, Ind.: University of Notre Dame Press, 1981), 3.

72. Ibid., 4.

CHAPTER 2

1. Aristotle, *The Metaphysics,* books I–IX, trans. Hugh Tredennick (London: William Heinemann, 1968), 87 (II.ii.1).

2. Ibid., 207 (IV.viii.8).

3. These are the ontological, cosmological, teleological, moral, and historical arguments. Horst Georg Pöhlmann, *Abriß der Dogmatik* (Gütersloh: Gerd Mohn, 1990), lists seven possible proofs for the existence of God, the additional two being a henological proof taken from Thomas's fourth argument (and probably best considered a variation of the cosmological argument) and an eudaemological proof., 122ff.

4. Cf. Anselm, *Proslogion: With a Reply on Behalf of the Fool by Gaunilo and the Author's Reply to Gaunilo,* trans. M. J. Charlesworth (Oxford: Clarendon Press, 1965), 117.

5. Ibid., 119.

6. Cf. René Descartes, *Meditationes de prima philosophia* (Paris: Librairie Philo-

sophique J. Vrin, 1967), Meditatio III, 34–52, and V, 62–70; and G. W. Leibniz, *Die philosophischen Schriften von G. W. Leibniz,* ed. C. J. Gerhardt, vol. 7 (Hildesheim: Georg Olms, 1960), 261ff.

7. Immanuel Kant, *The Critique of Pure Reason,* in *Great Books of the Western World,* vol. 42 (London: Encyclopaedia Britannica, 1952), 182.

8. For a basic statement of the various forms of this argument, see the first four of Aquinas's "five ways" in *Summa Theologica* (I.2.3) in *Basic Writings of Saint Thomas Aquinas,* vol. 1, ed. Anton Pegis (New York: Random House, 1945), 22f.

9. For this and the following see Kant, *Critique of Pure Reason,* 179.

10. Ibid., 180.

11. Ibid., 181.

12. For this and the following see ibid., 184.

13. For this and the following see ibid., 187ff.

14. Ibid., 190.

15. John Polkinghorne, *Science and Creation: The Search for Understanding* (Boston: Shambhala, 1989), 12.

16. The traditional arguments seem to be making somewhat of a comeback, however, among contemporary philosophers of religion. See, for instance, Richard Swineburne, who in his book *The Existence of God* (Oxford: Clarendon Press, 1979) makes use of a form of the cosmological argument and employs a teleological argument in a 1989 paper, "Argument from the Fine-Tuning of the Universe" (in *Physical Cosmology and Philosophy,* ed. John Leslie [London: Collier, 1990], 154–73)—in both cases making use of recent developments in physics and cosmology. Yet the arguments are intended to "render the existence of God . . . more probable than not," and not to prove the absolute necessity of such existence ("Argument," 172). Cf. also the works of John Leslie ("How to Draw Conclusions from a Fine-Tuned Universe," in *Physics, Philosophy, and Theology,* ed. R. Russell, W. Stoeger, and G. Coyne [Vatican City: Vatican Observatory, 1988], 297–312); Alvin Plantinga (*The Nature of Necessity* [Oxford: Clarendon Press, 1974]), and William L. Craig ("'What Place, Then, for a Creator?': Hawking on God and Creation," *British Journal for the Philosophy of Science* 41 [1990]: 473–91.

17. Ronald Gregor Smith, *J. G. Hamann 1730–1788: A Study in Christian Existence with Selections from his Writings* (New York: Harper Brothers, 1960), 253.

18. Søren Kierkegaard, *Philosophical Fragments,* trans. D. F. Swenson (Princeton, N.J.: Princeton University Press, 1936), 31.

19. Pierre Lecomte du Noüy, *Human Destiny* (New York: Longmans, 1947), 148.

20. Ibid., 188ff.

21. Edmund Whittaker, *Space and Spirit* (London: Thomas Nelson, 1947), 131f.

22. Ibid., 129ff.

23. Ibid., 131.

24. Siegfried Müller-Markus, *Wen Sterne rufen: Gespräch mit Lenin* (Wiesbaden: Credo, 1960), 83.

25. Ibid., 84.

26. Siegfried Müller-Markus, "Science and Faith," in *Integrative Principles of Modern Thought,* ed. Henry Margenau (New York: Gordon and Breach, 1972), 478, 486ff.

27. Ibid., 490.

28. For this and the following quote, see Freeman J. Dyson, "Science and Religion," in *Religion, Science and the Search for Wisdom,* ed. D. Byers (National Conference of Catholic Bishops, 1987), 60f.

29. Müller-Markus, "Science and Faith," 487.

30. Polkinghorne, *Science and Creation,* 47f.

31. See Charles Misner, "The Isotropy of the Universe," *Astrophysics Journal* 151 (February 1968): 431ff.

32. See Charles Misner, "Cosmology and Theology," in *Cosmology, History, and Theology,* ed. W. Yourgrau and A. Beck (New York: Plenum Press, 1977).

33. Cf. John Cobb and David Griffin, *Process Theology: An Introductory Exposition* (Philadelphia: Westminster Press, 1976); and L. S. Ford, "An Alternative to *creatio ex nihilo,*" in *Religious Studies* 19 (1983) for a discussion of creation out of chaos from the perspective of process theology.

34. Stephen Hawking, *A Brief History of Time: From the Big Bang to Black Holes* (New York: Bantam Books, 1988), 166.

35. Polkinghorne, *Science and Creation,* 50.

36. See M. Yoshimura, "Early Universe and GUT," in *Cosmology of the Early Universe,* ed. L. Z. Fang and R. Ruffini (Singapore: World Scientific, 1984). Yoshimura writes: "Near the Planck time (~10^{-64} sec.) the energy density must be fine-tuned to the critical density to the accuracy of 10^{-60}. A typical universe, instead, would recollapse soon after the Planck era, which makes our old universe an exception among infinite possibilities."

37. Hawking, *A Brief History of Time,* 125.

38. Roger Penrose, *The Emperor's New Mind: Concerning Computers, Minds, and the Laws of Physics* (Oxford: Oxford University Press, 1989), 343.

39. G. Whitrow, "Why Does Space Have Three Dimensions?" *British Journal for the Philosophy of Science* 6 (1955): 13ff.

40. John Barrow and Frank Tipler, *The Anthropic Cosmological Principle* (Oxford: Clarendon Press, 1986), 16.

41. Ibid.

42. Ibid., 21.

43. Ibid., 22.

44. Fred Hoyle, *Religion and the Scientists* (London: SCM Press, 1959).

45. Barrow and Tipler, *Anthropic Cosmological Principle,* 22.

46. Ibid.

47. Ibid., 23.

48. John Barrow, however, argues that although "Strong Anthropic coincidences cannot be the basis of a cogent argument for God's existence . . . they are

quite consistent with such a conclusion." John D. Barrow, *The World within the World* (Oxford: Oxford University Press, 1988), 365.

49. Hawking, *A Brief History of Time,* 126.

50. Ibid.

51. For this and the following see Paul Davies, *God and the New Physics* (New York: Simon and Schuster, 1983), 208f.

52. Richard Dawkins, *The Blind Watchmaker* (London: Longmans, 1986).

53. John Houghton, *Does God Play Dice?* (London: Inter-Varsity Press, 1988), 45.

54. Penrose, *The Emperor's New Mind,* 434.

55. Whittaker, *Space and Spirit,* 124.

56. Ibid., 125.

57. For this and the following quote see Misner, "Cosmology and Theology," 94f.

58. Ibid., 95.

59. Ibid., 95 and 97.

60. Max Planck, *The Universe in the Light of Modern Physics,* trans. W. Johnston (London: Allen and Unwin, 1937), 47.

61. Ibid., 48.

62. Cf. Robert J. Russell, "Quantum Physics in Philosophical and Theological Perspective," in *Physics, Philosophy, and Theology,* 349.

63. John Polkinghorne, *One World* (London: SPCK, 1986), 47.

64. Russell, "Quantum Physics," 349.

65. Cf. David Hume, *Dialogues Concerning Natural Religion* (Indiana: Bobbs Merrill, 1977), part 9, p. 177.

66. Cf. H. Everett III, "'Relative State' Formulations of Quantum Mechanics," *Review of Modern Physics* 29:3 (July 1957): 455–62.

67. Barrow and Tipler, *Anthropic Cosmological Principle,* 458.

68. Mary B. Hesse, "Physics, Philosophy, and Myth," in *Physics, Philosophy, and Theology,* 192ff.

69. Ibid., 192f.

70. Barrow and Tipler, *Anthropic Cosmological Principle,* 476.

71. Cited ibid., 476f.

72. Ibid., 106. Barrow and Tipler make this assessment apparently on the basis of comments Alfred North Whitehead made about "cosmic epochs" in *Process and Reality: An Essay in Cosmology* (New York: Macmillan, 1929). Whitehead believed that our cosmic epoch (that is, the present universe) "contains within itself other epochs" (148), and that "a chaos of diverse cosmic epochs" exists (171).

73. Frank Tipler, "The Many-Worlds Interpretation of Quantum Mechanics in Quantum Cosmology," in *Quantum Concepts in Space and Time,* ed. Roger Penrose and Chris J. Isham (Oxford: Clarendon Press, 1988), 214.

74. Richard Schlegel, "Quantum Physics and the Divine Postulate," *Zygon* 14:2 (June 1979): 177.

75. Davies, *God and the New Physics,* 173.

76. Hawking, *A Brief History of Time,* 136. The essential form of Hawking's model is based on theoretical work done in cooperation with American physicist James Hartle in 1983. Cf. James Hartle and Stephen Hawking, "Wave Function of the Universe," *Physical Review* D, 28, 3 (15 December 1983): 2960–75.

77. Hawking, *A Brief History of Time,* 135.

78. Ibid., 136.

79. Ibid., 140f.

80. Stephen Hawking, July 1985 interview with Renée Weber, in Weber, *Dialogues with Scientists and Sages: The Search for Unity* (London: Routledge & Kegan Paul, 1986), 209.

81. Bernulf Kanitscheider, "Gibt es einen absoluten Nullpunkt der Zeit?" *Praxis der Naturwissenschaft-Physik,* 4:40 (1991): 24.

82. Johannes Knöppler, "Welt ohne Schöpfer: von den theologischen Implikationen moderner Kosmologie," *Materialdienst* 54 (1 December 1991), 347.

83. G. Börner, from an unpublished manuscript presented at Bad Honnef (4 October 1990).

84. Thomas Becker, "A Review of Hawking's *A Brief History of Time,*" *Zygon* 24:4 (December 1989): 493.

85. Craig, "'What Place, Then, for a Creator?'" 474.

86. Hawking, *A Brief History of Time,* 175. This oft-cited passage from Hawking is an apparent allusion to Romans 11:33f.: "O the depth of the riches and wisdom of God! How unsearchable are his judgments and how unscrutable his ways! For who has known the mind of the Lord . . . ?"

87. Craig, "'What Place, Then, for a Creator?'"

88. Cited ibid.

89. Ibid., 475.

90. Thomas Aquinas, *Summa Theologica,* 453 (I.46.2).

91. Craig, "'What Place, Then, for a Creator?'" 475f. for this and the following.

92. Robin Le Poidevin, "Creation in a Closed Universe or, Have Physicists Disproved the Existence of God?" *Religious Studies* 27 (1991): 39.

93. Ibid.

94. Ibid., 40.

95. William Newton-Smith, *The Structure of Time* (London: Routledge and Kegan Paul, 1980), 55, 82. See also William Newton-Smith, "Space, Time and Space-Time: A Philosopher's View," in *The Nature of Time,* ed. R. Flood and M. Lockwood (Cambridge, Mass.: Basil Blackwell, 1986), 27ff.

96. Le Poidevin, "Creation in a Closed Universe," 40f.

97. Hawking, *A Brief History of Time,* 150.

98. Ibid., 152.

99. See Le Poidevin, "Creation in a Closed Universe," 47, for an explanation of why this is the case.

100. Cf. ibid., 41ff. for this and the following.

101. Ibid., 47.

102. Hawking, *A Brief History of Time,* 174.

103. Frank Tipler, "The Omega Point as *Eschaton:* Answers to Pannenberg's Questions for Scientists," *Zygon* 24:2 (June 1989): 250. Writes Tipler: "To emphasize the scientific nature of the Omega Point theory, let me state here that I consider myself an atheist."

104. Frank Tipler, *The Physics of Immortality* (New York: Doubleday, 1994), 205ff.

105. Tipler, "The Omega Point as *Eschaton,*" 217.

106. Ibid., 219.

107. Ibid., 221.

108. Ibid., 240f.

109. For this and the following quote see ibid., 243f.

110. Barrow and Tipler, *Anthropic Cosmological Principle,* 107.

111. Craig, "'What Place, Then, for a Creator?'" 475.

112. Hawking, *A Brief History of Time,* 141.

113. Willem Drees, *Beyond the Big Bang: Quantum Cosmologies and God* (La Salle, Ill.: Open Court, 1990), 192.

114. Davies, *God and the New Physics,* 47.

115. John Wheeler, "Genesis and Observership," in *Foundational Problems in the Special Sciences,* ed. R. Butts and K. Hintikka (Dordrecht: Reidel, 1977), 29.

116. C. M. Patton and J. Wheeler, "Is Physics Legislated by Cosmogony?" in *Quantum Gravity: An Oxford Symposium,* ed. C. Isham, R. Penrose, and D. Sciama (Oxford: Clarendon Press, 1975), 575.

117. John Wheeler, "Beyond the Black Hole," in *Some Strangeness in the Proportion: A Centennial Symposium to Celebrate the Achievements of Albert Einstein,* ed. H. Woolf (Reading, Mass.: Addison-Wesley, 1980), 342.

118. Barrow and Tipler, *Anthropic Cosmological Principle,* 108.

119. Hawking, *A Brief History of Time,* 122.

120. Steven Weinberg, *Dreams of a Final Theory: The Search for the Fundamental Laws of Nature* (London: Vintage, 1993), 195f.

121. Polkinghorne, *Science and Creation,* 13.

122. Ted Peters, "Cosmos as Creation," in *Cosmos as Creation,* ed. Ted Peters (Nashville: Abingdon Press, 1989), 55.

123. Barrow and Tipler, *Anthropic Cosmological Principle,* 107.

124. William Pollard, *Transcendence and Providence: Reflections of a Physicist and Priest* (Edinburgh: Scottish Academic Press, 1987), 189.

125. Ibid., 263f.

126. Arthur Peacocke, "God's Action in the Real World," *Zygon* 26:4 (December 1991): 461.

127. Schlegel, "Quantum Physics and the Divine Postulate," 164.

128. Schlegel seems especially impressed by the definitions of Karl Peters, "The Image of God as a Model for Humanization," *Zygon* 9 (June 1974): 98–125; and Charles Hartshorne and William Reese, *Philosophers Speak of God* (Chicago: University of Chicago Press, 1953), 15–25.

129. Schlegel, "Quantum Physics and the Divine Postulate," 175f. and 178. For an opposing point of view on the impact of quantum physics on the definition of God, see George Riggan, "Epilogue to the Symposium on Science and Human Purpose," *Zygon* 8 (September–December 1973): 443–81.

130. J. F. Donceel, *Natural Theology* (New York: Sheed and Ward, 1962), 107.

131. Drees, *Beyond the Big Bang,* 193.

132. Donceel, *Natural Theology,* 108.

133. Richard Morris, *The Edges of Science: Crossing the Boundary from Physics to Metaphysics* (New York: Prentice Hall, 1990), 221f.

134. Hesse, "Physics, Philosophy, and Myth," 200f.

CHAPTER 3

1. Cf. Wolfhart Pannenberg, *Systematische Theologie,* vol. 2 (Göttingen: Vandenhoeck & Ruprecht, 1991), 27f.

2. Gerhard von Rad, *Genesis: A Commentary* (Philadelphia: Westminster Press, 1972), 49.

3. See, for example, Claus Westermann, *Genesis 1–11: A Commentary,* trans. J. Scullion (Minneapolis: Augsburg, 1984). Westermann notes that the ideas of *creatio ex nihilo* versus ordering out of chaos "are foreign to both the language and thought of P." Further, "it is clear here that there can be no question of a *creatio ex nihilo;* our query about the origin of matter is not answered" (110, 121).

4. Karl Barth, *Church Dogmatics* III, 2, ed. G. Bromiley and T. F. Torrance (Edinburgh: T. & T. Clark, 1960), 154ff.

5. Paul Tillich, *Systematic Theology,* vol. 1 (Chicago: University of Chicago Press, 1951), 188.

6. Ibid., 189.

7. Norman Habel, *The Book of Job,* The Old Testament Library (Philadelphia: Westminster, 1985), 371. Habel notes that the biblical author, with the Hebrew word *tohu,* is referring not "to the chaos of waters but to the 'void' or 'nothing.'"

8. Cf. John R. Bartlett, *The First and Second Books of the Maccabees* (Cambridge: Cambridge University Press, 1973), 276; and Pannenberg, *Systematische Theologie* 2:28.

9. Jonathan Goldstein, *II Maccabees: A New Translation with Introduction and Commentary,* The Anchor Bible, vol. 41a (New York: Doubleday, 1983), 307.

See also in this regard Gerhard May, *Schöpfung aus dem Nichts: Die Entstehung der Lehre von der Creatio ex Nihilo* (Berlin: De Gruyter, 1978), 6ff.

10. C. E. B. Cranfield, *The Epistle to the Romans,* vol. 1, *The International Critical Commentary* (Edinburgh: T. & T. Clark, 1975), 244.

11. F. F. Bruce, *The Epistle to the Hebrews* (Grand Rapids: William B. Eerdmans, 1964), 281.

12. For a full discussion of the doctrine of *creatio ex nihilo* among the Ante-Nicene fathers, see May, *Schöpfung aus dem Nichts.*

13. Augustine, *Confessions,* trans. R. S. Pine-Coffin (New York: Penguin Books, 1961), 284f.

14. Barth, *Church Dogmatics* III, 2, 153.

15. Pannenberg, *Systematische Theology* 2:29.

16. Philip Hefner, "The Evolution of the Created Co-Creator," in *Cosmos as Creation: Theology and Science in Consonance,* ed. Ted Peters (Nashville: Abingdon Press, 1989), 226.

17. Friedrich Schleiermacher, *The Christian Faith* (Edinburgh: T. & T. Clark, 1986), 153.

18. Alfred North Whitehead, *Process and Reality: An Essay in Cosmology* (New York: Macmillan, 1929), 528f.

19. John Cobb and David Griffin, *Process Theology: An Introductory Exposition* (Philadelphia: Westminster Press, 1976), 66, suggest that as close as they can come to the traditional doctrine of *creatio ex nihilo* would be a "creation out of the nothingness of confusion," which they admit is quite different from a *creatio ex nihilo.*

20. Ibid., 65. See also in this regard Lewis S. Ford, "An Alternative to *creatio ex nihilo,*" *Religious Studies* 19 (1983): 205–13.

21. Cf. John Cobb, *A Christian Natural Theology, Based on the Thought of Alfred North Whitehead* (London: Lutterworth Press, 1965), 238ff.

22. Ibid., 193ff.

23. The view that a universe without a beginning and a creation out of nothing do not necessarily imply a contradiction seems also to have been held by Thomas's teacher, Albertus Magnus, and Maimonides. Cf. Richard Dales, *Medieval Discussions of the Eternity of the World* (Leiden: E. J. Brill, 1990), 91.

24. One sometimes reads the expression that "entropy never decreases," which would seem to imply that the total entropy in a system could theoretically remain constant. The catch, however, as Roger Penrose explains, is that this is true only in reversible systems. "It is only with irreversible systems that the entropy actually increases, rather than just remaining constant." Because the overall system of our universe "gives off heat" and has a thermodynamic direction of time, it is irreversible. As a practical matter, therefore, the second law is often summarized as "entropy always increases" when speaking of the universe as a whole. Cf. Roger Penrose, *The Emperor's New Mind: Concerning Computers, Minds, and the Laws of Physics* (Oxford: Oxford University Press, 1989), 309ff.

25. Cf. John Barrow and Frank Tipler, *The Anthropic Cosmological Principle* (Oxford: Clarendon Press, 1986), 173f.

26. J. Clerk Maxwell, *Theory of Heat* (London: Longmans, 1872), 208.

27. Barrow and Tipler, *Anthropic Cosmological Principle*, 174.

28. Cf. Penrose, *The Emperor's New Mind*, 302–17; Roger Penrose, "Big Bangs, Black Holes and 'Time's Arrow,'" in *The Nature of Time*, ed. R. Flood and M. Lockwood (Cambridge, Mass.: Basil Blackwell, 1986), 36–61; and Stephen Hawking, *A Brief History of Time: From the Big Bang to Black Holes* (New York: Bantam Books, 1988), 144ff.

29. Arthur Eddington, *The Nature of the Physical World* (London: Dent, 1935), 81.

30. Cf. E. Zermelo, "Ueber einen Satz der Dynamik und die mechanische Wärmetheorie," *Annalen der Physik und Chemie* 57:3 (25 February 1896): 485ff.; and "Ueber mechanische Erklärungen irreversibler Vorgänge. Eine Antwort auf Herrn Boltzmann's 'Entgegnung,'" *Annalen der Physik und Chemie,* 59:12 (15 November 1896): 793ff. This was a noteworthy accomplishment given the prevailing view that such a recurrence would essentially make the universe a perpetual motion machine, which the second law did not allow. Wrote Boltzmann in 1886: "Since a given system can never of its own accord go over into another equally probable state but only into a more probable one, it is likewise impossible to construct a system of bodies that after traversing various states returns periodically to its original state, that is a perpetual motion machine." Ludwig Boltzmann, "The Second Law of Thermodynamics," in *Ludwig Boltzmann: Theoretical Physics and Philosophical Problems,* ed. B. McGuinness (Dordrecht: D. Reidel, 1974), 30.

31. Barrow and Tipler, *Anthropic Cosmological Principle,* 174f.

32. Cited ibid., 175. Cf. Ludwig Boltzmann, "Zu Herrn Zermelo's Abhandlung 'Ueber die mechanische Erklärung irreversibler Vorgänge,'" *Annalen der Physik und Chemie* 60:2 (10 January 1897): 392–98.

33. Penrose, *The Emperor's New Mind,* 329.

34. Ibid., 329f.

35. Cf. Barrow and Tipler, *Anthropic Cosmological Principle,* 175.

36. Penrose, "Big Bangs, Black Holes and 'Time's Arrow,'" 39.

37. Arthur Eddington, *New Pathways of Science* (New York: Macmillan, 1935), 58f.

38. Ted Peters, "On Creating the Cosmos," in *Physics, Philosophy, and Theology,* ed. R. Russell, W. Stoeger, and G. Coyne (Vatican City: Vatican Observatory, 1988), 282.

39. Richard P. Feynman, *The Character of Physical Law* (Cambridge, Mass.: MIT Press, 1965), 115f., writes: "I think it is a ridiculous theory. . . . If there were a fluctuation, the prediction would be that if we looked at a place where we have not looked before, it would be disordered and a mess. . . . And since we always make the prediction that in a place where we have not looked we shall see stars in a similar condition, . . . the success [of this and other predictions]

indicates that the world did not come from a fluctuation, but came from a condition which was more . . . organized in the past than in the present time."

40. See, for example, A. Grünbaum, *Philosophical Problems of Space and Time* (New York: Knopf, 1963), 227f.; and H. Reichenbach, *The Direction of Time,* ed. Mary Reichenbach (Berkeley: University of California Press, 1971), 54ff.

41. For example, Fred Hoyle and Hermann Bondi.

42. See Barrow and Tipler, *Anthropic Cosmological Principle,* 384f., for a defense of the necessity of a large space for the appearance of life in the universe.

43. Penrose, *The Emperor's New Mind,* 343. Cf. also Penrose, "Big Bangs, Black Holes and 'Time's Arrow,'" 53f., where he comments regarding the incredible "aim" of a Creator: "I'm not saying that the Creator wasn't that clever. What I'm driving at is that we need a *law* which says that the universe had to be like that."

44. Penrose, *The Emperor's New Mind,* 344. For the complete analysis of the methods and mathematics involved in this calculation, see pages 339–44.

45. For this and the following cf. ibid., 317–22.

46. See Pius XII, "Modern Science and the Existence of God," *The Catholic Mind* (March 1952): 182–92.

47. Edmund Whittaker, *The Beginning and End of the World* (Oxford: Oxford University Press, 1942), 63.

48. Peters, "On Creating the Cosmos," 283.

49. In this same context Peters anticipates the charge of invoking a God-of-the-gaps and seeks to defend himself against it. He writes: "By speaking of *creatio ex nihilo* at this point the theologian can achieve some consonance without appealing to a crass God-of-the-gaps method. It is not the acknowledged limit to scientific conceptuality which is the point of departure here. Rather, it is the material content of the standard Big Bang theory" (ibid.). We must protest, however, that this seems like a bit of semantic maneuvering. What precisely is the difference between an "acknowledged limit" and the "material content" of a theory? Could one not have argued with equal conviction in the case of previous uses of God-of-the-gaps arguments that the presumed gap or "end of the line" was part of the content of the then-standard theory? Also, physicists themselves are not agreed that this actually is "the end of the line." In what sense then can such an assumption be said to be a part of "the material content" of the theory itself?

50. See, for example, Hermann Bondi, *The Universe at Large* (London: Heinemann, 1961), 47–55. The recent NASA Cobe discovery, however, of predicted fluctuations in the microwave background radiation of the universe seems to have gone a long way toward redeeming the Big Bang theory on this score. Cf. "Big Boost for the Big Bang," *Time* (4 May 1992): 23.

51. See, for example, within one short period in 1991, the appearance of such popular notices as Michael Lemonick, "Bang! A Big Theory May be Shot," *Time International* (14 January 1991): 46; Ron Cowan, "Quasar Clumps Dim Cosmological Theory," *Science News* 139 (26 January 1991): 52; and Jerome Cramer,

"New Challenge to the Big Bang?" *Time International* (15 April 1991): 50. All of these have informed armchair physicists the world over that the present version of the Big Bang theory may not be the final word on the origin and early history of our universe.

52. Whittaker, *The Beginning and End of the World*, 63.

53. Cf. Bernulf Kanitscheider, *Kosmologie: Geschichte und Systematik in philosophischer Perspekive* (Stuttgart: Philipp Reclam jun., 1984), 309, and Stephen Weinberg, *The First Three Minutes: A Modern View of the Origin of the Universe* (London: Trinity Press, 1977), 146. Weinberg writes that "we do not know enough about the quantum nature of gravitation even to speculate intelligently about the history of the universe before this time [10^{-24} sec]. We can make a crude estimate that the temperature of $10^{32°}$ K was reached some 10^{-43} after the beginning, but it is not really clear that this estimate has any meaning."

54. Kanitscheider, *Kosmologie*, 309.

55. The somewhat inaccurate portrayal of time as existing alongside of and separate from space rather than as part of an integrated space-time is not intended but is simply an unavoidable limitation of representing a four-dimensional space-time in a two-dimensional diagram.

56. Sten Odenwald, "A Modern Look at the Origin of the Universe," *Zygon* 25:1 (March 1990): 27f. This description, we might note, represents only the standard version of events from among several possibilities for the first seconds and milliseconds after the initial singularity. Even within this standard model of the very early universe, several important variations exist. Cf. Weinberg, *The First Three Minutes*, 133ff.

57. Augustine, *The City of God*, trans. Marcus Dods (New York: Random House, 1950), 350 (XI. 6). Augustine wrote: "If eternity and time are rightly distinguished by this, that time does not exist without some movement and transition, while in eternity there is no change, who does not see that there could have been no time had not some creature been made, which by some motion could give birth to change, as they cannot be simultaneous, succeed one another—and thus in these shorter or longer intervals of duration, time would begin. Since God . . . is the Creator and Ordainer of time, I do not see how He can be said to have created the world after spaces of time had elapsed . . . then assuredly the world was made, not in time, but simultaneously with time."

58. Weinberg, *The First Three Minutes*, 149.

59. Ernan McMullin, "How Should Cosmology Relate to Theology," in *The Sciences and Theology in the Twentieth Century*, ed. A. Peacocke (Notre Dame, Ind.: University of Notre Dame Press, 1981), 39.

60. A significant exception to this trend, which preserves (in most forms) an eternal universe of sorts, is the idea of an oscillating universe. Although seemingly disliked by theologians and physicists alike, various models of oscillating universes continue to find support. See, for instance, the work of two leading Russian cosmologists: M. A. Markov, "Some Remarks on the Problem of the Very Early

Universe," in *The Very Early Universe,* ed. G. Gibbons, S. Hawking, et al. (Cambridge: Cambridge University Press, 1983); and I. L. Rozental, *Big Bang Big Bounce: How Particles and Fields Drive Cosmic Evolution* (Berlin: Springer Verlag, 1988).

61. Frank Tipler, "The Omega Point as *Eschaton:* Answers to Pannenberg's Questions for Scientists," *Zygon* 24:2 (June 1989): 227.

62. Ibid.

63. Barrow and Tipler, *Anthropic Cosmological Principle,* 660.

64. Charles Misner, "Absolute Zero of Time," *Physical Review* 186,2:5 (25 October 1969): 1331.

65. Pannenberg, *Systematische Theologie,* 2:182.

66. Hawking, *A Brief History of Time,* 87.

67. Ibid., 134f.

68. Ibid., 139, and for the following quote, 136.

69. Cf. Hermann Bondi and Thomas Gold, "The Steady-State Theory of the Expanding Universe," *Monthly Notices of the Royal Astronomical Society* 108 (1948): 252–70.

70. Michael Berry, *Principles of Cosmology and Gravitation* (Cambridge: Cambridge University Press, 1976), 134.

71. Hermann Bondi, *The Universe at Large* (London: Heinemann, 1961), 42.

72. Cf. Gary Steigman, "Antimatter," in *Encyclopedia of Physics,* ed. R. Lerner and G. Trigg (New York: VCH, 1991), 42.

73. Cf., for instance, Peter Atkins, *The Creation* (Oxford: W. H. Freeman, 1981), 109.

74. Hawking, *A Brief History of Time,* 129.

75. It is not sufficient, as Peter Atkins argues in making a case for a creation out of nothing, that particles and antiparticles are created "out of essentially nothing." Atkins, *The Creation,* 109.

76. Stephen Hawking and G. Ellis, *The Large Scale Structure of Space-Time* (Cambridge: Cambridge University Press, 1973), 256–75 and 348–64.

77. Barrow and Tipler, *Anthropic Cosmological Principle,* 442.

78. Hawking and Ellis, *Large Scale Structure of Space-Time,* 364.

79. Cf. Stephen Hawking and Roger Penrose, "The Singularities of Gravitational Collapse and Cosmology," *Proceedings of the Royal Society of London* A314 (1970): 529–48.

80. Chris Isham, "Creation of the Universe as a Quantum Process," in *Physics, Philosophy, and Theology,* 398.

81. Edward P. Tryon, "Is the Universe a Vacuum Fluctuation?" *Nature* 246 (14 December 1973): 396.

82. Ibid., 397.

83. Odenwald, "A Modern Look at the Origin of the Universe," 36.

84. Tryon, "Is the Universe a Vacuum Fluctuation?" 396.

85. Odenwald, "A Modern Look at the Origin of the Universe," 36.

86. Details of Tryon's proposed model were filled in by R. Brout, F. Englert, and E. Gunzig in their article, "The Creation of the Universe as a Quantum Phenomenon," *Annals of Physics* 115:1 (1978): 78–106. They claimed that "the laws of quantum mechanics formulated in the general relativistic framework are perfectly consistent with the spontaneous creation of all the matter and radiation in the universe. This creation has as an inception some arbitrary space-time origin." The question they do not answer, however, is how the spontaneous creation of all matter and radiation can take place within some arbitrary point of space-time. Is not the spontaneous creation of space-time itself meant here? Or does the spontaneous creation of all matter presuppose some preexisting space-time?

87. Alexander Vilenkin, "Creation of Universes from Nothing," *Physical Letters* 117B:25 (4 November 1982): 26.

88. Alexander Vilenkin, "Birth of Inflationary Universes," *Physical Review* D, 27,3:12 (15 June 1983): 2849.

89. Vilenkin, "Creation of Universes from Nothing," 26.

90. Vilenkin, "Birth of Inflationary Universes," 2851.

91. Vilenkin, "Creation of Universes from Nothing," 27.

92. Ibid., 27f.

93. Alexander Vilenkin, "Boundary Conditions in Quantum Cosmology," *Physical Review* D, 33, 3:12 (1986): 3562.

94. Without the employment of imaginary numbers it is not possible to eliminate the need for an initial boundary in time; only with their use can the distinction between space and time directions be erased. The idea of a unified space-time, however, is not new to Hartle and Hawking, only the theories that show that such a unification can eliminate initial and final time boundaries within a "finite" universe. H. Minkowski, writing early in this century, was perhaps the first to truly recognize the significance of a unified space-time in light of Einstein's early theorems. Minkowski wrote somewhat prophetically in 1909, "henceforth space by itself, and time by itself, are doomed to fade away into mere shadows, and only a kind of union of the two will preserve an independent reality." H. Minkowski, "Space and Time," in *The Principle of Relativity,* ed. A. Sommerfeld, trans. W. Perret and G. Jeffrey (London, 1923), 75.

95. James Hartle and Stephen Hawking, "Wave Function of the Universe," *Physical Review* D, 28,3:12 (15 December 1983): 2961.

96. Ibid.

97. Isham, "Creation of the Universe as a Quantum Process," 401, believes that a true *ex nihilo* creation is described by the Hartle-Hawking model and, consequently, the nonoscillating feature is necessary to preserve this achievement. Writes Isham: "The creation out of nothing is precisely that. In particular, there is no sense of a bouncing or oscillating universe."

98. Cf. ibid., 398.

99. Ibid.

100. John Barrow, *Theories of Everything: The Quest for Ultimate Explanation* (Oxford: Clarendon Press, 1991), 67.

101. Cf. Willem Drees, *Beyond the Big Bang: Quantum Cosmologies and God* (La Salle, Ill.: Open Court, 1990), 72. Drees writes that "the theory gives a precise meaning to the notion of 'nothing' as the absence of other boundaries in the calculation. However this should not be misunderstood as appearance out of nothing."

102. That Hawking considers this a true boundary condition of the universe can be seen in two papers he coauthored in which he treats specifically the character of this "boundary condition." See Stephen Hawking and Julian Luttrell, "The Isotropy of the Universe," *Physics Letters* 143B: 1,2,3 (9 August 1984): 83ff.; and Jonathan Halliwell and Stephen Hawking, "Origin of Structure in the Universe," *Physical Review* D3, 31:8 (15 April 1985): 1777ff., which states that the quantum path integral over compact four-metrics "can be regarded as a boundary condition for the Wheeler-DeWitt equation for the wave function of the Universe" (1787).

103. Drees, *Beyond the Big Bang,* 72.

104. John Barrow, *The World within the World* (Oxford: Oxford University Press, 1988), 231.

105. Heinz Pagels, *Perfect Symmetry* (New York: Simon and Schuster, 1985), 347.

106. Barrow and Tipler, *Anthropic Cosmological Principle,* 444.

107. Cf. ibid., 499.

108. Ibid., 492f.

109. Cf. Tipler, "The Omega Point as *Eschaton*," 224ff.

110. Barrow and Tipler, *Anthropic Cosmological Principle,* 494.

111. John Polkinghorne, *Science and Creation: The Search for Understanding* (Boston: Shambhala, 1989), 59f.

112. Isham, "Creation of the Universe as a Quantum Process," 401.

113. Thus Atkins, *The Creation,* 119, after arguing that science has discovered a *creatio ex nihilo*, states that: "In the beginning was nothing. . . . By chance was a fluctuation and a set of points. . . . From absolute nothing, absolutely without intervention, there came into being rudimentary existence."

114. Cf. Bernulf Kanitscheider, "Gibt es einen absoluten Nullpunkt der Zeit," *Praxis der Naturwissenschaft—Physik* 4:40 (1991): 24.

115. Polkinghorne, *Science and Creation,* 60.

116. Isham, "Creation of the Universe as a Quantum Process," 404.

117. Hawking, *A Brief History of Time,* 173.

118. Cited in B. G. Kuznetsov, *Einstein: Leben, Tod, Unsterblichkeit,* trans. H. Fuchs (Basel: Birkhäuser, 1977), 285.

119. Hawking, *A Brief History of Time,* 174.

120. James Trefil, *The Moment of Creation: Big Bang Physics from Before the First Millisecond to the Present Universe* (New York: Charles Scribner's, 1983), 223.

121. Ian Barbour, *Religion in an Age of Science* (San Francisco: Harper & Row), 145.

122. Martin Luther, *Commentary on Genesis,* in *Luther's Work,* vol. 1 (St. Louis: Concordia, 1958), 16.

CHAPTER 4

1. Ian Barbour, *Issues in Science and Religion* (New York: Harper & Row, 1966), 384f.

2. Ibid., 385.

3. Langdon Gilkey, *Message and Existence* (New York: Seabury, 1980), 90.

4. Cf. John Cobb and David Griffin, *Process Theology: An Introductory Exposition* (Philadelphia: Westminster Press, 1976), 63ff.

5. Ted Peters, "Cosmos as Creation," in *Cosmos as Creation,* ed. Ted Peters (Nashville: Abingdon Press, 1989), 78.

6. Wolfhart Pannenberg, *Systematische Theologie,* vol. 2 (Göttingen: Vanden-hoeck & Ruprecht, 1991), 31.

7. Peters, "Cosmos as Creation," 82.

8. Cf. W. E. Barnes, *The Psalms* (London: Methuen, 1931), 492.

9. We recall, for example, the account of divine assistance given Joshua and the Israelites in battle against the Amorites in the so-called "long day" of Joshua. "The sun stopped in mid-heaven, and did not hurry to set for about a whole day" (Josh. 10:13b). Even more inexplicable than this apparent halting of the earth's rotation is the similar account in 2 Kings 20:11 in which the earth's rotation seems to have changed direction: "The prophet Isaiah cried to the Lord; and he brought the shadow back the ten intervals, by which the sun had declined on the dial of Ahaz."

10. Cf. Karl Barth, *Church Dogmatics* III, 2, ed. G. Bromiley and T. F. Torrance (Edinburgh: T. & T. Clark, 1960), 155f.

11. Pannenberg, *Systematische Theologie,* 2:31f.

12. Ralph P. Martin, *Colossians* (Exeter: Paternoster Press, 1972), 47.

13. Peter T. O'Brien, *Colossians, Philemon, Word Biblical Commentary,* vol. 44 (Waco, Texas: Word Books, 1982), 45.

14. Robert John Russell, "Contingency in Physics and Cosmology: A Critique of the Theology of Wolfhart Pannenberg," *Zygon* 23:1 (March 1988): 25. See also Robert John Russell, "Cosmology, Creation, and Contingency," in *Cosmos as Creation,* 180, for a similar claim.

15. Pannenberg, *Systematische Theologie,* 2:31.

16. E. O. Wilson, *On Human Nature* (Cambridge, Mass.: Harvard University Press, 1978), 171.

17. Philip Hefner, "The Evolution of the Created Co-Creator," in *Cosmos as Creation*, 227.

18. As noted earlier, the steady-state theory does not contain a true creation out of nothing inasmuch as the creation of new hydrogen atoms is dependent on already existing matter. Yet the theory also seems to have proposed something more profound than simple change or growth of already existing matter.

19. Hermann Bondi, *The Universe at Large* (London: Heinemann, 1961), 42.

20. John Polkinghorne, *Science and Creation: The Search for Understanding* (Boston: Shambhala, 1989), 54.

21. Russell, "Cosmology, Creation, and Contingency," 186.

22. Max Jammer, "Feldtheorie," in *Historisches Wörterbuch der Philosophie* (Darmstadt: Wissenschaftliche Buchgesellschaft, 1972), 923.

23. William Berkson, *Fields of Force: The Development of a World View from Faraday to Einstein* (London: Routledge and Kegan Paul, 1974), 50.

24. Michael Faraday, *Lectures on the Various Forces of Matter and Their Relations to Each Other* (London: Richard Griffen, 1861), 131.

25. Roger Penrose, *The Emperor's New Mind: Concerning Computers, Minds, and the Laws of Physics* (Oxford: Oxford University Press, 1989), 185.

26. Cf. Nancy Nessian, "Faraday's Field Concept," in *Faraday Rediscovered: Essays on the Life and Work of Michael Faraday, 1791–1867*, ed. D. Gooding and F. James (London: Macmillan Press, 1985), 183 and 175ff. Nessian discusses five different views regarding what Faraday's field concept actually was.

27. Cf. John Polkinghorne, *The Quantum World* (London: Longman, 1984), 7ff.

28. Cf. Penrose, *The Emperor's New Mind*, 153f.

29. Ibid., 289.

30. Max Jammer, *Concepts of Force: A Study in the Foundations of Dynamics* (Cambridge, Mass.: Harvard University Press, 1957), 250, for this and the following quotation.

31. T. F. Torrance, *Space, Time and Incarnation* (London: Oxford University Press, 1969), 70f.

32. Wolfhart Pannenberg, "The Doctrine of Creation and Modern Science," in *Zygon* 23:1 (March 1988): 13.

33. James Jeans, *Physics and Philosophy* (Cambridge: Cambridge University Press, 1944), 234.

34. Polkinghorne, *Science and Creation*, 58.

35. Pannenberg, "The Doctrine of Creation," 8.

36. Ibid., 12.

37. Ibid., 14.

38. Pannenberg, *Systematische Theologie*, 2:104.

39. Ibid.

40. Ibid., 111.

41. Pannenberg, "The Doctrine of Creation," 15.

42. Ibid.

43. Pannenberg, *Systematische Theologie,* 2:129.

44. John Polkinghorne, *Reason and Reality: The Relationship between Science and Theology* (Philadelphia: Trinity Press International, 1991), 93.

45. Pannenberg, "The Doctrine of Creation," 12.

46. Ibid., 13.

47. Jeffrey Wicken, "Theology and Science in the Evolving Cosmos: A Need for Dialogue," in *Zygon* 23:1 (March 1988): 48, 51.

48. Ibid., 52.

49. Cf. Albert Einstein, Boris Podolsky, and Nathan Rosen, "Can Quantum-Mechanical Description of Physical Reality Be Considered Complete?" *Physical Review* 47:10 (15 May 1935): 777ff.

50. Cf. Polkinghorne, *The Quantum World,* 72f.

51. Einstein, Podolsky, and Rosen, "Can Quantum-Mechanical Description of Physical Reality Be Considered Complete?" 778.

52. Ibid., 779f.

53. Cf. Niels Bohr, "Can Quantum-Mechanical Description of Physical Reality Be Considered Complete?" *Physical Review* 48 (18 October 1935): 696.

54. Cf. ibid., especially 699ff., where Bohr explains his concept of "complementarity."

55. Ibid., 702.

56. Max Jammer, *The Philosophy of Quantum Mechanics: The Interpretations of Quantum Mechanics in Historical Perspective* (New York: John Wiley & Sons, 1974), 254.

57. Cited ibid.

58. John Bell, "On the Einstein-Podolsky-Rosen Paradox," (1964) in J. Bell, *Speakable and Unspeakable in Quantum Mechanics: Collected Papers on Quantum Philosophy* (Cambridge: Cambridge University Press, 1987), 14.

59. The delayed choice version of the experiment (first proposed as an addition to the EPR thought experiment) is accomplished by switching the orientation of the measuring devices at the last moment, after the particles have split but before they reach the detectors. It is based on the assumption in quantum theory that the measurement itself determines the orientation of the spin.

60. Penrose, *The Emperor's New Mind,* 282.

61. Donald M. MacKay, *Science, Chance and Providence* (Oxford: Oxford University Press, 1978), 30.

62. Cf. Bell, "On the Einstein-Podolsky-Rosen Paradox," 17ff.

63. Kevin Sharpe, "Relating the Physics and Religion of David Bohm," *Zygon* 25:1 (March 1990): 107.

64. Henry Pierce Stapp, "Quantum Mechanics, Local Causality, and Process Philosophy," ed. William Jones, *Process Studies* 7:3 (Autumn 1977): 173f.

65. Bell, "On the Einstein-Podolsky-Rosen Paradox," 20.

66. Cf. Alain Aspect, Jean Dalibard, and Gérhard Roger, "Experimental Test

of Bell's Inequalities Using Time-Varying Analyzers," *Physical Review Letters* 49,2:25 (20 December 1982): 1807.

67. Alain Aspect, transcript of BBC radio interview, in Paul C. W. Davies and J. R. Brown, *The Ghost in the Atom: A Discussion of the Mysteries of Quantum Physics* (Cambridge: Cambridge University Press, 1986), 42.

68. Nick Herbert, *Quantum Reality: Beyond the New Physics* (New York: Doubleday Press, 1985), 245.

69. David Bohm, B. J. Hiley, and P. Kaloyerou, "An Ontological Basis for the Quantum Theory," *Physics Reports* 144 (1987): 340f.

70. David Bohm and B. J. Hiley, "Non-Locality and Locality in the Stochastic Interpretation of Quantum Mechanics," *Physics Reports* 172 (1989): 95.

71. David Bohm, *Wholeness and the Implicate Order* (London: Routledge & Kegan Paul, 1980), 84.

72. Ibid., 149.

73. Sharpe, "Relating the Physics and Religion of David Bohm," 105.

74. It is uncertain what Bohm may mean by his caution about the limited application of nonlocality, even within quantum physics, when he then proceeds to build an entire cosmology and quasi-religious philosophy on the concept. From the standpoint of physics, Bohm admits that nonlocality may only apply "over relatively short distances for simple systems." Yet he believes that the theory of implicate order and holomovement that he has built on these perhaps limited instances of nonlocality "has brought together questions of the nature of the cosmos, of matter in general, of life, and of consciousness. All of these have been considered to be projections of a common ground. This we may call the ground of all that is" (*Wholeness and the Implicate Order*, 212). A long way indeed from a nonlocality that may only apply over short distances within certain simple quantum systems!

75. David Bohm and B. J. Hiley, "Some Remarks on Sarfatti's Proposed Connection between Quantum Phenomena and the Volitional Activity of the Observer-Participator," *Psychoenergetic Systems* 1 (1976): 178.

76. John Polkinghorne, "The Quantum World," in *Physics, Philosophy and Theology*, ed. R. Russell, W. Stoeger, and G. Coyne (Vatican City: Vatican Observatory, 1988), 340.

77. Barth, *Church Dogmatics*, III.3, 185.

78. Albrecht Ritschl, *Unterricht in der christlichen Religion* [1875] (Gütersloh: Gerd Mohn, 1966), 21 (Section 15).

79. Barth, *Church Dogmatics* III.3, 101f.

80. Ian Stewart, *Does God Play Dice? The New Mathematics of Chaos* (London: Penguin Books, 1990), 1.

81. For purposes of reference, the Schrödinger equation is: $i\hbar \partial/_{\partial t} | \psi \rangle = H | \psi \rangle$, where $\hbar$ is Dirac's version of Planck's constant, $\partial/_{\partial t}$ is the operator acting on ψ that denotes the rate of change of ψ with respect to time, and H is the quantum version of the classical Hamiltonian function.

82. Roger Penrose, *The Emperor's New Mind,* 288.

83. Stephen Hawking, *A Brief History of Time: From the Big Bang to Black Holes* (New York: Bantam Books, 1988), 166.

84. Davies and Brown, *The Ghost in the Atom,* 30.

85. Cf., for example, Penrose, *The Emperor's New Mind,* 167ff. and 431ff.; and John Barrow, *Theories of Everything: The Quest for Ultimate Explanation* (Oxford: Clarendon Press, 1991), 125ff.

86. Roger Penrose, "Big Bangs, Black Holes and 'Time's Arrow,'" in *The Nature of Time,* ed. R. Flood and M. Lockwood (Cambridge, Mass.: Basil Blackwell, 1965), 60.

87. Cf. Davies and Brown, *The Ghost in the Atom,* 30.

88. O. E. Rössler, "How Chaotic Is the Universe?" in *Chaos,* ed. Arun V. Holden (Manchester: Manchester University Press, 1986), 317.

89. Cf. Robert John Russell, "Quantum Physics in Philosophical and Theological Perspective," in *Physics, Philosophy and Theology,* 349.

90. Gary Zukav, *The Dancing Wu Li Masters: An Overview of the New Physics* (New York: William Morrow, 1979), 213.

91. Stewart, *Does God Play Dice?* 1.

92. Heinz Georg Schuster, *Deterministic Chaos: An Introduction* (Weinheim: Physik-Verlag, 1984), 1f.

93. Penrose, *The Emperor's New Mind,* 431.

94. Ibid., 353ff. and 431f.

95. Erwin Schrödinger, "Die gegenwärtige Situation in der Quantummechanik," *Die Naturwissenschaften,* vol. 23 (1935): 807–12, 823–28, 844–49. English translation taken from "The Present Situation in Quantum Mechanics," trans. J. Trimmer, in *Quantum Theory and Measurement,* ed. J. Wheeler and W. Zurek (Princeton: Princeton University Press, 1983), 157.

96. Penrose, "Big Bangs, Black Holes and 'Time's Arrow,'" 58.

97. Schrödinger, "The Present Situation in Quantum Mechanics," 157, explains that he intended his cat paradox as an example of "a ridiculous case . . . [in which] an indeterminacy originally restricted to the atomic domain becomes transformed into macroscopic indeterminacy, which can then be resolved by direct observation. That prevents us from so naively accepting as valid a 'blurred model' for representing reality. In itself it would not embody anything unclear or contradictory. There is a difference between a shaky or out-of-focus photograph and a snapshot of clouds and fog banks."

98. Davies and Brown, *The Ghost in the Atom,* 30.

99. Ibid., 31; and Penrose, *The Emperor's New Mind,* 293ff.

100. For this and the following see Barth, *Church Dogmatics* III.3, 98ff.

101. Stewart, *Does God Play Dice?* 2.

102. Hawking, *A Brief History of Time,* 122.

103. Arthur Peacocke, *Theology for a Scientific Age: Being and Becoming—Natural and Divine* (Oxford: Basil Blackwood, 1990), 182.

104. Ibid.

105. G. F. Woods, among others, has convincingly argued that the so-called *momentum theologicum* does not necessarily follow from the occurrence of a "miraculous" violation of natural law. "When it is assumed that a miracle has a cause and that this cause is in some sense above or beyond the normal system of natural causes, we are not confined to the view that this supernatural cause must be the work of God. It may have other origins." G. F. Woods, "The Evidential Value of Miracles," in *Miracles: Cambridge Study in Their Philosophy and History,* ed. C. F. D. Moule (London: A. R. Mowbray, 1965), 26.

106. David Hume, "Of Miracles," in *David Hume: The Philosophical Works,* vol. 4, ed. T. Green and T. Grose (London, 1882), 93 and n. 1.

107. Theologians who have attempted to resolve the apparent dispute with the natural sciences by rejecting the possibility of miracles have inevitably, when they remained consistent, rejected traditional interpretations of incarnation and resurrection, interpreting these as "spiritual," "psychological," or "mythological" events that violated no natural laws. Cf., for instance, Rudolf Bultmann, "Zur Frage des Wunders," in Bultmann, *Glauben und Verstehen,* vol. 1 (Tübingen: J. C. B. Mohr, 1966), 214. Bultmann wrote: "The understanding of a wonder as miracle has become impossible for us today because we understand natural occurrences to be events which are regulated by natural law and we understand miracles to be an interruption of the laws which regulate natural occurrences." It seems only consistent, therefore, that Bultmann "denies . . . also the reality of the incarnation and resurrection of Jesus as *novum* in the history of our world." So Hans Schwarz, *Das Verständnis des Wunders bei Heim und Bultmann* (Stuttgart: Calwer Verlag, 1966), 202.

108. Richard Feynman, *The Character of Physical Law* (Cambridge, Mass.: MIT Press, 1965), 13.

109. For this and the following quotation see ibid., 159.

110. Ahron Katchelsky, "Thermodynamics of Flow and Biological Organization," *Zygon* 6:2 (June 1971): 101.

111. Hawking, *A Brief History of Time,* 122.

112. Richard Swineburne, *The Concept of Miracle* (London: Macmillan, 1970), 2f.

113. Erwin Schrödinger, *What Is Life? The Physical Aspect of the Living Cell* (Cambridge: Cambridge University Press, 1944), 10.

114. George G. Stokes, *Natural Theology* (London: Adam and Charles Black, 1891), 24.

115. Mary Hesse, "Miracles and the Laws of Nature," in *Miracles: Cambridge Study,* 37.

116. Ibid., 38.

117. Ibid.

118. Swineburne, *The Concept of Miracle,* 30.

119. The implications of this change in the worldview of physics have yet to be fully grasped—even by theologians who, like physicists, sometimes find it difficult to move beyond the deterministic worldview of classical physics. Ironically, Bultmann's rejection of miracles, although intended to make the Gospel accounts comprehensible in the modern, scientific age, was based on the causalistic, deterministic worldview of the nineteenth century—a worldview that the advent of quantum mechanics had already brought into question in Bultmann's time. Cf. Schwarz, *Das Verständnis des Wunders bei Heim und Bultmann,* 48.

120. Hawking, *A Brief History of Time,* 46.

121. Peacocke, *Theology for a Scientific Age,* 183.

122. Polkinghorne, *Science and Creation,* 35.

123. Cf., for example, Brevard Childs's comment on the exodus in which he points out that "the direct intervention of God is pictured in terms of 'natural' causes such as the blowing of the east wind, the impeding of chariot wheels, and the panicking of the Egyptian army." *The Book of Exodus: A Critical, Theological Commentary* (Philadelphia: Westminster, 1974), 228.

124. William Pollard, *Chance and Providence: God's Action in a World Governed by Scientific Law* (New York: Charles Scribner's Sons, 1958), 83. Pollard considers, however, the original creation, the incarnation, and the resurrection to be true miracles.

125. Hesse, "Miracles and the Laws of Nature," 41f.

126. For this and the following quote see Robert John Russell, "Entropy and Evil," *Zygon* 19:4 (December 1984): 457.

127. Paul Tillich, *Systematic Theology,* vol. 2 (Chicago: University of Chicago Press, 1957), 60.

128. In the Boltzmann formula S represents entropy, which is seen to increase in isolated systems; k is the Boltzmann universal constant; and P is probability.

129. Cf., for example, Charles Misner, "Neutrino Viscosity and the Isotropy of Primordial Blackbody Radiation," *Physical Review Letters* 19 (28 August 1967): 533–37, and *Astrophysics Journal* 151 (1968): 431ff.

130. Cf. Irenaeus, *Against Heretics,* in *The Ante-Nicene Fathers,* vol. 1, *Justin Martyr and Irenaeus* (Grand Rapids: Eerdmans, 1979), 558 (book iv, xxix.1 and iv, xxxix.1).

131. John Hick, *Evil and the God of Love* (London: Macmillan, 1966), 237.

132. Cf., for example, Kenneth Denbigh, *An Inventive Universe* (New York: Braziller, 1975), and Katchelsky, "Thermodynamics of Flow and Biological Organization," 99ff., both of whom, recalling Boltzmann's formulaic linkage of entropy with increased probability, find here also increased possibilities for organized states that assume a necessary amount of entropy.

133. Philip Hefner, "God and Chaos: The Demiurge Versus the Ungrund," *Zygon* 19:4 (December 1984): 483. Cf. also Nicolas Berdyaev, *The Destiny of Man* (New York: Harper, 1960), for a similar view.

134. Russell, "Entropy and Evil," 465. The structural similarity with Ernan McMullin's oft-quoted comment on the relationship between Big Bang cosmologies and creation theology is intended.

135. Cf. Hick, *Evil and the God of Love*, 236ff., for a concise description of the distinctions between these two streams within Christian theodicy.

136. Cf. Horst Georg Pöhlmann, *Abriß der Dogmatik* (Gütersloh: Gerd Mohn, 1990), 154.

137. Cf. Hick, *Evil and the God of Love*, 38–89.

138. Cf. Hermann von Helmholz, "On the Interaction of the Natural Forces," in *Popular Scientific Lectures*, ed. M. Line (New York: Dover, 1961).

139. John Barrow and Frank Tipler, *The Anthropic Cosmological Principle* (Oxford: Clarendon Press, 1986), 166.

140. Cf. James Jeans, *The Universe around Us* (Cambridge: Cambridge University Press, 1929); and Arthur Eddington, *The Nature of the Physical World* [1928] (London: Dent, 1935).

141. Eddington, *Nature of the Physical World*, 71 and 84.

142. Ibid., 91f.

143. Cf. Irenaeus, *Against Heresies*, book 4, 29.1.

144. Friedrich Schleiermacher, *The Christian Faith* (Edinburgh: T. & T. Clark, 1986), 337.

145. Barrow and Tipler, *Anthropic Cosmological Principle*, 174f.

146. Ibid., 178.

147. W. J. Cocke, "Statistical Time Symmetry and Two-Time Boundary Conditions in Physics and Cosmology," *Physical Review* 160:2 (1967): 1165–70; and John Wheeler, *Frontiers of Time* (Amsterdam: North-Holland, 1978), 54–73.

148. Zukav, *The Dancing Wu Li Masters*, 213.

149. Ilya Prigogine and Isabelle Stengers, *Order out of Chaos: Man's New Dialogue with Nature* (Boulder, Colo.: New Science Library, 1984), 297f.

150. Cf. Ilya Prigogine, *From Being to Becoming* (New York: W. H. Freeman, 1980).

151. Russell, "Entropy and Evil," 465.

152. Hefner, "God and Chaos," 473.

153. Katchelsky, "Thermodynamics of Flow and Biological Organization," 107.

154. Ibid., 121ff.

155. Consider, for instance, Voltaire's famous satire *Candide*, which is a parody of the philosophy of Dr. Pangloss (Leibniz). Ignoring the seemingly overwhelming evil and suffering around him, Pangloss continues to maintain that we live in the best of all possible worlds (Voltaire, *Candide* [New York: Random House, 1956]). *Candide* closes with Dr. Pangloss's concluding argument: "All events are linked up in this best of all possible worlds; for, if you [Candide] had not been expelled from the noble castle, . . . if you had not been clapped into the Inquisi-

tion, if you had not wandered about America on foot, [etc.] . . . you would not be eating candied citrons and pistachios here" (188f.).

156. Carl Friedrich von Weizsäcker, *Zum Weltbild der Physik* (Stuttgart: S. Hirzel Verlag, 1963), 160.

157. Ibid., 160f.

158. Ibid., 161.

159. Cf. Gottfried Wilhelm von Leibniz, *The Philosophical Works of Leibniz,* ed. G. Duncan (London, 1890), 101, where he writes: "The present state of the universe exists because it follows from the nature of God that he should prefer the most perfect."

160. Barrow and Tipler, *Anthropic Cosmological Principle,* 476.

161. Ibid., 62f.

162. Cf. John Wheeler, "Beyond the Black Hole," in *Some Strangeness in the Proportion: A Centennial Symposium to Celebrate the Achievement of Albert Einstein,* ed. H. Woolf (Reading, Mass.: Addison-Wesley, 1980), especially 359ff.

163. Willem Drees, *Beyond the Big Bang: Quantum Cosmologies and God* (La Salle, Ill.: Open Court, 1990), 125.

164. Cited in B. G. Kuznetsov, *Einstein: Leben, Tod, Unsterblichkeit,* trans. H. Fuchs (Basel: Birkhauser, 1977), 285.

165. Hawking, *A Brief History of Time,* 174.

166. Peacocke, *Theology for a Scientific Age,* 176.

167. Cf., for instance, Romans 8:21: "the creation itself will be set free from its bondage to decay and will obtain the freedom of the glory of the children of God."

168. Russell, "Entropy and Evil," 462.

169. Wilson, *On Human Nature,* 171.

CHAPTER 5

1. Hermann von Helmholtz, "On the Interaction of the Natural Forces" [1854], in *Popular Scientific Lectures,* ed. M. Kline (New York: Dover, 1961).

2. Cf. James Jeans, *The Universe around Us* (Cambridge: Cambridge University Press, 1929); and Arthur Eddington, *The Nature of the Physical World* (London: Dent, 1935).

3. By "scientific eschatology" we mean visions of the future of the physical universe based on scientific investigation and theory. No specific theological or metaphysical implications are implied by the term. The term seems to make its first tentative appearance in theological literature in Karl Heim's *Weltschöpfung und Weltende* (Hamburg: Im Furche-Verlag, 1952), 114, as "naturwissenschaftliche Eschatologie." (Cf. English translation, *The World: Its Creation and Consummation,* trans. Robert Smith [Edinburgh: Oliver and Boyd, 1962], 89, where the term "scientific eschatology" is used.) In scientific literature "wissenschaftliche

Eschatologie" seems to have first been used to describe the emerging worldview of a universal "heat death" in an 1880 lecture by the physicist and historian of science Emil du Bois-Reymond titled "Die sieben Welträthsel." (Cf. *Über die Grenzen des Naturerkenntnis. Die sieben Welträthsel.* Zwei Vorträge, Leipzig: Veit, 1903). Heim appears to have taken the term from Bois-Reymond's lecture.

4. John Barrow and Frank Tipler, *The Anthropic Cosmological Principle* (Oxford: Clarendon Press, 1986), 658.

5. Freeman J. Dyson, "Time without End: Physics and Biology in an Open Universe," *Reviews of Modern Physics* 51:3 (July 1979): 447. Some of Dyson's eschatological ideas have been more fully developed in nontechnical language in his book *Infinite in All Directions* (New York: Harper and Row, 1988).

6. Barrow and Tipler, *Anthropic Cosmological Principle,* 658.

7. Dyson, *Infinite in All Directions,* 447.

8. Steven Weinberg, *The First Three Minutes: A Modern View of the Origin of the Universe* (London: Trinity Press, 1977), 154.

9. Milton K. Munitz, *Cosmic Understanding: Philosophy and Science of the Universe* (Princeton: Princeton University Press, 1986), 138f.

10. Karl Heim (*The World: Its Consummation and Creation,* see note 3 above) and Wolfhart Pannenberg ("Theological Questions to Scientists," and *Systematische Theologie,* vol. 2, see notes 43 and 68 below) are notable exceptions, though neither addresses the subject extensively.

11. Karl Heim, *The World: Its Creation and Consummation. The End of the Present Age and the Future of the World in the Light of the Resurrection* [1952], trans. Robert Smith (Edinburgh: Oliver and Boyd, 1962), 85.

12. Cf. Ron Cowan, "Hubble: A Universe without End and a Search for Dark Matter," *Science News* 141:5 (1 February 1992): 79.

13. Cf. Robin Mckie, "Has Man Mastered the Universe?" *The Sunday Observer* (26 April 1992): 8f.; Andrew Berry, "Scientists Find Holy Grail of the Cosmos in First Sign of Creation," *The Daily Telegraph* (24 April 1992): 1; and "Big Boost for the Big Bang," *Time International* (4 May 1992): 23.

14. Cf. McKie, "Has Man Mastered the Universe?" 9.

15. Cf. Stephen Hawking, *A Brief History of Time: From the Big Bang to Black Holes* (New York: Bantam Books, 1988), 42ff.

16. P. C. W. Davies, "The Thermal Future of the Universe," *Monthly Notices of the Royal Astronomical Society* 161:1 (1973): 4.

17. Dyson, "Time Without End," 448. Dyson has elsewhere contended that "if the universe is open and infinite in time, the world of life and consciousness is inexhaustible too." Dyson, "Comment on the Topic 'Beyond the Black Hole,'" in *Some Strangeness in the Proportion: A Centennial Symposium to Celebrate the Achievements of Albert Einstein,* ed. H. Woolf (Reading, Mass.: Addison-Wesley, 1980), 80.

18. Ibid.

19. Dyson, "Time without End," 447f.

20. Ibid., 450.

21. Dyson, *Infinite in All Directions,* 111f.

22. Dyson, "Time without End," 448.

23. Ibid., 449.

24. Ibid., 453.

25. John Barrow and Frank Tipler, "Eternity Is Unstable," *Nature* 276 (30 November 1978): 453ff. and 458.

26. Steven Frautschi, "Entropy in an Expanding Universe," *Science* 217: 4560 (13 August 1982): 597.

27. Dyson, "Comment on the Topic 'Beyond the Black Hole,'" 378.

28. Dyson, "Time without End," 453f.

29. Ibid., 455.

30. Willem Drees, *Beyond the Big Bang: Quantum Cosmologies and God* (La Salle, Ill.: Open Court, 1990), 123.

31. Dyson, "Time without End," 455f.

32. Cf. Frautschi, "Entropy in an Expanding Universe," 598. The idea of towing black holes as a feasible method of obtaining energy was first mentioned in 1975 by L. Wood, T. Weaver, and J. Nuckolls, in *Annals of the New York Academy of Science* 251 (1975): 623.

33. Another method of obtaining energy from black holes is by gathering it from the rotational energy of a spinning black hole, an idea apparently first suggested by Roger Penrose (cf. David Block, "Black Holes and Their Astrophysical Implications," *Sky and Telescope* [July 1975]: 21f.) and developed further in regard to its implications for the long-term survival of life by Jamal Islam, "The Ultimate Fate of the Universe," *Sky and Telescope* (January 1979): 17f.

34. Frautschi, "Entropy in an Expanding Universe," 598.

35. Islam, "The Ultimate Fate of the Universe," 18, calculates that no black hole will be left in an open universe after 10^{100} years.

36. Ibid., 15.

37. Hawking, *A Brief History of Time,* 105.

38. Dyson, "Time without End," 459.

39. Ibid., 456.

40. Frank Tipler, "The Omega Point Theory: A Model of an Evolving God," in *Physics, Philosophy, and Theology,* ed. R. Russell, W. Stoeger, G. Coyne (Vatican City: Vatican Observatory, 1988), 313–31; "The Omega Point as *Eschaton:* Answers to Pannenberg's Questions for Scientists," *Zygon* 24:2 (June 1989): 217–53; and *The Physics of Immortality* (New York: Doubleday, 1994).

41. Tipler, "The Omega Point as *Eschaton*," 222.

42. Ibid., 250, n. 2.

43. Wolfhart Pannenberg, "Theological Questions to Scientists," in *The Sciences and Theology in the Twentieth Century,* ed. Arthur Peacocke (Notre Dame, Ind.: University of Notre Dame Press, 1981), 14f.

44. Tipler, "The Omega Point as *Eschaton*," 220.

45. Because the ability to communicate across the tremendous expanses of an open universe is ruled out by Tipler as impossible "because the redshift implies that arbitrarily large amounts of energy must be used to signal," he predicts, in light of his Omega Point theory (which requires that intelligent life fill every part of the universe and maintain contact at the Omega Point of the universe), that the universe must be closed (Tipler, "The Omega Point Theory," 321).

46. Barrow and Tipler, *Anthropic Cosmological Principle,* 659.

47. John Polkinghorne, *Science and Providence: God's Interaction with the World* (London: SPCK, 1989, 95.

48. For this and the following see Tipler, "The Omega Point as *Eschaton,*" 226ff.

49. Barrow and Tipler, *Anthropic Cosmological Principle,* 676f.

50. Ibid., 682.

51. Tipler, "The Omega Point Theory," 331, n. 14.

52. John Wheeler, "Beyond the Black Hole," in *Some Strangeness in the Proportion,* 362f.

53. Ibid., 362.

54. C. M. Patton and J. Wheeler, "Is Physics Legislated by Cosmogony?" in *Quantum Gravity: An Oxford Symposium,* ed. C. Isham, R. Penrose, and D. Sciama (Oxford: Clarendon Press, 1975), 543.

55. See similarly Tipler, *The Physics of Immortality,* 153ff., where he contends that the Omega Point, as the final state of the universe is approached, becomes omnipresent, omnipotent, and omniscient.

56. For this and the following see Tipler, "The Omega Point as *Eschaton,*" 229ff.

57. Ibid., 230.

58. Tipler, *The Physics of Immortality,* 220.

59. Wolfhart Pannenberg, "Theological Appropriation of Scientific Understandings: Response to Hefner, Wicken, Eaves, and Tipler," *Zygon,* vol. 24, no. 2 (June 1989): 265.

60. For this and the following see ibid., 267f.

61. Polkinghorne, *Science and Providence,* 96.

62. Ian G. Barbour, *Religion in an Age of Science* (San Francisco: Harper & Row, 1990), 151f. Although Barbour is certainly correct in his overall criticism, his reference to "the work of a personal God *as well as humanity*" seems to imply a syncretism in the eschatological work of ushering in the reign of God that is foreign to the Bible. As Rudolf Bultmann wrote concerning the eschatological message of the New Testament: "The coming of the reign of God is a miraculous [*wunderbares*] occurrence which is achieved alone by God without the help of humans." Rudolf Bultmann, *Theologie des Neuen Testaments* (Tübingen: J. C. B. Mohr, 1965), 3.

63. Pannenberg, "Theological Appropriation of Scientific Understandings," 268.

64. Pannenberg, "Theological Questions to Scientists," 14.

65. Barbour, *Religion in an Age of Science,* 152.

66. Karl Peters, "Eschatology in Light of Contemporary Science," an unpublished paper presented to the Theology and Science Group of the American Academy of Religion, November 1988, 2f.

67. For this and the following see ibid., 9ff.

68. Wolfhart Pannenberg, *Systematische Theologie,* vol. 3 (Göttingen: Vandenhoeck & Ruprecht, 1993), 635.

69. Revelation 21:1 provides a good example of this focus. Alan Johnson, *The Expositor's Bible Commentary,* vol. 12, ed. F. Gaebelein (Grand Rapids: Zondervan, 1987), 592, writes that the "first heaven and earth refers to the whole order of life in the world—an order tainted by sin," and that "John's emphasis on heaven and earth is not primarily cosmological but moral and spiritual." Similarly, James Blevins, *Revelation as Drama* (Nashville: Broadman, 1984), 134f., sees in this text a portrayal of the realms of heaven and earth in which "heaven and earth will be joined," with heaven becoming an extension of the earth for the purpose of creating a dwelling place for God's people.

70. The writer of the pseudepigraphal book of Enoch seemed to have held precisely such a view of the "end" of the world. In Enoch 45:4f. we read: "I will transform the heaven, and make it an eternal blessing and light. And I will transform the earth and make it a blessing."

71. Emil Brunner, *The Christian Doctrine of the Church, Faith, and the Consummation,* Dogmatics, vol. 3, trans. David Cairns (Philadelphia: Westminster, 1962), 375, 377.

72. Heim, *The World: Its Creation and Consummation,* 86.

73. Ibid., 89f. and 97.

74. Ted Peters, "On Creating the Cosmos," in *Physics, Philosophy, and Theology,* 282.

75. Weinberg, *The First Three Minutes,* 150f.

76. Arthur Eddington, "The Arrow of Time, Entropy and the Expansion of the Universe," in *The Concepts of Space and Time,* ed. Milic Capek (Dordrecht: D. Reidel, 1976), 465.

77. E. A. Milne, *Modern Cosmology and the Christian Idea of God* (Oxford: Clarendon Press, 1952), 146.

78. Ibid., 147ff.

79. For this and the following see ibid., 150ff.

80. In an intriguing aside Milne raises the question of what the existence of intelligent life on other planets would mean for the Christian faith. His tentative answer, while extremely speculative, is nevertheless intriguing and, if nothing else, consistent with the missionary spirit of Christianity. Milne writes: "What . . . of the possible denizens of other planets, if the Incarnation occurred only on our own? . . . There is no prima facie impossibility in the expectation that first of all the whole solar system, secondly our own group of galaxies, may by inter-

communication become one system. In that case there would be no difficulty in the uniqueness of the historical event of the Incarnation. For knowledge of it would be capable of being transmitted by signals to other planets and the reenactment of the tragedy of the crucifixion in other planets would be unnecessary" (153f.).

81. Ibid., 153.

82. Islam, "The Ultimate Fate of the Universe," 14f.

83. The portrayal of the glory of God, in one form or another, as light is not unique to this passage. Cf., for example, Exodus 34:29 and Ezekiel 43:2 for the expression of similar concepts.

84. Wilhelm Bousset, Die Offenbarung Johannis (Göttingen: Vandenhoeck & Ruprecht, 1906), 451.

85. R. H. Charles, A Critical and Exegetical Commentary on the Revelation of St. John, vol. 2 (Edinburgh: T. & T. Clark, 1920), 171f.

86. George E. Ladd, A Commentary on the Revelation of St. John (Grand Rapids: Eerdmans, 1972), 284.

87. Barrow and Tipler, Anthropic Cosmological Principle, 650.

88. Cf. Barrow and Tipler, "Eternity Is Unstable," 453.

89. I. L. Rozental, Big Bang Big Bounce: How Particles and Fields Drive Cosmic Evolution (Berlin: Springer Verlag, 1988), 128.

90. Hawking, A Brief History of Time, 88.

91. Ibid., 89.

92. Although the concept of a cyclic cosmology is to be found in most ancient cultures, the idea is developed most explicitly among the Greeks. Especially of interest is the cosmology of Empedocles, who maintained that the universe is continually being created and destroyed. Cf. G. Lloyd, "Greek Cosmologies," in Ancient Cosmologies, ed. C. Blacker and M. Loewe (London: George Allen & Unwin Ltd., 1975), 207.

93. Patton and Wheeler, "Is Physics Legislated by Cosmology?" 556f.

94. John Wheeler, "Beyond the End of Time," in C. Misner, K. Thorne, and J. Wheeler, Gravitation (San Francisco: W. H. Freeman, 1970), 1214.

95. George Gamow, "Modern Cosmology," in The New Astronomy, ed. The Scientific American editorial board (New York: Simon and Schuster, 1955), 23.

96. Eddington, "The Arrow of Time, Entropy and the Expansion of the Universe," 466.

97. Eddington, The Nature of the Physical World, 92.

98. The fact that this point has so often been misunderstood was noted by Rudolf Bultmann, who wrote: "It is the paradox of the Christian message . . . that the eschatological event is not genuinely understood in its own sense—at least as Paul and John understood it—if it is interpreted as an event that brings an end to the visible world through a cosmic catastrophe rather than as an occurrence within history." Rudolf Bultmann, Geschichte und Eschatologie (Tübingen: J. C. B. Mohr, 1964), 180f.

99. Barrow and Tipler, *Anthropic Cosmological Principle*, 248f.

100. Weinberg, *The First Three Minutes*, 154. Ian Barbour correctly notes, however, that although "one would expect from the law of entropy that there could have been only a finite rather than an infinite number of oscillations, . . . under such conditions the applicability of the law is uncertain." Barbour, *Religion in an Age of Science*, 129. Thus the possibility that an oscillating universe can exist for an eternity of cycles cannot be entirely dismissed.

101. Among recent and current supporters of an oscillating universe (assuming, of course, that the universe is indeed closed) we might list John Wheeler, "Beyond the End of Time"; I. L. Rozental, *Big Bang Big Bounce;* M. A. Markov, "Some Remarks on the Problem of the Very Early Universe" in *The Very Early Universe*, ed. G. Gibbons, S. Hawking et al. (Cambridge: Cambridge University Press, 1983); and George Gamow, "Modern Cosmology," especially 23ff.

102. Cf. Stanley Jaki, "The History of Science and the Idea of an Oscillating Universe," in *Cosmology, History, and Theology*, ed. Wolfgang Yourgrau and Allen Beck (New York: Plenum Press, 1977), 238; and Tipler, *The Physics of Immortality*, 74ff.

103. Origen, *De Principiis*, in *The Ante-Nicene Fathers*, vol. 4, ed. A. Roberts and J. Donaldson (Grand Rapids: Eerdmans, 1979), 341f. (III.V.3).

104. Ibid., 272f. (II.III.4,5).

105. See ibid., 240 (preface, 4), for example, where he writes: "There is one God, who created all things, and who, when nothing existed, called all things into being—God from the first foundation of the world."

106. Could this be what Origen meant when he wrote that "there was one beginning; and . . . there spring from one beginning many differences and varieties"? Ibid., 261 (I.VI.2).

107. Cf. ibid., 341f. (III.V.3).

108. Cf. Barrow and Tipler, *Anthropic Cosmological Principle*, 576ff.

109. See Patton and Wheeler, "Is Physics Legislated by Cosmology?" 557, for this and the following quote.

110. See, for example, John Whitcomb and Henry M. Morris, *The Genesis Flood: The Biblical Record and Its Scientific Implications* (Philadelphia: Presbyterian & Reformed, 1970), 232ff.; and Henry M. Morris, *The Twilight of Evolution* (Grand Rapids: Baker, 1963), chap. 3.

111. Joel Friedman, "The Natural God: A God Even an Atheist Can Believe in," *Zygon* 21:3 (September 1986): 378.

112. Cf. Charles Hartshorne, *The Divine Relativity* (New Haven: Yale University Press, 1964).

113. In a sense all eschatology, whether scientific or theological, remains by nature speculative, simply because the future has not yet taken on final form. As Karl Heim has written, "As long as the event is still future, it is uncertain; only when it hardens into the past does it assume a fixed form." (Heim, *The World: Its Creation and Consummation*, 85.)

114. Polkinghorne, *Science and Providence,* 97. The Scripture quotations are taken, respectively, from 2 Corinthians 5:4 and Romans 8:21.

115. Weinberg, *The First Three Minutes,* 154.

116. Heim, *The World: Its Creation and Consummation,* 97f.

CHAPTER 6

1. Ian Barbour, *Religion in an Age of Science* (San Francisco: Harper & Row, 1990), has identified four alternative models of relating science and religion that are advocated today. (1) Science and religion are in conflict. (2) Science and religion are independent, having different methodologies and language and having essentially nothing to do with each other. (3) Science and religion stand in a relationship of dialogue with each other. (4) Science and theology are capable of being integrated. Cf. also Ian Barbour, "Ways of Relating Science and Theology," in *Physics, Philosophy, and Theology,* ed. R. Russell, W. Stoeger, and G. Coyne (Vatican City: Vatican Observatory, 1988).

Russell Kleckley has likewise identified four alternative models of the relationship between science and theology, all of which exhibit various degrees of animosity/patronization toward theology. They are: (1) Science eliminates theology. (2) Science defines the limits of theology. (3) Theology is anthropology. (4) Theology is teleology. Russell Kleckley, "The Concept of God and the Place of Religion in Recent Popular Cosmologies," in *Glaube und Denken: Jahrbuch der Karl-Heim-Gesellschaft* (Moers: Brendow, 1992), 36.

Harold Oliver, "The Complementarity of Theology and Cosmology," *Zygon* 13:1 (March 1978): 19–33, has suggested a simpler and more useful description of the range of relationships between theology and natural science: (1) Conflict theory of relationship; (2) compartment theory (both science and theology have their own separate compartments of interest and little or no overlap exists); (3) complementarity theory of relationship.

2. As Richard Morris has written: "The boundaries between physics and metaphysics have become blurred. Questions that would have been considered metaphysical in another age enter into discussions of the origin of the universe, and physicists speak of anthropic principles, which sometimes seem to be more philosophical than scientific. Meanwhile, some all-embracing theories are proposed that yield unverifiable conclusions, and appear similar to the metaphysical systems constantly proposed by nineteenth century philosophers." (Richard Morris, *The Edges of Science: Crossing the Boundary from Physics to Metaphysics* [New York: Prentice Hall, 1990], 221f.)

3. Wolfhart Pannenberg, "Theological Questions to Scientists," in *The Sciences and Theology in the Twentieth Century,* ed. A. R. Peacocke (Notre Dame, Ind.: University of Notre Dame Press, 1981), 3.

4. Thomas F. Torrance, *Reality and Scientific Theology* (Edinburgh: Scottish Academic Press, 1985), 33.

5. John Polkinghorne, *Science and Creation: The Search for Understanding* (Boston: Shambhala, 1989), 86.

6. John Barrow and Frank Tipler, *The Anthropic Cosmological Principle* (Oxford: Clarendon Press, 1986), 107.

7. Cf. Joel Friedman, "The Natural God: A God Even an Atheist Can Believe In," *Zygon* 21:3 (September 1986): 378.

8. It is no accident, therefore, that the recent revival of design type arguments based on the results of modern physics has been expressed in such a way that the transcendence of God is emphasized. As Ernan McMullin has written, these arguments "point to a transcendent Creator, not to a world-soul or even an all-powerful Craftsman. The agent who brings the universe into being is not itself limited to that universe." Ernan McMullin, "Natural Science and Belief in a Creator," in *Physics, Philosophy, and Theology,* 71.

9. Hans Schwarz, "God's Place in a Space Age," *Zygon* 21:3 (September 1986): 364.

10. Cf. Ernan McMullin, "Natural Science and Belief in a Creator: Historical Notes," 66f.

11. Stephen Hawking, *A Brief History of Time: From the Big Bang to Black Holes* (New York: Bantam Books, 1988), 175.

12. As Freeman Dyson, who wishes to make eschatology a respected field of scientific enquiry, has confessed: "Like the majority of scientists in this century, I have not concerned myself seriously with theology. Theology is a foreign language which we have not taken the trouble to learn." Freeman Dyson, *Infinite in All Directions* (New York: Harper & Row, 1988), 119.

13. Kleckley, "The Concept of God," 39.

14. Ted Peters, "Cosmos as Creation," in *Cosmos as Creation,* ed. Ted Peters (Nashville: Abingdon Press, 1989), 56f.

15. Kleckley, "The Concept of God," 45.

16. Jeffrey Wicken, "Theology and Science in the Evolving Cosmos: A Need for Dialogue," *Zygon* 23:1 (March 1988): 48.

Selected Bibliography

Atkins, Peter. *The Creation*. Oxford: W. H. Freeman, 1981.

Barbour, Ian G. *Issues in Science and Religion*. New York: Harper & Row, 1966.

_____. *Religion in an Age of Science*. San Francisco: Harper & Row, 1990.

_____. "Ways of Relating Science and Religion." In *Physics, Philosophy, and Theology*, ed. R. Russell, W. Stoeger, and G. Coyne. Vatican City: Vatican Observatory, 1988.

Barrow, John. *Theories of Everything: The Quest for Ultimate Explanation*. Oxford: Clarendon Press, 1991.

_____. *The World within the World*. Oxford: Oxford University Press, 1988.

Barrow, John, and Frank Tipler. *The Anthropic Cosmological Principle*. Oxford: Clarendon Press, 1986.

_____. "Eternity Is Unstable." *Nature* 276 (30 November 1978): 453–59.

Bell, John. "On the Einstein-Podolsky-Rosen Paradox." *Physics* 1:3 (1964): 195ff.

Bohm, David. "The Implicate Order: A New Order for Physics," ed. Dean Fowler. *Process Studies* 8 (Summer 1978): 73–102.

_____. *Wholeness and the Implicate Order*. London: Routledge & Kegan Paul, 1980.

Bohm, David, and B. J. Hiley. "Non-Locality and Locality in the Stochastic Interpretation of Quantum Mechanics." *Physics Reports* 172 (1989): 94–122.

_____. "Some Remarks on Sarfatti's Proposed Connection between Quantum Phenomena and the Volitional Activity of the Observer-Participator." *Psychoenergetic Systems* 1 (1976): 177ff.

Bohm, David, B. J. Hiley, and P. N. Kaloyerou. "An Ontological Basis for the Quantum Theory." *Physics Reports* 144 (1987): 321–75.

Bohr, Niels. "Can Quantum-Mechanical Description of Physical Reality Be Considered Complete?" *Physical Review* 48 (18 October 1935): 696–702.

Bondi, Hermann. "Religion Is a Good Thing." In *Lying Truths*, ed. R. Duncan and M. Weston Smith. Oxford: Pergamon, 1979.

_____. *The Universe at Large*. London: Heinemann, 1961.

Brout, R., F. Englert, and E. Gunzig. "The Creation of the Universe as a Quantum Phenomenon." *Annals of Physics* 115:1 (1978): 78–106.

Byers, D., ed. *Religion, Science and the Search for Wisdom*. National Conference of Catholic Bishops, 1987.

Capek, Milic, ed. *The Concepts of Space and Time*. Dordrecht: D. Reidel, 1976.

Capra, Fritjof. *The Turning Point*. New York: Simon and Schuster, 1982.

Craig, William L. "'What Place, Then, for a Creator?': Hawking on God and Creation." *British Journal for the Philosophy of Science* 41 (1990): 473–91.

Davies, Paul C. W. *God and the New Physics.* New York: Simon and Schuster, 1983.

_____. *The Mind of God: Science and the Search for Ultimate Meaning.* London: Simon and Schuster, 1992.

_____. "The Thermal Future of the Universe." *Monthly Notices of the Royal Astronomical Society* 161:1 (1973): 2–4.

Davies, Paul C. W., and J. R. Brown. *The Ghost in the Atom: A Discussion of the Mysteries of Quantum Physics.* Cambridge: Cambridge University Press, 1986.

Dawkins, Richard. *The Blind Watchmaker.* London: Longmans, 1986.

Donceel, J. F. *Natural Theology.* New York: Sheed and Ward, 1962.

Drees, Willem. *Beyond the Big Bang: Quantum Cosmologies and God.* La Salle, Ill.: Open Court, 1990.

_____. "Quantum Cosmologies and the 'Beginning.'" *Zygon* 26:3 (September 1991): 373–96.

Dyson, Freeman J. "Comment on the Topic 'Beyond the Black Hole.'" In *Some Strangeness in the Proportion: A Centennial Symposium to Celebrate the Achievements of Albert Einstein,* ed. H. Woolf. Reading, Mass.: Addison-Wesley, 1980.

_____. *Infinite in All Directions.* New York: Harper and Row, 1988.

_____. "Science and Religion." In *Religion, Science and the Search for Wisdom,* ed. D. Byers. National Conference of Catholic Bishops, 1987.

_____. "Time without End: Physics and Biology in an Open Universe." *Reviews of Modern Physics* 51:3 (July 1989): 447–60.

Eddington, Arthur. "The Arrow of Time, Entropy and the Expansion of the Universe." In *The Concepts of Space and Time,* ed. Milic Capek. Dordrecht: D. Reidel, 1976.

_____. *The Nature of the Physical World.* London: Dent [1928], 1935.

_____. *New Pathways of Science.* New York: Macmillan, 1935.

Einstein, Albert, Boris Podolsky, and Nathan Rosen. "Can Quantum-Mechanical Description of Physical Reality Be Considered Complete?" *Physical Review* 47:10 (15 May 1935): 777–80.

Feynman, Richard. *The Character of Physical Law.* Cambridge, Mass.: MIT Press, 1965.

Flood, R., and M. Lockwood, eds. *The Nature of Time.* Cambridge, Mass.: Basil Blackwell, 1986.

Frauenknecht, Hans. *Urknall, Urzeugung und Schöpfung: Ein Informationsbuch zum Dialog zwischen Naturwissenschaften und Glauben.* Wiesbaden: Brockhaus, 1976.

Frautschi, Steven. "Entropy in an Expanding Universe." *Science* 217:4560 (13 August 1982): 593–99.

Friedman, Joel. "The Natural God: A God Even an Atheist Can Believe In." *Zygon* 21:3 (September 1986): 369–88.

Gamow, George. "Modern Cosmology." In *The New Astronomy,* ed. *The Scientific American* editorial board. New York: Simon and Schuster, 1955.

Halliwell, Jonathan, and Stephen Hawking. "Origin of Structure in the Universe." *Physical Review* D3, 31:8 (15 April 1985): 1777–91.

Hartle, James, and Stephen Hawking. "Wave Function of the Universe." *Physical Review* D, 28,3:12 (15 December 1983): 2960–75.

Hawking, Stephen. *A Brief History of Time: From the Big Bang to Black Holes.* New York: Bantam Books, 1988.

——————. "The Edge of Spacetime." *New Scientist* 103 (16 August 1984): 10–14.

——————. July 1985 interview with Renée Weber. In *Dialogues with Scientists and Sages: The Search for Unity.* London: Routledge & Kegan Paul, 1986.

Hawking, Stephen, and G. Ellis. *The Large Scale Structure of Space-Time.* Cambridge: Cambridge University Press, 1973.

Hawking, Stephen, and Julian Luttrell. "The Isotropy of the Universe." *Physics Letters* 143B:1,2,3 (9 August 1984): 83–86.

Hawking, Stephen, and Roger Penrose. "The Singularities of Gravitational Collapse and Cosmology." *Proceedings of the Royal Society of London* A314 (1970): 529–48.

Hefner, Philip. "The Evolution of the Created Co-Creator." In *Cosmos as Creation,* ed. Ted Peters. Nashville: Abingdon Press, 1989.

——————. "God and Chaos: The Demiurge Versus the Ungrund." *Zygon* 19:4 (December 1984): 469–85.

Heim, Karl. *The World: Its Creation and Consummation: The End of the Present Age and the Future of the World in the Light of Resurrection,* trans. Robert Smith. Edinburgh: Oliver and Boyd [1952], 1962.

Heisenberg, Werner. *Physics and Beyond.* New York: Harper & Row, 1971.

Herbert, Nick. *Quantum Reality: Beyond the New Physics.* New York: Doubleday, 1985.

Hesse, Mary B. "Miracles and the Laws of Nature." In *Miracles,* ed. C. F. D. Moule. London: A. R. Mowbray, 1965.

——————. "Physics, Philosophy, and Myth." In *Physics, Philosophy, and Theology,* ed. R. Russell, W. Stoeger, and G. Coyne. Vatican City: Vatican Observatory, 1988.

Hiebert, Erwin. "Modern Physics and Christian Faith." In *God and Nature,* ed. D. Lindberg and R. Numbers. Berkeley: University of California Press, 1986.

Honner, John. "Not Meddling with Divinity: Theological Worldviews and Contemporary Physics." *Pacifica* 1 (1988): 251–72.

Hoyle, Fred. *Religion and the Scientists.* London: SCM Press, 1959.

Isham, Chris. "Creation of the Universe as a Quantum Process." In *Physics, Philosophy, and Theology,* ed. R. Russell, W. Stoeger, and G. Coyne. Vatican City: Vatican Observatory, 1988.

Isham, Chris, Roger Penrose, and Denis Sciama, eds. *Quantum Gravity: An Oxford Symposium*. Oxford: Clarendon Press, 1975.

Islam, Jamal. "The Ultimate Fate of the Universe." *Sky and Telescope* (January 1979): 13–18.

Jaki, Stanely L. "The History of Science and the Idea of an Oscillating Universe." In *Cosmology, History, and Theology*, ed. W. Yourgrau and Allen Beck. New York: Plenum Press, 1977.

_____. "Miracles and Physics." *Asbury Theological Journal* 42:1 (Spring 1987): 5–42.

Jammer, Max. *Concepts of Force: A Study in the Foundations of Dynamics*. Cambridge, Mass.: Harvard University Press, 1957.

_____. *The Philosophy of Quantum Mechanics: The Interpretations of Quantum Mechanics in Historical Perspective*. New York: John Wiley & Sons, 1974.

Jastrow, Robert. *God and the Astronomers*. New York: W. W. Norton, 1978.

Jeans, James. *Physics and Philosophy*. Cambridge: Cambridge University Press, 1944.

_____. *The Universe around Us*. Cambridge: Cambridge University Press, 1929.

Kanitscheider, Bernulf. "Gibt es einen absoluten Nullpunkt der Zeit?" *Praxis der Naturwissenschaft—Physik* 4:40 (1991): 19–24.

_____. *Kosmologie: Geschichte und Systematik in philosophischer Perspekive*. Stuttgart: Philipp Reclam jun., 1984.

Kleckley, Russell. "The Concept of God and the Place of Religion in Recent Popular Cosmologies." *Glauben und Denken: Jahrbuch der Karl-Heim-Gesellschaft* 4 (Moers: Brendow, 1992): 36–48.

Lecomte du Noüy, Pierre. *Human Destiny*. New York: Longmans, 1947.

Le Poidevin, Robin. "Creation in a Closed Universe or, Have Physicists Disproved the Existence of God?" *Religious Studies* 27 (1991): 39–48.

Leslie, John. "How to Draw Conclusions from a Fine-Tuned Universe." In *Physics, Philosophy, and Theology*, ed. R. Russell, W. Stoeger, and G. Coyne. Vatican City: Vatican Observatory, 1988.

_____, ed. *Physical Cosmology and Philosophy*. London: Collier, 1990.

Margenau, Henry, ed. *Integrative Principles of Modern Thought*. New York: Gordon & Breach, 1972.

_____. *The Nature of Physical Reality*. New York: McGraw-Hill, 1950.

Markus, S. M. (also Siegfried Müller-Markus). *Der Gott der Physiker*. Basel: Birkhäuser, 1986.

McMullin, Ernan. "How Should Cosmology Relate to Theology?" In *The Sciences and Theology in the Twentieth Century*, ed. A. Peacocke. Notre Dame, Ind.: University of Notre Dame Press, 1981.

_____. "Natural Science and Belief in a Creator." In *Physics, Philosophy, and Theology*, ed. R. Russell, W. Stoeger, and G. Coyne. Vatican City: Vatican Observatory, 1988.

Milne, E. A. *Modern Cosmology and the Christian Idea of God.* Oxford: Clarendon Press, 1952.

Misner, Charles. "Absolute Zero of Time." *Physical Review* 186,2:5 (25 October 1969): 1328–33.

_____. "Cosmology and Theology." In *Cosmology, History, and Theology,* ed. W. Yourgrau and Allen Beck. New York: Plenum Press, 1977.

Morris, Richard. *The Edges of Science: Crossing the Boundary from Physics to Metaphysics.* New York: Prentice Hall, 1990.

Müller-Markus, Siegfried (also S. M. Markus). "Science and Faith." In *Integrative Principles of Modern Thought,* ed. Henry Margenau. New York: Gordon & Breach, 1972.

_____. *Wen Sterne rufen: Gespräch mit Lenin.* Wiesbaden: Credo, 1960.

Munitz, Milton K. *Cosmic Understanding: Philosophy and Science of the Universe.* Princeton: Princeton University Press, 1986.

Nebelsick, Harold P. *Circles of God: Theology and Science from the Greeks to Copernicus.* Edinburgh: Scottish Academic Press, 1985.

Newton, Isaac. "Four Letters to Dr. Bentley Containing Some Arguments in Proof of a Deity." In *Isaac Newton's Papers and Letters on Natural Philosophy,* ed. Bernard Cohen. Cambridge, Mass.: Harvard University Press, 1978.

Newton-Smith, William. *The Structure of Time.* London: Routledge and Kegan Paul, 1980.

_____. "Space, Time and Space-Time: A Philosopher's View." In *Nature of Time,* ed. R. Flood and M. Lockwood. Cambridge, Mass.: Basil Blackwell, 1986.

Odenwald, Sten. "A Modern Look at the Origin of the Universe." *Zygon* 25:1 (March 1990): 25–45.

Oliver, Harold. "The Complementarity of Theology and Cosmology." *Zygon* 13:1 (March 1978): 19–33.

Pagels, Heinz. *Perfect Symmetry.* New York: Simon and Schuster, 1985.

Pannenberg, Wolfhart. "The Doctrine of Creation and Modern Science." *Zygon* 23:1 (March 1988): 3–21.

_____. *Systematische Theologie,* vols. 2 and 3. Göttingen: Vandenhoeck & Ruprecht, 1991 and 1993.

_____. "Theological Questions to Scientists." In *The Sciences and Theology in the Twentieth Century,* ed. A. R. Peacocke. Notre Dame, Ind.: University of Notre Dame Press, 1981.

Peacocke, Arthur R. "God's Action in the Real World." *Zygon* 26:4 (December 1991): 455–76.

_____, ed. *The Sciences and Theology in the Twentieth Century.* Notre Dame, Ind.: University of Notre Dame Press, 1981.

_____. *Theology for a Scientific Age: Being and Becoming—Natural and Divine.* Oxford: Basil Blackwood, 1990.

Penrose, Roger. "Big Bangs, Black Holes and 'Time's Arrow.'" In *The Nature of*

Time, ed. R. Flood and M. Lockwood. Cambridge, Mass.: Basil Blackwell, 1965.

_____. *The Emperor's New Mind: Concerning Computers, Minds, and the Laws of Physics*. Oxford: Oxford University Press, 1989.

Peters, Ted. "Cosmos as Creation." In *Cosmos as Creation*, ed. Ted Peters. Nashville: Abingdon Press, 1989.

_____. "On Creating the Cosmos." In *Physics, Philosophy, and Theology*, ed. R. Russell, W. Stoeger, and G. Coyne. Vatican City: Vatican Observatory, 1988.

_____, ed. *Cosmos as Creation: Theology and Science in Consonance*. Nashville: Abingdon Press, 1989.

Planck, Max. *The Universe in the Light of Modern Physics*, trans. W. Johnston. London: Allen and Unwin, 1937.

Polkinghorne, John. *One World*. London: SPCK, 1986.

_____. *The Quantum World*. London: Longman, 1984.

_____. "The Quantum World." In *Physics, Philosophy, and Theology*, ed. R. Russell, W. Stoeger, and G. Coyne. Vatican City: Vatican Observatory, 1988.

_____. *Reason and Reality: The Relationship between Science and Theology*. Philadelphia: Trinity Press International, 1991.

_____. *Science and Creation: The Search for Understanding*. Boston: Shambhala, 1989.

_____. *Science and Providence: God's Interaction with the World*. London: SPCK, 1989.

Pollard, William. *Chance and Providence: God's Action in a World Governed by Scientific Law*. New York: Charles Scribner's Sons, 1958.

_____. *Transcendence and Providence: Reflections of a Physicist and Priest*, Edinburgh: Scottish Academic Press, 1987.

Prigogine, Ilya. *From Being to Becoming*. New York: W. H. Freeman, 1980.

_____. "The Rediscovery of Time." *Zygon* 19:4 (December 1984): 433–41.

Prigogine, Ilya, and Isabelle Stengers. *Order out of Chaos: Man's New Dialogue with Nature*. Boulder, Colo.: New Science Library, 1984.

Reichenbach, Hans. *The Direction of Time*, ed. Mary Reichenbach. Berkeley: University of California Press, 1971.

_____. "The Philosophical Significance of the Theory of Relativity." In *Albert Einstein: Philosopher-Scientist*, ed. Arthur Schlipp. London: Cambridge University Press, 1970.

Rozental, I. L. *Big Bang Big Bounce: How Particles and Fields Drive Cosmic Evolution*. Berlin: Springer Verlag, 1988.

Russell, Robert John. "Contingency in Physics and Cosmology: A Critique of the Theology of Wolfhart Pannenberg." *Zygon* 23:1 (March 1988): 23–43.

_____. "Cosmology, Creation, and Contingency." In *Cosmos as Creation,* ed. Ted Peters. Nashville: Abingdon Press, 1989.

_____. "Entropy and Evil." *Zygon* 19:4 (December 1984): 449–68.

_____. "Quantum Physics in Philosophical and Theological Perspective." In *Physics, Philosophy, and Theology,* ed. R. Russell, W. Stoeger, and G. Coyne. Vatican City: Vatican Observatory, 1988.

Russell, Robert John, William Stoeger, and George Coyne, eds. *Physics, Philosophy, and Theology: A Common Quest for Understanding.* Vatican City: Vatican Observatory, 1988.

Schlegel, Richard. "Quantum Physics and the Divine Postulate." *Zygon* 14:2 (June 1979): 163–85.

_____. "The Return of Man in Quantum Physics." In *The Sciences and Theology in the Twentieth Century,* ed. A. R. Peacocke. Notre Dame, Ind.: University of Notre Dame Press, 1981.

Schrödinger, Erwin. *What Is Life?: The Physical Aspect of the Living Cell, with Mind and Matter and Autobiographical Sketches.* Cambridge: Cambridge University Press, 1967.

Schuster, Heinz Georg. *Deterministic Chaos: An Introduction.* Weinheim: Physik-Verlag, 1984.

Schwarz, Hans. "God's Place in a Space Age." *Zygon* 21:3 (September 1986): 353–68.

_____. "Science in Need of Religion?" *Sophia: A Journal for Discussion in Philosophical Theology* (1988): 45–55.

_____. *The Search for God: Christianity—Atheism—Secularism—World Religions.* Minneapolis: Augsburg Press, 1975.

Sharpe, Kevin J. "Relating the Physics and Religion of David Bohm." *Zygon* 25:1 (March 1990): 105–22.

Stapp, Henry Pierce. "Quantum Mechanics, Local Causality, and Process Philosophy," ed. William Jones. *Process Studies* 7:3 (Autumn 1977): 173–82.

Stewart, Ian. *Does God Play Dice? The New Mathematics of Chaos.* New York: Penguin Books, 1990.

Swineburne, Richard. "Argument from the Fine-Tuning of the Universe." In *Physical Cosmology and Philosophy,* ed. John Leslie. London: Collier, 1990.

_____. *The Existence of God.* Oxford: Clarendon Press, 1979.

Thum, Beda. "Theologie und Kosmophysik." *Kairos: Zeitschrift für Religionswissenschaft und Theologie* 26:1,2 (1984): 108–24.

Tipler, Frank. "The Many-Worlds Interpretation of Quantum Mechanics in Quantum Cosmology." In *Quantum Concepts in Space and Time,* ed. Roger Penrose and Chris J. Isham. Oxford: Clarendon Press, 1988.

_____. "The Omega Point as *Eschaton:* Answers to Pannenberg's Questions for Scientists." *Zygon* 24:2 (June 1989): 217–53.

_____. "The Omega Point Theory: A Model of an Evolving God." In

Physics, Philosophy, and Theology, ed. R. Russell, W. Stoeger, and G. Coyne. Vatican City: Vatican Observatory, 1988.

_____. *The Physics of Immortality.* New York: Doubleday, 1994.

Torrance, Thomas F. *Reality and Scientific Theology.* Edinburgh: Scottish Academic Press, 1985.

Tracy, David, and Nicholas Nash, eds. *Cosmology and Theology.* Edinburgh: T. & T. Clark, Concilium, 1983.

Trefil, James. *The Moment of Creation: Big Bang Physics from Before the First Millisecond to the Present Universe.* New York: Charles Scribner's Sons, 1983.

Tryon, Edward P. "Is the Universe a Vacuum Fluctuation?" *Nature* 246 (14 December 1973): 396–97.

Vilenkin, Alexander. "Birth of Inflationary Universes." *Physical Review* D 27,3:12 (15 June 1983): 2848–55.

_____. "Boundary Conditions in Quantum Cosmology." *Physical Review* D 33,3:12 (1986): 3560–69.

_____. "Creation of Universes from Nothing." *Physical Letters* 117B:25 (4 November 1982): 25–28.

Weinberg, Steven. *Dreams of a Final Theory: The Search for the Fundamental Laws of Nature.* London: Vintage, 1993.

_____. *The First Three Minutes: A Modern View of the Origin of the Universe.* London: Trinity Press, 1977.

Weizsäcker, Carl Friedrich von. *Zum Weltbild der Physik.* Stuttgart: S. Hirzel Verlag, 1963.

Wheeler, John. "Beyond the Black Hole." In *Some Strangeness in the Proportion: A Centennial Symposium to Celebrate the Achievements of Albert Einstein,* ed. H. Woolf. Reading, Mass.: Addison-Wesley, 1980.

_____. "Genesis and Observership." In *Foundational Problems in the Special Sciences,* ed. R. Butts and K. Hintikka. Dordrecht: Reidel, 1977.

Whitehead, Alfred North. "The Philosophical Aspects of the Principle of Relativity." In *The Interpretation of Science: Selected Essays,* ed. A. H. Johnson. New York: Bobbs-Merrill, 1961.

_____. *Process and Reality: An Essay in Cosmology.* New York: Macmillan, 1929.

Whittaker, Edmund. *The Beginning and End of the World.* Oxford: Oxford University Press, 1942.

_____. *Space and Spirit.* London: Thomas Nelson, 1947.

Wicken, Jeffrey. "Theology and Science in the Evolving Cosmos: A Need for Dialogue." *Zygon* 23:1 (March 1988): 45–55.

Yourgrau, Wolfgang, and Allen Beck, eds. *Cosmology, History, and Theology.* New York: Plenum Press, 1977.

Zukav, Gary. *The Dancing Wu Li Masters: An Overview of the New Physics.* New York: William Morrow and Company, 1979.

Index (of main text and extended notes)